Advance praise for
Why CRM Doesn't Work:
How to Win by Letting Customers Manage the Relationship
BY FREDERICK NEWELL

"Fred Newell raises relationship marketing to a new level, beyond database marketing, loyalty programs, targeted advertising, and customer relationship marketing. **Read this before your competitors do.**"

—PHILIP KOTLER

SC Johnson & Son Distinguished Professor of International Marketing

Northwestern University Kellogg School of Management

"In this competitive world, hanging onto customers is critical. Fred Newell's new book is a commonsense approach to helping you do just that."

—JACK TROUT

President, Trout & Partners Ltd.

"Frederick Newell has hit the CRM nail on the head. A lot of company managers thought you could create profits by buying CRM software and building an expensive data warehouse. Fred has pointed out that they were wrong. **You cannot predict or modify customer behavior with CRM. What you can do is waste a lot of money.** What you need is a customer database and intelligent customer communications, which come from creative strategies, not a piece of software."

—ARTHUR MIDDLETON HUGHES

Vice President for Business Development

CSC Advanced Database Solutions

"Fred Newell does a wonderful job of helping us understand why so few companies get the return from CRM initiatives that they expect. *Why CRM Doesn't Work* makes a compelling case for putting the customer in the driver's seat and allowing the customer to manage the relationship. **The book is filled with practical examples and tips and is an ideal solution for business executives intent on avoiding 'CRM backlash.'** In the process, Newell addresses a host of relevant topics ranging from

wireless technologies to brand building to permission marketing in a cogently written and easy-to-read treatise. Newell moves beyond the buzz and quickly gets to the essence of what companies need to do if they expect to win the 'hearts and minds' of customers. A must-read for any manager in an enterprise focused on improving its profitability, as well as the quality of its customers' lives."

—JONATHAN COPULSKY
Lead Partner, Customer and Channel Strategy Practice
Deloitte Consulting

"Fred Newell, in his trademark easy-to-read style, showers us with ideas and examples to illustrate his message that 'it's not technology that drives CRM, it's intelligence about the customer.' He rightly reminds us that the customers must truly be placed at center stage and that we must listen with both ears to their stated and unstated needs. As a recent definition of CRM states, 'Customers Really Matter.' Fred's book is **timely for all businesses**."

BRIAN WOOLF
Author, *Loyalty Marketing: The Second Act*

"CRM has been promoted as the answer to customer development and loyalty. Fred addresses head on why this has failed for so many companies that have spent heavily and had such big expectations for CRM. Importantly, Fred now takes customer development and loyalty to a new level—beyond CRM—by redefining and empowering the customer. **This is the way to build a successful customer-focused business.** Fred is always ahead of the curve."

—CHARLES J. BEECH
Chairman & CEO, Message Factors, Inc.

"If you're struggling with a CRM initiative in your company, get this book. It can set you straight clearly, easily, quickly and, most of all, through a very readable format. Fred Newell has taken a beacon to the 'black hole of CRM.' Grab a flashlight and follow along."

—DON SCHULTZ
Professor, Medill School of Journalism, Northwestern University

Why CRM Doesn't Work

A complete list of our titles is available at
www.bloomberg.com/books

Why CRM Doesn't Work

How to Win by Letting Customers
Manage the Relationship

FREDERICK NEWELL

Bloomberg Press
Princeton, New Jersey

This publication contains the author's opinions and is designed to provide accurate and authoritative information. It is sold with the understanding that the author, publisher, and Bloomberg L.P. are not engaged in rendering legal, accounting, investment planning, business management, or other professional advice. The reader should seek the services of a qualified professional for such advice; the author, publisher, and Bloomberg L.P. cannot be held responsible for any loss incurred as a result of specific investments or planning decisions made by the reader.

First edition published 2003
1 3 5 7 9 10 8 6 4 2

Library of Congress Cataloging-in-Publication Data

Newell, Frederick
    Why CRM doesn't work : how to win by letting customers manage the relationship / Frederick Newell.-- 1st ed.
        p. cm.
Includes index.
    ISBN 1-57660-132-3 (alk. paper)
    1. Customer relations--Management. I. Title

HF5415.5 .N49 2003
658.8'12--dc21   2002153916

Acquired by Jared Kieling
Edited by Tracy Tait

Don't believe what your eyes are telling you.
All they show is limitation.
Look with your understanding,
find out what you already know,
and you'll see the way to fly.

—*Jonathan Livingston Seagull*
Richard Bach

To the pioneers of customer relationship building from whom I have learned so much and to the many marketers who truly want to make life better for their customers—with the hope that some of these words will help you to look beyond today's limitations, find out what you already know, and see the way to fly.

Contents

WHAT NEEDS TO CHANGE

HOW TO CHANGE

A LOOK AHEAD

Acknowledgments

M Y SINCERE THANKS to all the companies that cared enough to share stories, numbers, and insights. Special thanks to the many fine people at the companies I work with throughout the year. They have taught me more than I have been able to teach them, and I continue to learn from every visit.

Many individuals deserve my heartfelt thanks for their professional contributions. First among these is Loren Lemon who spent hours reading early drafts, always providing exactly the right incisive comments and suggestions.

Equal thanks to Professor Katherine Lemon, author of *Customer Equity—How Customer Lifetime Value is Reshaping Corporate Strategy*, my coauthor of *Wireless Rules* (and my delightful daughter), for adding the text that ties the customer management of relationships to the development of customer equity.

For the foreword I went to the one professional who really pioneered the concept of transferring power to the customer with his earliest thoughts about permission marketing. My sincere thanks to Seth Godin for accepting the challenge.

Thanks to my agent, Ed Knappman of New England Publishing Associates for finding the good folks at Bloomberg Press, to Jared Kieling, editorial director, for his dedicated counsel, and, above all, to my editor, Tracy Tait, who brought order out of chaos in the kindest possible way to help me sharpen my thoughts throughout the book. Special thanks to my associate, Devon Wylie, for her quiet patience, sound advice, and dedicated research.

I especially want to acknowledge the following executives who shared stories, quotes, and ideas: Héctor Bajac of Johnny Walker, Richard Barlow of Frequency Marketing, Bob Brand of the *Newtown Bee*, Susan Cohen of increMETRICS, Deborah Galea of email replies.com, Barton Goldenberg of ISM, Bernice Grossman of the

DMRS Group, Sandra Gudat of the Customer Communication Group, Guara Verma and Todd Hollowell of informationweek.com, Kenneth Kanady of KANA, John Lawlor of Spectra Marketing, Federico Tapper of BancoRio, and Paco Underhill of Envirosell.

Finally, most special thanks to my wife, Harriette, for her unwavering support and encouragement, and thanks to our three great children for their enthusiastic advocacy.

The quote on pages 74–75 is reprinted with the permission of Simon & Schuster Adult Publishing Group from *Why We Buy*, by Paco Underhill. Copyright © 1999 by Obat, Inc.

The sidebar on pages 140–141 is reprinted with permission, CMP MEDIA LLC, *Information Week*, February 18, 2002, "CRM Makes Strides in Self Service," Guarav Verma and Todd Hollowell. All rights reserved.

The text in Chapter 17 from *Driving Customer Equity* appears with permission from the publisher. *Driving Customer Equity: How Customer Lifetime Value is Reshaping Corporate Strategy*, by R. T. Rust, V. A. Zeithaml, and K. N. Lemon. Copyright © 2000 by Roland T. Rust, Valarie A. Zeithaml, and Katherine N. Lemon. Reprinted with permission of The Free Press, an imprint of Simon & Schuster Adult Publishing Group.

Foreword

YOU'RE NOT IN CHARGE. Sorry. Someone had to say it. The delusion that you are still in charge of what your prospects (and consumers) see and think and do is costing you money. Consumers have a real choice today. They can choose to ignore your ads, your messages, your follow-up messages, your phone calls, your coupons, and your begging.

CRM, if you haven't noticed, appears to stand for "Consultants (making) Real Money." It's positioned as an arcane black art, something both technical and artistic, and something that you couldn't possibly understand without their help.

But that's not true. CRM isn't hard. It isn't complicated. It's just foggy. It's foggy because too many companies persist in believing that CRM is just a tactic, something to be installed. Once companies get it nailed, they believe they can go back to business as normal.

All you need to do to really get it, of course, is to abandon that thinking. Realize that a sea change has occurred, that "permission" is not just a buzzword invented to get you to buy books and stuff. Instead, recognize that the empowered consumer is here to stay and we all better get used to it. That realization, together with a large dose of common sense (provided for you here by Fred Newell) gets you almost all the way there.

Last thought: quit studying the issue and go try something. You can set up a simple e-mail solution on your desk for a dollar. See what happens when you interact with 100 consumers a day by e-mail—treating them like real people and doing what you need to do to grow their business. The results will surprise you.

—SETH GODIN
Author, *Permission Marketing*

Preface

A QUICK SEARCH of online bookseller Amazon.com lists close to one hundred books on customer relationship management (including three of mine) with specialty titles covering Canada, Western Europe, Central Europe, Japan, and Latin America. Why does the world need one more? Because all ninety-eight—including mine, I'm not afraid to admit—have gotten it wrong. The very phrase explained in these books—CRM, or "customer relationship management"—implies that companies can manage the customer relationship by targeting specific customers for specific product offerings. How audacious! How impudent! How wrong!

Most reports show that only 25 to 30 percent of companies implementing CRM initiatives feel that they are getting the return they expected. Too many executives want CRM deployed quickly and broadly because they think it will bring a rapid return on their investment. Not only do these executives underestimate the magnitude of the task, but they also fail to understand what the customer really wants from a business relationship. As a result, the very things they are doing to try to build and manage relationships with customers are all too often the things that are destroying those relationships. Customers don't want to be targeted like hunted animals. This is seen in studies of marketing channel use and as increased numbers of consumers opt out of mailing lists. Consumers want companies to make their lives easier and less stressful by not forcing them to do anything they don't want to do. With product and service options exploding on the Internet and through multichannel purchase opportunities, the balance of power has shifted to the customer, and the customer wants control.

The time has passed for customer relationship management (CRM); it's time to transition to customer empowerment and switch to customer management of relationships (CMR). CMR gives the customer the power to tell us what he's interested in and not interested in. For a customer relationship building initiative to be effective, it should be a well-managed process of turning control over to the customer. And that means letting customers tell you what kind of information they want, what level of service they want to receive, and how they want you to communicate with them—where, when, and how often.

Why CRM Doesn't Work is written to speak directly to the executives in companies of every size who are concerned with achieving a profitable return on their investments in building and maintaining customer relationships. It is an ideal solution for business people at all levels in all industries who want to stay ahead of the curve. This book will show you how to create business strategies and processes that put customers first and will help you develop a clearly defined plan for profitable return on customer-centric marketing investments.

Projecting a step beyond CRM, to CMR, this book shows by lesson and example how companies can improve the quality of peoples' lives while, at the same time, improving corporate profits. You'll find out why the current CRM isn't working, what needs to change, and how to apply the CMR philosophy at your company. You will learn why so many initiatives fail, a new view of customer service, and a new definition of permission marketing.

Part I of *Why CRM Doesn't Work*, "What's Not Working," takes you through the essential errors in CRM thinking, from not recognizing that the power is in the hands of the customer, to misunderstanding what CRM is all about, to misplacement of technology's role. This section explains the problems caused by failure to change from a culture of product-based management, and by lack of commitment from senior management. The case histories cover different marketing challenges and provide ideas that any business can put into action.

Part II, "What Needs to Change," explains specific alterations that must be made to current CRM programs and why. You will learn the new power of permission marketing, the most profitable role for e-mail in building customer relationships, and important rules for e-mail marketing. The ten commandments of personalization will show you how to balance personalization with privacy. In Chapter 10 you will learn the new role of loyalty cards. Chapter 12 shows how the traditional market-speak of branding hasn't helped most companies and how the new CMR can build strong brands one customer at a time.

Part III, "How to Change," is about updating both your mind-set and your approach to customer relations, and deciding whether or not CRM is important—or even right—for your business. You will see why "best customer service" can be a cause of failure for a CMR program and why you can't let every customer manage the relationship. In Chapter 15 you will learn the questions and rules for evaluating customers, and Chapter 16 has eight steps for your transition to CMR. Chapter 17 shows how you can transition to CMR without additional expense, and how to get a true return on investments in relationship-building initiatives.

Part IV, "A Look Ahead," will stretch your thinking about your market, and will show you what customers really want from mobile messaging. Chapter 22 demystifies customer lifetime value and shows how your company's stock can earn a higher multiple based on it's price-to-customer-relationship ratio. The Conclusion suggest the big-picture changes that will occur in a move to CMR, and directs the actions you can take today.

Throughout the book, you will learn from packaged goods giants like Kraft Foods, Procter & Gamble, and Budweiser; financial service leaders Charles Schwab and Fidelity; technology influentials Dell, IBM, and Hewlett-Packard; hospitality and travel firms Ritz-Carlton, Hilton Hotels, and EasyRentaCar; and retail champions Lands' End, Norm Thompson, Sports Authority, Radio Shack, Staples, Tower Records, eBags—even upscale retailer Prada. With examples from airlines, booksellers, banks, telecoms, newspapers, supermarkets, shopping centers, and theme parks, this book has an important message for everyone whose success depends on selling to customers: consumers, business-to-business, internal clients—any kind of customer.

Switching to the new CMR is a process of realizing you are not in charge and allowing the customer to guide your efforts. That's the only way companies will be able to build and sustain profitable relationships with customers. That shift is what this book is all about.

PART ONE

What's Not Working

Why Doesn't CRM Work?   1

Does the customer really want to be managed?

I'm not stupid. I read about what you guys call customer relationship management. Why doesn't it work for me? Companies ask for my preferences and I tell them what I want from them. Still, each offer is more meaningless than the last. Why doesn't your so-called CRM make my life easier?

MARKETERS HEAR THIS from so many customers that the question becomes, who's the enemy? Is the customer the enemy or was Pogo right: "We have met the enemy, and he is us"? Our customers are crying out for us to understand their individual needs. They tell marketers what they want, but we keep bothering them with irrelevant offers.

In the preface to *loyalty.com* (McGraw-Hill, 2000), my book about CRM and Internet marketing, I said: "CRM is now moving to the center of corporate strategy as a process of learning to understand the values that are important to individual customers and using that knowledge to deliver benefits the customer really wants and making it easier for the customer to do business with the company."

No one would question the fact that CRM has since moved to the center of corporate strategy. A Jupiter Media Metrix study reports that 74 percent of U.S. businesses spent more money on CRM infrastructure in 2001 than they did in 2000, with a majority increasing their spending by 25 to 50 percent. A Gartner Dataquest survey forecast that CRM services revenue would increase 15 percent in 2002.[1] A similar Gartner, Inc. survey reports 52 percent of respondents rated CRM as their highest business priority.[2] The same is true in Europe where a Cap Gemini Ernst & Young and Gartner survey of 242 senior marketing executives from 145 firms reports that 67 percent of respondent companies launched a CRM initiative between 1999 and 2001, and over one third consider CRM a top priority.

Taken together, what do these statistics mean? The acceptance of CRM has been confirmed. The enthusiasm for CRM has been proven. The investment in CRM has been quantified. But why have so many firms that have embarked on CRM initiatives failed to realize the kind of results they anticipated? In 2001 only one in five of all CRM solution providers actually realized a profit. As a group, solution providers lost $8.8 billion dollars, spending three dollars for every two dollars in revenue.[3] CRM has obviously not been the panacea many had hoped.

Is CRM Really About the Customer?

One reason CRM practice is at a standstill and why so many companies are failing to see a return on their CRM investment is that, because of its celebrity, the label "CRM" has been loosely (and often incorrectly) applied to anything that suggests customer-centricity. It is almost impossible to hear a common definition of CRM from industry experts, even among executives within the same company.

Some think CRM is a matter of technology. Some still believe it's just the process of segmenting customers. Some think it's a matter of selling efficiency. Many marketers still think CRM is just an advanced stage of database marketing—using your customer database to find which customers would be the right ones for a specific product offering. They don't yet understand that relationship building must start with an understanding of the customer's needs. They talk about "share of wallet" but fail to realize that you can't get access to the customer's wallet if you don't first have access to the customer's heart and mind. As our customer said in the beginning of this chapter, CRM ought to be about making her life easier. Do that first, and then you'll gain access to your customer's heart and mind.

CRM Practice at a Standstill

Industry consultant David Raab says, "Customer relationship management has now reached the awkward stage in its adoption cycle. The concept and its benefits are widely accepted, but few complete implementations are in place. What's lagging is CRM practice." It may just be that we're going about customer relationship management in all the wrong ways. Len Ellis, executive vice president of enterprise strategy, Wunderman, New York, says all the talk about CRM reminds him of what Voltaire said about the Holy Roman Empire:

> It's not holy, Roman or an empire. There's a certain degree to which CRM is not about the customer nor is it about relationships—at least not how it's practiced now. Marketing automation is fine, but it's not about the customer. Most marketing automation is about costs and speed. Selling efficiency is not about the customer, it's just about leveraging your resources. Value maximization, in terms of figuring out which of your customer segments are going to deliver the most top or bottom line, that's not about the customer. So a lot of the benefits that are claimed for CRM are really benefits that accrue to the enterprise, but have nothing to do with the customer.[4]

Handing Over the Car Keys

The fact that marketers must recognize the power of the customer is not a new concept. As far back as 1936 the American Marketing Society began publishing the semiannual *Journal of Marketing*. In the first issue John Benson, then president of the American Association of Advertising Agencies, talked about looking ahead after difficult days. Except for his outdated use of the personal pronoun, this excerpt could have been written today:

As a form of commercial intelligence advertising must keep abreast of this fast moving world. One has to run pretty fast these days to keep from falling back.

The depression undermined much that we had thought was solid as a rock. Seven lean and desperate years put all tradition to the test; billions of property lost; millions of people without jobs. Such a collapse could not occur without business itself being put to a drastic test. Our ideas of doing business have been challenged and are being weighed in the light of a new point of view as to what is economically sound.

...The common man is out for an equal chance to win; the buyer, be he large or small, wants full value for his money as much as anybody gets; and as you well know, the consumer is king.

Perhaps hereafter we shall use less ingenuity in the way of fanciful appeal and more in finding out what people really want. The consumer himself is boss.[5]

Today new technologies have given even greater power and freedom to customers. Customers, not companies, control the purchasing process today by having access to more information, and having it in real time. The Internet has given them unprecedented research tools. A customer shopping for a car today may enter a dealership with more knowledge about models, options, and price than the salesman on the showroom floor may be aware of—if she hasn't already made the purchase on the Web. What does this mean for marketers? That we need even greater ingenuity in finding out what people really want—and giving them control—than we did sixty-some years ago when John Benson gave us this advice.

People are more comfortable when they feel they are in command. We see this in simple things. For example, when I feel the first sign of a cold coming on, I start taking cold pills. For some reason I don't feel comfortable with the promise of the extended twelve-hour tablet. If I use the four-hour version, I feel more empowered to control the dosage. In a similar manner, customers want to determine the channels and dosage of marketing they receive. In a recent Yankelovitch study of marketing channel use, the need to control channels was constantly in the background of consumers' responses.[6] Larry Kimmel, chairman and CEO of Grey Direct talks about this consumer desire for control, giving his belief why both direct mail and catalogs remain in such high favor with consumers, even though responding via telephone and online or e-mail channels requires less effort.

Direct mailings and catalogs can be viewed when convenient, or easily ignored by a customer. "They're controllable," Kimmel says. "In the phone situation there is a possibility of being talked into upgrading. Some consumers don't want to engage in that."[7]

MOVING TOWARD CMR

Customers have shown they don't want to be hunted like prey. They don't want to be managed; they just want companies to make their lives easier and less stressful. They're not removing their names from mailing lists for defensive reasons. Rather it's an offensive lifestyle management tactic aimed at reconfiguring and improving— not severing—their connection with marketers.[8]

The time has passed for customer relationship management, which has been trying to make business better for the company. It's time to recast the discipline of CRM as one of greater customer empowerment. Customer management of relationships (CMR) makes doing business better for the customer. As a business strategy, CMR requires management change, not change management. CMR also requires operational and process changes that will allow the company to respond to individual customer's needs. Within your enterprise, CMR will touch every business and cultural area, every human relationship, and every technology.

CMR is not about launching yet another campaign, and it is not about formulating one more promotion. It is much more, even, than the sum of database marketing, targeted advertising, collecting information about customers, and offering new services. It is about creating an experience, personalizing the interaction with individual customers in ways directed by the customer, and thereby developing relationships.

Paul Greenburg, executive vice president of LiveWire Inc., talked about this customer empowerment in *CRM at the Speed of Light:*

CRM	CMR
The company is in control	The customer is in control
Makes business better for the company	Makes business better for the customer
Tracks customers by transaction	Understands customer's unique needs
Treats customers as segments	Treats customers as individuals
Forces customers to do what you believe they'll want	Lets customers tell you what they care about
Customers feel stalked	Customers are empowered
Organized around products and services	Organized around customers

Capturing and Keeping Customers in Internet Real Time (McGraw-Hill, 2001): "What is empowering is not forcing customers to do anything they don't want. Let the customers tell you what they care about." The new CMR is a process of turning power over to the customer: allowing the customer to tell us what she's interested in and not interested in, what kind of information she wants, what level of service she wants to receive, and how she wants us to communicate with her—where, when, and how often.

And customers will tell us what they care about. According to a 2001 survey sponsored by Teradata, a division of NCR, 80 percent of Americans are willing to share personal information with companies if it means getting more personal service. Sixty percent of those surveyed said companies that provide personal offers combining online and offline information about their shopping preferences offer an advantage that "makes life easier."[9] But customers will be disappointed if they never see a benefit from the information they give. If you are asking customers for sensitive information and aren't putting that information rapidly to use to make their lives easier, stop asking those questions. Collecting information that may some day prove useful is not just bad CRM; it is the opposite of what CRM should be.

UPDATING THE CONCEPT

Corporate boards have been swept away with enthusiasm for CRM because customer relationship management appeared to meet three of business's fundamental needs:

1 Understanding customers' buying behavior for better targeting of offers
2 Spreading customer information across the enterprise to allow customer-facing personnel to be more efficient
3 Creating greater operational efficiency to reduce expense

CRM still meets the three fundamental needs listed above, but the model has lost its luster. Companies that have failed to achieve benefits from CRM are beginning to realize their efforts have failed to meet the fundamental needs of the customer. David Bradshaw, an analyst at Ovum, likens CRM to a fashion industry. "Last year it seemed that CRM was all the rage. It was the hottest solution and companies spent millions to get a piece of it. Now, about one year later these same companies have a high-priced outfit that barely fits. But I tend to agree with the analysts, authors, and other industry pundits—CRM is not an outdated leisure suit. It's merely stumbled on the catwalk and with a little time it will prove to be as essential as the little black dress."[10]

Fulfilling Bradshaw's forecast will require more than just a little time. It will call for a re-examination and re-evaluation of the CRM concept. Finding ways to empower the customer in the adoption cycle of a new CMR suggests a reappraisal of objectives. Companies that started CRM efforts to improve efficiency are now looking for ways to increase effectiveness. They are seeking new ways to do the right thing rather than just doing things right.

COMMON CAUSES OF FAILURE

Before starting on the new journey to CMR it will be a helpful exercise to review some of the causes of companies' failures to achieve benefits from existing CRM initiatives. Though the goal of the new CMR takes relationship building to a new level, the process relies on many of the same disciplines required for the old CRM, and we can learn a lot from past failures.

Too often executives want these initiatives deployed quickly and broadly because they want to see a prompt return on their investment. They see CRM as an easy solution to their business problems. It is only after the initiatives begin to unfold and become tangible that these individuals begin to realize the gaps in their expectations.

It's Not About the Technology

Sure, CRM means obtaining customer information, understanding what different customers are worth, treating different customers differently, and improving efficiency. But none of these goals should define the route to success.

In 1998 three professors, Susan Fournier, Susan Dobscha, and David Glen Mick, wrote an article called "The Premature Death of Customer Relationship Management." They said in part:

> Companies profess to do relationship marketing in new and better ways every day. Unfortunately, a close look suggests that relationships between companies and consumers are troubled at best. When we talk to people about their lives as consumers, we do not hear praise for their so-called partners. Instead, we hear about the confusing, stressful, insensitive and manipulative marketplace in which they feel trapped and victimized. Companies may delight in learning more about their customers than ever before and in providing features and services to please every possible palate. But customers delight in neither. Customers cope.[11]

In the four years since that article appeared little has changed. One of the reasons that so little has changed is that businesses continue to try to implement CRM as a technology, not as a marketing practice—a one-dimensional exchange of money for goods that one writer described as luring marketers ever further down a cul-de-sac. This is, all too often, due to the automation of obsolete processes and people believing that technology alone can change results without having to change what they really do or what they really believe.

For results to change, there needs to be a change in the process and the philosophy behind it.

The Challenge of Management Culture

In many companies, product-based management is so entrenched in management culture that the switch to anything different is a significant challenge. More than half of CRM failures have been blamed on the challenges of company politics, inertia, and implementing organizational change—not software and not budgets.

A study by CRM-Forum detailed the significance of nine different causes of failures for CRM initiatives:[12]

Organizational change	29%
Company politics and inertia	22%
Lack of CRM understanding	20%
Poor planning	12%
Lack of CRM skills	6%
Budget problems	4%
Software problems	2%
Bad advice	1%
Other	4%

None of these causes suggests external reasons for CRM failure. With 29 percent of failures caused by problems with organizational change, it's clear that the most difficult step for customer-based initiatives is the cultural change required.

In most companies, parts and pieces of the customer information base are sequestered in separate departmental silos, and department heads can be like tribal chieftains. The marketing tribe has its culture, IT another, and financial, operations, merchandising, human resources, and product managers still more. Turf wars have been the undoing of CRM, and will prove to be even more of an obstacle for CMR initiatives.

Remaking a company to be genuinely customer-centric is new and uncharted territory for many, and as with anything new, there is always resistance to change. CMR requires new ways of thinking for everyone. It's not something that can happen in a vacuum; it will affect the whole business. Companies must encourage the exchange of information, not just with customers but within the enterprise, yet it has been reported that only 5 percent of investments being made into CRM are going toward change management.

Sounds easy, and might be were it not for politics. In companies, politics polarize people and groups as people feel they may lose power, or even their jobs. Change often forces people to regress to what they know, and protect what they have always been comfortable with.

CRM Misunderstood

Even when companies survive the challenges of organizational change, company politics, and inertia, another fifth stumble on their understanding of what CRM is all about. Some think it's all about technology and fail to align technology with strategy. Some think it's all about targeting customers and customer groups for special offers. They see CRM as a simple matter of capturing names and addresses and linking this identification to customer transactions to cross-sell and up-sell. They don't understand the importance of the customer in the process. META Group has reported that many of the CRM initiatives in the largest companies are in "serious risk of failure" because few are using applications that enable proper collaboration with customers. Gartner Group reports that although CRM will remain a key initiative within many enterprises, 65 percent will fail "to align senior executive, IT, management, functional/departmental management and customer outcomes."

Lack of Planning

Poor planning is often the result of fuzzy strategy. The first question a focused strategy must address is who are the right customers for your business. Who are the customers that can provide you with the business rewards you need to grow, and which are the ones you can successfully serve? Where can you find them and what activities will you require to capture and keep them? Can you align CMR with your profitable growth objectives and company goals?

Goals are the broad statements about what you want your company to be when it grows up. Objectives are the specific measurable actions that will support your strategies. Financial objectives might include: increase incremental revenue, reduce operating costs, improve profitability, and provide a quantifiable process improvement. Sales and marketing objectives might include: increase sales and marketing efficiency and effectiveness; increase average customer purchase dollars; increase customer purchases; increase number of products per purchase; increase customer profitability; increase customer loyalty, retention, and lifetime value; and gain and sustain competitive advantage. Specific objectives translate the larger goal into measurable tasks. For example, if the goal is retention, the specific objective might be to reduce attrition by 15 percent in the most profitable customer segment.

Poor planning affects the company's view of its interaction with customers and increases the opportunity of implementing an initiative that addresses the wrong issues. Planning for CMR must be based on creating new initiatives that will make doing business better for the customer. As you will see in Chapter 18, CMR planning includes taking small steps to reach the larger goal. The only good thing that can be said about poor planning is that without a strategy and a plan, failure comes as a surprise, saving you fear and worry.

Lack of Skills

The lack of CRM skills is understandable. Sales managers, product managers, sales personnel, and others interacting with customers have all grown in their jobs selling whatever the company wants to sell to as many customers as possible. Many companies are creating sophisticated customer relationship management technology without realizing that such sophisticated tools require sophisticated users and that their users will need training. For CMR they must develop new skills to create offerings based on customer needs and to develop customer-centric service strategies—a giant leap. To make the leap successfully, the right tools must be in the hands of line-level personnel who have been trained to use the tools for the customers' benefit.

A recent study of 400 CRM implementations worldwide concluded that 25 percent of the explained variation between successful and unsuccessful CRM initiatives is due to variations in line-level training and support.[13]

Inadequate Budget

Budget problems are only 4 percent of the causes of CRM failure. Six or seven-figure budgets, multiyear implementations, and swelling IT staffs are not inevitable. A study by the Seattle, Washington–based Data Warehouse Institute shows that 13 percent of companies surveyed spent over $10 million on CRM solutions, but 40 percent spent less than $500,000 and 16 percent of the companies studied are spending under $100,000 to realize measurable benefits.[14]

Inefficient Software

So much progress has been made in recent years that we now see the software issues as a very small part of the challenge. Still some failures come from companies asking the in-house IT team to reinvent the wheel—creating a proprietary query tool that often ends up as an extension of transaction processing and fails to provide the analysis and intelligence that deliver the real value. With so many tried and true solutions available in the market today, good out-of-the-box programs exist for companies of almost any size. The few software problems we see today are not coming from faulty software but are a result of attempting to automate faulty processes. Most often it's the process that needs to be fixed, not the software.

CRM-Forum's Richard Forsyth likes to say, "If a company's fundamental premise is that the customer is a bleeding nuisance, then all the software packages in the world are not going to improve the situation. All that's going to happen is that the lousy customer service stance will become more automated so that companies can be indifferent to their customers more easily."[15]

ROI Expectations

There are more than enough elements with which to build an ROI (return on investment) model: incremental improvement in "share of wallet," customer retention, increased margin, or expense savings. Telecom companies will want to reduce customer churn that can be up to 40 percent, and to sell more data and other communication services. Financial services companies will want to cross-sell more products, and reduce transaction costs. Insurance firms will want to increase customer retention. Retailers will want customers to increase their basket value. Yet, a study that interviewed CRM heads at fifty companies reported that 90 percent of them have no ROI model in place.[16] This may be because so many CRM vendors tout their solutions as "plug and play." In any event, the lack of measurable metrics—a lack of definition of what return on investment is expected—established at the start has been the cause of many failures. The importance of establishing metrics for the ROI model is discussed in detail in Chapter 17.

Lack of Commitment

Without a solid and total commitment from the most senior management, any CRM project will fail. The company must change its core strategy to focus on customer-centricity if the shift is to be made to customer control. This means the program must have a dedicated senior executive with the strength to sell the program throughout the organization as its champion, assuring the company's commitment.

Profit from CMR will grow over time. CMR will require patience and a belief in the durability of the customer-centric concept. Without a champion to sustain this belief, the project will fail.

A LOOK AT CRM INITIATIVES

Companies in almost every industry are trying to use customer information to manage relationships. The proliferation of loyalty programs is one example. More recently the ease of customer communication through the use of e-mail has spawned a torrent of attempts to develop what some marketers consider CRM dialog. Few of these efforts have been developed with an understanding of their CMR potential.

Loyalty Programs

The airline industry provides the best and the worst examples of current initiatives. It introduced the concept of loyalty cards long before anyone talked about CRM or database marketing. When American Airlines launched its AAdvantage Program in 1981 the term *frequent flyer* was born and loyalty marketing was changed forever.

In the earlier days of the airlines' loyalty programs, American and United and the others who soon followed tracked little more than flight miles customers could accumulate for free award flights. Over the years as they have captured more and more knowledge about their millions of customers, the airlines have adopted the fundamental rules of CRM:

- Obtain individual information about customers
- Understand what different customers are worth
- Treat different customers differently

They have done this in outstanding fashion with the creation of valuable perks for the best customers. This year I will complete five million miles with American Airlines, and American knows it. Like other Executive Platinum AAdvantage members I get to board early while there is still room in the overhead for my roll-a-board, and I get frequent upgrades. I save time at check-in with the Executive Platinum line, and since 9/11 American has added VIP Executive Platinum lines at the security checkpoints at some airports.

Beyond Executive Platinum status my multimillion-mile history earns special surprise gifts sent personally by Michael Gunn, American's senior vice president of marketing: ice-cream toppings, interesting books, even crystal glassware from Tiffany, all greatly appreciated. This is neat stuff and certainly indicates American's desire to manage customer relationships (CRM), but it's not yet customer management of relationships (CMR).

As beguiling as these perks are, they have not been personalized. All Executive Platinum members get the same early boarding and upgrade privileges, and it is safe to assume that whatever percentage of flyers are selected for the special gifts, they all receive the same books and glassware. Going one step further—with CMR—would mean delivering services that address my personal desires. I enjoy a drink now and then on long flights, but I don't care for Bombay Sapphire or Tanqueray. How thoughtful would it be for American to stock Beefeaters, my favorite gin, when they know I will be on a flight, just as they already can provide me with a vegetarian special meal? Or for them to include the current issue of *Yachting* magazine aboard my flights because they know I am a sailing fanatic.

Please believe me, I'm not picking on American Airlines. My flying experience makes me believe American Airlines is the best. I've logged over a million miles on several other airlines and they, too, offer perks that show me they are treating different customers differently. But the industry's customer differentiation is still designed around their product and their services, not around individual customer needs. Customers don't want to be treated equally. They want to be treated individually.

It's as if companies believe the technologies that allow them to capture customer data will allow them to change results without having to change what they do. They haven't, yet, invited customers to be part of the process, understanding that the customer can add value to the product.

They ask if I'll need a rental car (a purely generic offer). Why can't they know my limousine preference and book my limo right along with the flight? Why can't they know my first hotel choice is Hilton and offer to reserve my preferred room near the elevator as part of the airline reservation—maybe even include the wake-up call? In the true sense of CMR, they should be able to allow me to manage my complete travel experience, with their help, with a single phone call or mouse click. Some could argue that this is asking the airlines to function as travel agents. Since all of the airlines have now reduced or, in many cases eliminated, travel agents' commissions, forcing agents to charge service fees, perhaps the airlines could even add a small charge for this extra customer service. As the

How Much Empowerment Is Too Much?

Here is one of the most creative stories I could find about a customer looking for empowerment. It's a letter from a long-time customer of a bank.[17]

Dear Sir:

I am writing to thank you for bouncing the check with which I endeavored to pay my plumber last month. By my calculations some three nanoseconds must have elapsed between his presenting the check, and the arrival in my account of the funds needed to honor it.

I refer, of course, to the automatic monthly deposit of my entire salary, an arrangement which, I admit, has only been in place for eight years. You are to be commended for seizing that brief window of opportunity, and also for debiting my account with $50 by way of penalty for the inconvenience I caused to your bank. My thankfulness springs from the manner in which this incident has caused me to rethink my errant financial ways.

You have set me on the path of fiscal righteousness. No more will our relationship be blighted by these unpleasant incidents, for I am restructuring my affairs this year taking as my model the procedures, attitudes and conduct of your very bank. I can think of no greater compliment, and I know you will be excited and proud to hear it.

To this end, please be advised about the following changes. I have noticed that whereas I personally attend to your telephone calls and letters, when I try to contact you I am confronted by the impersonal, ever-changing, prerecorded, faceless entity which your bank has become.

From now on I, like you, choose only to deal with a flesh and blood person. My mortgage and loan repayments will, therefore and hereafter, no longer be automatic, but will arrive at your bank, by check, addressed personally and confidentially to an employee of your branch, whom you must nominate. You will be aware that it is an offense under the Postal Act for any other person to open such an envelope.

Please find attached an Application for Authorized Contact Status which I require your chosen employee to complete. I am sorry it runs to eight pages, but in order that I know as much about him or her as your bank knows about me, there is no alternative.

Please note that all copies of his or her medical history must be countersigned by a Justice of the Peace, and that the mandatory details of his/her financial situation (income, debts, assets and liabilities) must be accompanied by documented proof.

In due course I will issue your employee with a PIN number which he/she must quote in all dealings with me. I regret that it cannot be shorter than 28 digits but, again, I have modeled it on the number of button presses required to access my account balance on your phone bank service. As they say, imitation is the sincerest form of flattery.

Let me level the playing field even further by introducing you to my new telephone system, which you will notice, is very much like yours. My Authorized Contact at your bank, the only person with whom I will have any dealings, may call me at any time and will be answered by automated voice.

Press buttons as follows:

1 To make an appointment to see me
2 To query a missing payment
3 To transfer the call to my living room in case I am there
4 To transfer the call to my bedroom in case I am sleeping
5 To transfer the call to my toilet in case I am attending to nature
6 To transfer the call to my mobile phone in case I am not at home
7 To leave a message on my computer, a password to access my computer is required: password will be communicated at a later date to the Authorized Contact
8 To return to the main menu and listen carefully to options 1 through 7
9 To make a general complaint or inquiry. The Authorized Contact will then be put on hold, pending the attention of my automated answering service. While this may on occasion involve a lengthy wait, uplifting music will play for the duration. This month I've chosen a refrain from "The Best of Woody Guthrie":

> "Oh, the banks are made of marble,
> With a guard at every door,
> And the vaults are filled with silver,
> That the miners sweated for."

After twenty minutes of that, our mutual Contact will probably know it by heart. On a more serious note, we come to the matter of cost. As your bank has often pointed out, the ongoing drive for greater efficiency comes at a cost, a cost which you have always been quick to pass on to me.

Let me repay your kindness by passing some costs back. First, there is the matter of advertising material you send me. This I will read for a fee of $20 per page. Inquiries from your Authorized Contact will be billed at $5 per minute of my time spent in response. Any debits to my account, as, for example, in the matter of the penalty for the dishonored check, will be passed back to you. My new phone service runs at 75 cents a minute (even Woody Guthrie doesn't come for free), so you would be well advised to keep your inquiries brief and to the point.

Regrettably, but again following your example, I must also levy an establishment fee of 2% of my balance or $50 (whichever is more) to cover the setting up of this new arrangement.

May I wish you a happy, if ever-so-slightly less prosperous, New Year.

Your humble client.

You may say that's a bit more empowerment than you are ready for, but this client didn't wait for his bank to initiate CMR. He took over the management of the relationship on his own.

Teradata survey indicated, customers would be willing to answer questions and give personal information in order to get these more personalized services.

This is the magic of bringing the customer into the process to help manage the relationship—added value for the customer and added value for the company. The customer's life is made simpler and the company develops new revenue streams.

E-Mail

I really shouldn't pick on the airlines when there are firms in many other sectors that are worse offenders. I don't spend as much at Neiman Marcus as I do with the airlines but I do have a relationship with them. When I open my e-mail in the morning I really don't care about the "new sunny looks" from the N/M resort collections. I don't think any of the hot swimwear, straw totes, fresh fashions, or romantic sandals are right for me. I wonder why someone at Neiman's thinks they are, and wish they would ask me what I am interested in.

There are folks who do just that. And some do it badly. For example, one bookseller I deal with sent the following request:

Hello, Fred Newell

Hmm. We were unable to find any titles to recommend after looking at your purchase history.

Help us create useful recommendations for you by telling us about your interests with the Recommendations Explorer.

I did what they asked, and the next screen said,

WELCOME TO
Your Recommendations

Exploring products or interests that you are familiar with and clicking "I own it" or "not interested" will help us generate recommendations personalized for you. To refine your results, click "more like this."

I did exactly as they asked, checking off my preferences for several categories of business books and some on sailing. I have gotten several offers since that dialog but all have been offers for Tea of the Month, *Snow White and the Seven Dwarfs*, *The Mummy Returns* DVD, *The Best of Martha Stewart Living*, and the latest Diana Krall CD—none of which match preferences on my list!

For all their good words about wanting to create useful recommendations for me, this company is not letting me manage the relationship. They still come across as trying to do more for their sales curve than trying to do more for their customer. If they are asking customers for sensitive information and aren't using that information to the customer's benefit, they should stop asking those questions.

It Won't Be Easy

If all of this sounds like CMR is hard, that's because it is. The problems inherent in implementing a customer relationship management project pale in comparison to the challenge of achieving benefits from customer management of relationships. It's a giant step from CRM with its goal of making business better for the company to CMR, trying to make life better for the customer. It will require a clear understanding of what CMR is and a willingness for companies to change the ways they interact with customers.

It's Not a Question of the Chicken or the Egg 2

It's not technology that drives relationships

THE KEY LESSONS FOR CRM SUCCESS have not been technical, but organizational. Software problems rank low on the list of causes for failure of CRM initiatives. And yet, our experience working with organizations of every size has been that companies want to start with the technology decisions.

They spend a tremendous amount of time and energy looking for a technological solution without having first established a clear business case with goals and objectives and metrics to identify the results they hope to achieve. They don't understand it's not technology that drives CRM, it's intelligence about the customer. James Goodnight, CEO of SAS Institute, the world's largest privately held software company, says, "Take customer relationship management but leave the intelligence behind and what do you have? Just a fancy Rolodex."[1]

Technology vendors are often responsible for this disconnect. At the CRM Expo in New York City in August 2002, keynoter Martha Rogers, Ph.D., founding partner of the Peppers and Rogers Group, hammered home the point that strategy comes first, before technology. Yet, on the floor of the Javits Center, where the Expo was held, vendors talked only of the technology with no mention of an overarching strategy.[2]

THE IMPORTANCE OF PLANNING

The customer management of relationships is a combination of processes, people, and technology. Notice that technology is the last of these. Despite the fact that 74 percent of U.S. businesses spent more on CRM technology in 2001 than they did in 2000 (as much as 50 percent more), fewer than half of IT managers surveyed by Unisys Corporation report a positive return on their IT spending. The survey of IT executives at 200 businesses reports 44 percent show a positive return on IT investments, 42 percent report a level return, and 14 percent a negative return.[3]

Don Neal, senior vice president of marketing at Rapp Collins Worldwide, may say it best: "Whereas companies have much to gain from CRM, the pitfalls of spending before planning are real and perilous. Those that apply a great deal of rigor in analyzing their CRM goals and objectives will be the most successful."[4]

Certainly identifying, extracting, and transforming customer data into usable information to achieve critical business objectives requires technology. But the business objectives must be defined before the search for the technological solution starts.

STRATEGY

Through analyst fieldwork with their clients, research and consulting firm Gartner, Inc. saw that successful enterprises have become more aware of focusing on customer satisfaction rather than technological applications. Gartner identified eight distinct layers or building blocks used by the world's leading businesses to reach excellence in CRM.

- **Vision:** leadership, market position, value proposition
- **Strategy:** objectives, segments, effective interaction
- **Valued experience for the customer**
- **Organizational collaboration**
- **Processes:** customer life cycle, knowledge management
- **Information:** data, analysis, one view across channels
- **Technology:** applications, architecture, infrastructure
- **Metrics:** retention, satisfaction, loyalty, cost to serve[5]

Note that they ranked CRM technology next to last. They also conclude that too many CRM initiatives suffer from an inward focus on the enterprise, whereas the point of CRM is to achieve a balance between value to shareholders or stakeholders and value to customers for a mutually beneficial relationship. Their long-range prediction reinforces the argument for getting the strategy right before searching for the technology: "Through 2005, enterprises that use a strategic CRM framework to estimate, plan and promote their CRM initiatives while building up their capabilities in small piloted steps are twice as likely to achieve planned business benefits as enterprises that pursue projects without a framework."[6]

Others agree the question of technology comes at the end. Professor Adrian Payne of the Cranfield School of Management in the United Kingdom puts questions about the CRM process in this order:

- **Process 1: strategic development process.** Where are we and what do we want to achieve? Who are the customers that we want, and how should we segment them?
- **Process 2: value creation process.** How should we deliver value to our customers? How should we maximize the lifetime value of the customers we want?
- **Process 3: the multichannel integration process.** What are the best ways for us to get to customers and for customers to get to us? What does the outstanding customer experience, deliverable at an affordable cost, look like?
- **Process 4: information management process.** How should we organize information on customers? How can we 'replicate' the mind of the customer?
- **Process 5: performance assessment process.** How can we create increased profits and shareholder value? How should we measure our results, set standards, and improve our performance?[7]

Again, the technology issue is addressed near the end, right before final performance assessment. All of what David Scholes called the "good common marketing sense" comes first.

A Good Example

One of the best examples of a company moving successfully to CMR comes from a Seklemian/Newell retail client. The company has a long and profitable history of efficient database marketing that produced sales, but those activities have not moved customers up the loyalty ladder and have not resulted in increased customer retention. When the firm made the decision to develop a CMR initiative, they did not start by looking for a simple technology solution; they began by taking a careful look at the current business environment and making a business case for CMR.

The company established goals and objectives at the start based on the company's vision, a definition of the customers the company wanted, the current experience these customers were having with the company, and the customer experience the company hoped to deliver to the specified group. A study of current business requirements, work flow, operational processes, and their interdependencies helped to create a road map. From here they could see the factors critical for success, establish the strategic imperatives, and identify the management change that would be required.

Only after the new business plan, strategy, and deliverables were confirmed did the company start to identify gaps in the functionality of its existing technology. It was a full year of such planning before the company was ready to take their CMR initiatives to customers, and another six months of small pilot tests to prove their capabilities before any enterprisewide activities were considered.

As this is written, the company is about to roll the program out on a broader scale. They are confident that these preliminary steps—the rigorous analysis of goals and objectives and understanding of the management and process change required—will assure success of their CMR initiative.

Successful CMR initiatives must start with such a thorough analysis and a clear definition of business objectives to make a strong business case for the project. This must be followed by a study of the organizational and operational changes that will be required to enable your company to empower customers. Only after this strategic CMR framework is in place is it time to look for the final technology solution.

"One Girl in a Convertible..." 3

It takes more than a database

MARKETING TO CUSTOMERS based on their purchase history data was what we did with CRM, and it worked for what we were trying to do—sell more of what we wanted to sell. But marketing based on the transaction database alone is not enough for CMR, where we are trying to serve the consumers or businesses by getting them to show us the solutions that will serve their needs.

This chapter's title comes from a Warren Buffett letter to shareholders in which he said, "One girl in a convertible is worth five in the phone book." He was explaining why he avoided the allure of the dot-com stock boom and kept his investments in companies with proven performance. For marketers it might be changed to: One customer who will communicate personal needs to us is worth five names in our database.

CONNECTING

The world changed after September 11, 2001, challenging marketers to reflect—as *human beings*, not just as marketers—on what their customer messages should be going forward. The United States was already mired in a recession, unemployment levels had risen, retail sales were flat, consumer debt remained high, and now the country was at war.

In times like these it would be presumptuous and foolish to believe that a transactional database could still provide the correct guidance for reaching our very confused and frightened customers. Never before in our history has the need been greater for establishing, nurturing, and creating strong relationships—and this holds true for both business-to-consumer relationships and business-to-business relationships. Customers want a sense of security; that can't be achieved solely through targeted offers.

At the start of a chapter in his excellent book, *All-to-One* (McGraw-Hill, 2002), Steve Luengo-Jones quotes John McKean of the Center for Information Based Competition in Ohio. The quote captures our challenge: "Some 70 percent of delivering customer value is about making the customer feel like a human being. This is the most profoundly simple idea that everyone in the customer arena seems to miss."[1] Steve goes on in that chapter to reinforce the point: "You have to get close to your customers, as close as possible, understand them, direct at each one of them all the good and appropriate benefits your company has to offer, communicate with each one of them in all the ways open to you, find out what each one wants or needs or both, then provide it for them."[2]

That's what CMR requires; getting as close to your customers as possible and using customer intelligence, not just collecting customer data, but connecting. And connecting means more than being available on the Web.

ASKING THE RIGHT QUESTIONS

The results of ignoring customer intelligence and relying solely on customer data have been compared by one writer to steering a tanker by observing its wake. That's what CRM practitioners have been doing for years, and it has often created problems. CRMGuru.com reports the story of a vice president of a large auto manufacturer who increased production of lime green cars after noticing a spike in quarterly sales numbers for such cars. It turned out that dealers were slashing prices of the hard-to-sell cars to get them off the lot. The company lost millions. If the VP had asked the right questions, he would have received the right intelligence.[3]

We had a similar experience with one of our retail clients. I was talking about what we could learn by tracking sales of trend items. One of the buyers left the room and came back with the report that a swimsuit with a zipper down the front had sold twenty-three units the day before. He immediately reordered, only to learn later that the twenty-three units sold in one day were a result of a high school swim team selecting the suit as the team uniform. Just as in the first example, if the buyer had asked the right questions, he would have received the right information.

Personalization

Research shows that the critical element in providing a positive customer experience lies in personalized and proactive service. Nearly 75 percent of one study's participants said that personalization was a major factor in their "most satisfying" purchase experience, on or off the Web. Seventy-three percent of the most positive customer experiences were due to personalization such as self-service, personalized voice or e-mail interactions, the ability to track purchases and requests, and knowledgeable customer service. Thirty-four percent of respondents cited a lack of personalized customer care in their "least satisfying" customer experience.[4]

Connecting with the customer and finding ways to provide a positive customer experience go far beyond the initial transaction. The more you can "delight" customers the more they will come back. Denny Hatch, contributing editor of *Target Marketing*, tells the story of a man who bought a $45,000 Lexus and experienced something memorable on his way home from the dealership when he turned on the radio and discovered a very small bit of personalized proactive service.

Hatch reports,

> His favorite classical music station came on in splendid quadraphonic sound. He pushed the second button; it was his favorite news station. The third button brought his favorite talk station that kept him awake on long trips. The fourth button was set to his daughter's

favorite rock station. Every button was set to his specific tastes. The new owner knew the car was smart, but was it psychic? No, the mechanic at Lexus took the trouble to note the radio setting on his trade-in and duplicated them on the new Lexus. What this technician did cost Lexus nothing—not one red cent. Yet it solidified the relationship. Customer delight? More like customer delirium. During the coming years, Lexus would have to screw up real time to negate that divine moment and cause the owner to switch to a Jag, a Mercedes or a Caddie.[5]

Dallas-based ClubCorp, a company operating 115 private golf courses, understands this kind of proactive service. Its employees work hard to learn things about their customers that will enable the company to empower them, like whether they want to be the driver or the passenger in the cart. With this knowledge they know ahead of time how to load up the cart. They even try to learn customers' drink preferences so the right beverage is on the cart when the golfers arrive or is available for them on the roaming drink cart.[6]

Customer Loyalty

I learned a lot about empowerment and customer loyalty from Kenneth Kanady, education enablement manager of KANA, a leading provider of external-facing CRM solutions in Natick, Massachusetts. Kanady wrote a thoughtful paper he called, "Confessions of a Loyal Customer...When Being Satisfied Is Just No Longer Satisfying." His paper is both a personal and professional perspective from a very, very loyal customer who also happens to be a corporate enablement manager within the CRM industry. He starts with six important messages:

1 Customer loyalty is influenced as much by your customer's emotions and learning capacity as your own company's products, services, processes, and prices.

2 Customer loyalty is a rare gift given to only a few over a lifetime.

3 Customer loyalty is not normally admitted aloud because its roots are not very well understood even by customers themselves.

4 The three key elements of customer loyalty are: engagement, enablement, and empowerment. The presence of all three can be significantly differentiating—the lack of one can be devastating.

5 Whereas customer satisfaction and customer confidence can be well managed and measured up close, customer loyalty is not really manageable at all and is best assessed from afar.

6 Stop offering special deals designed to get loyalty. Such things just don't work.

Kanady defines engagement as the capacity that "helps me feel connected and affiliated .... Being able to engage them whenever, wherever and how I choose, conveys to me they are growing, open and accessible." He explains that enablement creates the state of "achieving desired outcomes through the use of a business's products or services," and saves his strongest words for empowerment:

> Empowerment is the feeling that customers develop 'about them-selves' as a result of interacting with a company through its people, products, processes or services. Empowerment is what differentiates a 'repeat' customer from a loyal customer. I view customer loyalty as the steadfast emotional allegiance or commitment given to a business, product, brand or person. As such, loyalty is an emotional state of empowerment. It's empowerment that keeps me coming back for more ... keeps me loyal.[7]

Customer Empowerment

The advertising agency Brann Worldwide agrees that customers have taken control and says, "We're not helping sellers sell anymore. We're helping buyers buy." The following case history explains how the company's approach has changed:[8]

Bermuda was facing stiff competition for tourists from other islands, cruises, and even Europe. Although general media coverage had raised awareness of Bermuda's appeal, conversion of leads was still lagging. The tourism industry was able to reverse a ten-year decline by connecting with customers and giving them the information they wanted, the way they wanted it.

In the past when prospects called 1-800-BERMUDA, the phone reps asked only for their name and address and processed the callers' requests by sending generic materials, the same information to each prospect.

With Brann's help, the call center has been transformed into a customer-oriented service center that interacts with the prospects to determine what sort of vacation they are considering. A customized print-on-demand package is created around each prospect's individual interests. With 11,000 possible variations, each package offers prospects the exact information they want. An e-mail is sent to those with Web access directing them to their own personalized Bermuda website which the system builds on the fly. The process of connecting with the customer continues with follow-up communications immediately after the customer's visit to the island and even an "anniversary-of-your-visit" mailing to encourage a return trip.

By probing for details of callers' lifestyles, learning what callers really want from their vacation, and using that intelligence for connecting with the customer, Brann has created a completely personalized buyer's experience, giving power to the customer.

And it's the customer experience that counts. Good customer experiences drive satisfaction, trust, and loyalty. Poor customer experiences have the opposite effect and can do great harm. According to a Brann Worldwide study "Marketing Practices That Drive Customers Away," up to 50 percent of customers surveyed are so irked by common experiences of marketing, sales, and customer service practices that they're ready and willing to stop doing business with the companies. Poor customer experiences often come from simple things: irrelevant offers, uninformed sales people, delays in answering—or even failure to answer—inquiries. It doesn't take much to annoy customers.

"It's no secret that companies are alienating current and potential customers," says Nancy Hallberg, executive vice president and North American insight director at Brann. "Our findings suggest that the depth of the problem is much greater than most companies realize. If even a percentage of disgruntled customers vote with their wallets, many companies will experience losses ranging from 15 to 30 percent."[9]

When customers get fed up, they aren't just leaving—they are also engaging in anti-advocacy, warning friends, coworkers, and family about bad experiences through word of mouth, e-mail campaigns, and Internet chat rooms. Yet one more reason to take a fresh look at how we improve customer relationships and win loyalty.

The Internet Community

In the above context, the Internet is an enemy, but it can also be a friend. It is important to remember that the original intent of the World Wide Web was to facilitate interaction among people of similar interests. We now call this community. Because people are more loyal to communities than they are to companies, community on the Internet can be a powerful force.

For example, when NASA set out to produce a map of Mars, it invited the Internet community to help identify more than 40,000 craters on the Martian surface. In a single day, more than 90,000 entries were recorded—1.9 million in two months. NASA called the work of these volunteers "virtually indistinguishable from the input of a geologist with years of experience in identifying Mars craters."[10] The "customers" responded primarily to the opportunity to be part of that 90,000, not out of loyalty to NASA. But now they feel they have a special relationship with that agency.

Companies like Mercury Interactive, which provides indexes of business-to-business software products and services, are creating online communities where customers can gather to trade tips on how to fix problems and how to make best use of a product. The businesses can essentially eavesdrop on such discussions to get smarter about dealing with customers. Analysts say that by setting up and monitoring these online communities, companies can reduce customer service inquiries and sift through the dialog to glean valuable information from customers more efficiently than in the past.[11]

The folks at Dell understand this. On Dell's Web-based service site you get access to a community of other Dell owners who ask questions and provide helpful answers. Of course, this is not surprising since Michael Dell founded his company on the principle of finding out precisely what the customers want and allowing them to have it exactly their way.

Another successful company, eBags, which sells luggage and over 4,000 related products, has had monthly sales growth of 50 percent since its launch in 1999. Their interactive site asks customers to return thirty days after purchasing to rate the products they bought, and more than 30 percent do. To reward this behavior, eBags posts all of their shoppers' opinions on price/value, appearance, durability, and overall performance (good or bad), and whether the buyers would purchase the product again. Close to one quarter of eBags's customers offer testimonials, and these are also shared with the community.[12]

Both eBags and Dell were ranked tops in their category by the Direct Marketing Association study, *The Merchandising Scan*, released in January 2002; and in June 2002 in the 3rd Annual I.Merchants Awards, eBags tied with Orvis for website of the year.

To help companies develop this sense of community for customers, a San Diego company called Akonix has developed a way for online shoppers to talk to each other in addition to sales associates. People can see who is logged into a store's site as well as who is looking at a specific item. Shoppers can trade information about products and about their experiences with the company or its goods.

Akonix founder Dimitry Shapiro says, "Since the beginning of human time we have relied on the opinions of other people to help in our decision-making process." That's the kind of reassurance we need, but all that's missing online. Shapiro reports that the human interaction increases sales because it gives people a sense of community within a website. "Right now," he says, "people don't feel any loyalty or obligation to make purchases online because they can easily leave a website."[13]

Communities help us tap into the emotions of consumers. Kjell Nordstrom of the Stockholm School of Economics says, "Emotion is the great differentiator in a world where sameness increasingly rules. In an excess economy, success comes from attracting the emotional consumer, not the rational one. Companies can tap into the emotions of consumers by focusing on a specific tribe."[14]

In their preface to *Emotion Marketing: The Hallmark Way of Winning Customers for Life* (McGraw-Hill, 2001), Scott Robinette and Claire Brand write, "If there's one thing we've learned after nearly

The Kraft Online Community

One company that understands the power of community is Kraft Foods. At www.kraftfoods.com you'll see things like a place to store recipes, personalized tools to create meal plans to meet calorie requirements, the ability to update personal profiles or to request recipes by e-mail, and even a section called "The Wisdom of Mom," with shared ideas like these:

Sally—Wilbraham, Massachusetts:

We turn the heat up, get out our picnic blanket and our bathing suits and have a summer picnic in the living room, complete with grilled hot dogs, macaroni salad, and lemonade while the snow falls outside.

Gladine—Bolivar, Pennsylvania:

To make my mac&cheese extra fancy and dress it up a little bit, I put it in a casserole dish and layer Kraft singles over the top. Put it in a warm oven until the singles melt.

Kraft has customers doing the work that used to be done by its promotions department.

90 years of leadership in the relationship business, it's that *emotion matters*. From brand building and employee satisfaction to product leadership and customer loyalty, nearly every major success at Hallmark can be traced to effective creation, utilization, delivery, or exchange of emotional value."[15]

BEATING THE COMPETITION

Connecting to customers, listening to customers, and letting customers connect to each other have never been so important, and are all critical to CMR. Except under exceptional circumstances customers will accept only the products and services that fit their lifestyles, so the process of connecting means knowing more about your customer than current CRM practices make possible. It's not enough to know just what the customers buy, but also their preferences, aspirations, habits, and interests. You are allowing customers to manage the relationship when you know enough to offer products and services, on an individual basis, that you know to be useful to them personally. You will not only have a reason for the offering; you can also explain the reason to them.

In *The Myth of Excellence: Why Great Companies Never Try to Be the Best at Everything* (Crown Business, 2002), Fred Crawford and Ryan Mathews support this argument for the importance of connecting with customers. They talk of "Consumer Relevancy," suggesting that the new way for businesses to create a bond with their customers is to reflect fundamental human values such as trust, respect, dignity, and ease in their offerings. Customers, they say, are looking for human values showcased in every product or service the company offers. They want to be treated like human beings and not just a $26.95 transaction. They want respect, honesty, trust, and recognition as individual human beings, not just a 30 percent discount.

These authors head in the right direction, suggesting that through a focus on customer relevancy companies discover the difference that matters to consumers and develop a program for investments that are more productive and that improve financial performance. Their conclusion is that today's best companies select one of five attributes (price, product, service, experience, or access) on which to dominate the competition, add a second attribute on which to differentiate, and at least meet industry standards on the remaining three.[16]

We can build on such an approach, yet even it is still too generalized to take us to the level of individual customers—the signal weakness of most CRM initiatives today. Within any company's family of customers, different customers seek different levels of experience with the company. It's no longer good enough for a business to base its strategy on the "average" purchasing experience of price, product, service, or access. A successful business strategy must be based on empowering individual customers to allow them to develop the experience with the company on their terms.

Almost forty years ago, management guru Ted Levitt, talking about the purpose of a business being to create and keep a customer, advocated that the modern firm should "view the entire business process as consisting of a tightly integrated effort to discover, create, arouse, and satisfy customers' needs." Today, "customers" can best be amassed by offering "singular" service—presenting many relevant offerings to one customer, rather than settling for the subset of prospects who find one offer relevant. That requires creating a dialog with that one girl in the convertible and keeping her happy by meeting her unique needs.

Why Do We Have Two Ears and Only One Mouth? 4

The importance of dialog

W HY WOULD A BOAT BUILDER invite its customers for three- to four-day getaways? Because boating is an industry where customer relationships are most difficult to maintain. Due to the expense and difficulty of boating, 70 percent of boaters sell their boats after three years.

The makers of Sea Ray boats have learned the importance of listening to customers. They engage customers in relationship-building rendezvous at marinas and planned activities such as golf outings, mansion tours, and boat hopping. They even have a personal concierge service tending to boat owners' needs, checking in to see how they can help, even planning weekend jaunts. They know communication means a lot more than just talking *to* customers. That may be why Sea Ray's customer retention rate is the highest in the industry, nearly twice that of its closest competitor.

Customers are tired of being talked to based on information from a company's transaction database. Customers are now beginning to say, "Stop relying on information *about* me and start listening and paying attention to information *from* me."

Lester Wunderman, chairman emeritus of Wunderman Worldwide, a member of Young & Rubicam Global Communications Network in New York, says, "CRM is a process that builds more information, understanding and dialog between sellers and buyers. CRM is not advertising. It's not one-way anything. It implies dialog."[1]

GETTING STARTED

Getting your customers to talk to you doesn't require trendy, hi-tech stuff. One of our clients with a strong commitment to dialog has a firm policy: always ask one question in any customer communication. The company doesn't use complicated surveys. It asks simple questions, but does so on every account statement, every catalog, and even some sale notices. Surprisingly, they get more than a 20 percent response rate. When customers share their interests on returned postcards, on the phone, or via e-mail, the company learns a lot about what individual customers want and they deliver CMR.

Retail

Saks, Inc. entices its most valuable customers by offering a 10 percent discount on the next purchase for answers to a few simple questions. Their involvement allows customers to tell Saks, Inc. how they want the relationship to grow.

When Sears developed The Great Indoors (TGI), their highly successful new chain of stores, they started by having conversations with their female customers to understand exactly what frustrates them about shopping for home décor. They didn't ask what the customer wanted. They asked what frustrates her.

They learned the average customer spends twenty-five hours a week for eight weeks, visiting sixteen stores and making purchases in 3.8 of those stores in the process of redecorating a room. From dialog with customers, TGI also learned that customers didn't talk about faucets and tile and towels. They talked about rooms. From that simple feedback TGI planners merchandised the stores by rooms. There is no towel department or hardware department; there is a bathroom department that includes bath furniture, bath hardware, bath and accent rugs, shower curtains, spa products, and towels.

CEO Bob Rodgers credits the success of the stores to these conversations with customers. And to be sure the dialog continues, store buyers are required to spend 25 percent of their time on the floor listening to customers.

Banking

The Woolrich, a bank in the United Kingdom, engages customers in dialog to learn the savings objectives of its customers. The bank then allows each customer to set up as many as fifteen separate savings accounts they call "jam jars" so customers can save for different needs while getting an interest rate based on the combined balance. Each "jam jar" is christened by the customer and this name is then used in every communication, including ATM transactions. By letting its customers manage the relationship, The Woolrich has become known as "the bank with the memory."

Finland's largest bank, MeritaNordbanken, has established online open pages geared to building up life-event combinations rather than offering straight deposits, loans, and payment products. They approach CMR from a person's life events: going abroad, retirement, or the need to move. Merita has 600,000 Finnish e-banking customers, 500,000 of whom use the service on a monthly basis (representing 42 percent of its retail customer base in Finland). By getting customers to tell them about their activities and plans, the bank is able to begin the kind of dialog that creates customer knowledge.

Healthcare/Pharmaceutical

Pharmaceutical companies are now spending significant advertising dollars to tell consumers the benefits of their prescription drugs. But studies show that less than one-third of 1 percent of health information seekers exposed to these ads ever get on the prescription-compliance track. A patient on average persists in taking an antidepressant for only 3.5 months. For an oral diabetes drug, it is only 5.6 months. Among a group of patients taking a drug for a chronic condition, only 16 percent are still on the medication after a year.[2] Industry sources believe this is because without actually interacting with these customers, pharmaceutical companies can't build the learning relationships necessary for repeat purchases and long-term revenue growth. This is not a healthy prognosis for either the patients or the industry.

RealAge, an online, permission-based health-marketing intermediary, has a solution. They use interactive communication to point their 3.4 million members toward healthy living choices. The company's objective is to help pharmaceutical companies build dialog with end-users. RealAge conducted a six-week test with 400 members whose profiles indicated a high cholesterol risk compared with general health-oriented communications, and their compliance to a control group whose members were not exposed to the dialog. The members of the dialog group filled their prescriptions and took the medication as prescribed in five times greater number than the control group. Rich Benci, president of RealAge, says, "This is proof that an ongoing dialog about a specific topic to a specified group of people is much more valuable than hitting different groups of people one message at a time."[3]

RealAge asked customers what they knew about their condition, their feelings about specific drugs, and their relationship with their doctors. They created a dialog to gain enough information to let the customer manage the relationship by having their specific questions answered. If this can be accomplished for companies that have always had to wade through numerous intermediaries in order to reach the end-user of their product, think what dialog with your direct customers can do for you.

THE POWER OF INFORMATION

Never underestimate the customer's desire for information. The Kaiser Foundation, an independent firm focusing on major health issues, finds that 68 percent of young adults between the ages of fifteen and twenty-four in the United States have searched online for health information.[4] This is not just an online phenomenon, and it's not just a health-care issue. People value information. OAG, a company that provides flight schedule information to airlines, airports, and travel agencies and publishes the *Official Airline Guides*, made more money in 2001 than all of the U.S. airlines combined. Information is more important than product and is an important ingredient of the dialog required to help customers manage your relationship.

You can't determine what information to share with customers until you understand how they think your company can add value to their lives. Effective dialog requires changing the way you do business, moving from transactions to solutions, from getting the order to helping the customer. It means building an interdependent relationship between the customer and the company in which each relies on the other for solutions and successes. The customer values the relationship and believes in it. The company creates a common bond with the individual customer based on trust and a shared win-win approach.

As a company develops this CMR partnership, customers begin to initiate more interactions. The customer can suddenly choose where and when to contact the company, where and when to do business with the company, even which channels to use. The customer becomes partly responsible for the company's marketing strategy. The customer begins to engage in more self-service activities, gaining a greater level of perceived control while, at the same time, saving the company some expense. Customers start to offer opinions or advice on products and services and in that process find new solutions for themselves and for the company. As the relationship grows, customers engage in new types of dialog that provide extensive knowledge of the customer by the company and a new level of input into the company's business approaches by the customer.

Baseball's Seattle Mariners, with exciting new stars such as Ichiro Suzuki, set a team attendance record in 2001 by drawing more than 3.5 million fans. One reason behind this could be because they understand the importance of dialog. They listen to their fans at the ballpark and at the fan forum on their website. The Mariners responded to the fans' complaint on opening day of 2001 that there was no sauerkraut for their hot dogs, something the team hadn't considered very important. The concession stands started serving sauerkraut, and a customer's potential problem was solved. The fans feel important when they are listened to, which will help to ensure continuing support for the team.

Why is this kind of attention to customer sentiment important? In today's I-want-it-now world, real-time communication can mean the difference between a great customer experience and an irrecoverable service failure. Sometimes adding something as simple as sauer-

---

Winning the Game

How will you know if you are winning the dialog game, if your customer is truly interacting with you or just reacting to you? Here are some questions to ask:

- What share of the communications do you initiate and what share do customers initiate?
- What is the frequency and intensity of the conversations you have with your customer?
- How easy is it for your customer to communicate with you?
- Can customers easily get the information they need?
- What can you improve? You can gauge the strength of your customer dialog by monitoring the quality of the information you gain. How much is the customer willing to tell you about his or he preferences, needs, and desires? Develop a scale and rank customers by relationship values, just as you do by the values of their transactions.

---

kraut can turn a service failure to a delightful customer experience and the word-of-mouth that results, but you have to listen to your customers to find the secret ingredient.

Finally, for the payoff in sales, constantly measure the extent to which customers take advantage of your personalized offers. You will quickly learn the value your customers place on customized communications—customized by content, by context, and by time.

Creating dialog with customers is more high-touch than high-tech. It's a simple matter of asking customers to tell you what they value in your relationship and what more you can do for them. It's not rocket science. It's not even difficult. But it does mean using your two ears more than your one mouth.[5]

PART TWO

What Needs to Change

It's No Longer Good Enough to Ask Forgiveness Rather Than Permission

5

One person's relevance
is another person's intrusion

S O NOW YOU ARE LISTENING with both ears. Your dialog is giving you all kinds of valuable information. Beyond that, you're using the Internet as what John McCarthy of Forrester Research calls a super-recorder. He tells us, "In the virtual world we can track everywhere you go. With wireless, companies not only know where someone surfs on the Web, they know where he walks around and uses his cell phone and PDA. So you have another pool of data that can be potentially abused."[1]

Now it's time to remember that you promised your customer you would use this information to help her manage your relationship. It will be critical for you to make the customer part of the information gathering and dissemination process, which brings us to the matters of privacy and permission.

We have to accept the fact that privacy is a growing customer concern. Warnings of consumers' concern about how businesses use and share their information abound. Richard Barlow, president of Frequency Marketing, puts it well: "One man's relevance is another man's intrusion. Big Brother has arrived—with a grin and a fist full of coupons—and many customers are less than overjoyed."[2]

Privacy Concerns

In October 2001, Harris Interactive released a survey showing privacy concerns sky-high on consumers' radar. The survey found more Americans are concerned about loss of personal privacy (56 percent) than health care (54 percent), crime (53 percent), or taxes (52 percent).[3]

While announcing the naming of IBM's first chief privacy officer in November 2001, IBM Chairman Louis Gerstner, Jr. said, "We know that one of the great conundrums of e-business is that it gives enterprises a powerful new capability to capture and analyze massive amounts of customer information so they can serve individuals more effectively. Yet this very capability troubles some people, who see it as a means to disclose or exploit their personal information. These are legitimate concerns, and they must be addressed if the world of e-business is to reach its full potential. At its core, privacy is not a technology issue; it is a policy issue. And the policy framework that's needed here must involve the technology industry, the private sector in general, and public officials."[4]

Some in the private sector take the position that honesty and integrity in the collecting, using, and even sharing customers' personal information is not merely good business, but is actually a customer service. Privacy is an important part of Royal Bank Financial Group's customer relationship management. Employees explain Web cookies to customers. The bank shows its concern for security by offering cell phones with special encryption chips for wireless transactions, and it has a pilot program through which it offers free firewalls and other security products to customers.

Peter Cullen, chief privacy officer at the Toronto-based bank, says, "There's profit in privacy. It's one of the key drivers of a customer's level of commitment and has a significant contribution to overall demand [for our services]."[5]

Protecting Your Customers

A consumer's view of how a business should be able to use and share customer information does not always agree with the business's view. The action of two major companies illustrates some of these issues.

In August 2001, Amazon.com put out a new privacy policy acknowledging that it uses customer data to let partners send e-mail marketing pitches to consumers. Amazon's view was that such a practice isn't an invasion of privacy; it's the grease that lubricates the wheels of e-business. A spokesperson explained, "We want to make it as easy as possible for our customers to find whatever they want to buy online. The way to do that is by using recommendations or their buying histories.[6]

Not good enough, say privacy advocates. The Amazon privacy policy dropped the ball because it also dropped the customer's option to tell Amazon, "Never sell information about me." The company has been lambasted for that policy switch by privacy advocates such as Jason Catlett, president of Junkbusters Corp., a privacy group in Green Brook, New Jersey.

Sean Carton, managing partner of Carton Donforio Interactive, said, "Amazon is making a stupid decision. Their belief that they own the data is understandable, however keeping the consumer in control is paramount to running a successful e-commerce business."[7] Amazon isn't the only dot-com resisting the tide toward greater protection of online customer privacy, and one reporter says, "It's not surprising that some e-businesses will resist limiting their use of private customer information. After all, telling e-marketers that they shouldn't use customer data to cross-sell, up-sell or personalize their sites is like telling kids that candy's not for eating."[8]

When DoubleClick acquired offline direct marketer Abacus Direct in 1999 there were plans to merge Abacus Direct's vast database of consumer buying habits, culled from 1,100 merchandise catalogs, with DoubleClick's websurfing information. When privacy groups complained, DoubleClick backed off. That was not enough to stop the FTC from investigating and consumer groups from instigating lawsuits. Finally, in 2001, the FTC closed its probe concluding that the firm had not violated its own privacy policy and had not engaged in deceptive practices. But a California state court ruled a California class action could go forward unless the parties settled.

DoubleClick announced a settlement in March 2002. As part of the settlement, the company agreed to include in its privacy policy easy-to-read explanations of its online ad serving services, and promised no new personal information the company collects will be merged with previous information it has on the user without an opt-in approval from the user. The company also ensured that users' online data will not be used in ways different from what is outlined in the settlement, even if the privacy policy under which it was collected changes.

The company agreed to launch a consumer education effort, serving 300 million consumer privacy banner ads, asking consumers to learn more about how to protect their online privacy. The company agreed to have an independent accounting firm conduct annual reviews for the next two years to assure compliance.[9] One can only hope others in the online advertising industry will see this case as setting a standard for the future.

Interestingly, most of the discussion of privacy in the trade press concentrates on privacy as an e-business issue. As we examine the process of turning the management of relationships over to the customer, we must address the issue at all business levels if, to paraphrase Louis Gerstner, any business is to reach its full potential. The consumer's concern for privacy isn't going to go away.

Gathering Information

The Gartner Group predicted, "Adequately addressing privacy concerns will be a top business priority as part of customer relationship marketing in 2002. Enterprises will be forced to rethink how information is gathered, how customers access and control it, and how enterprises can safeguard it from parties who might want it, but shouldn't have it."[10]

Microsoft had to rethink a technology that Bill Gates had described as "probably the most important ... building block service" of the company's history, due to resistance from customers. .Net My Services, previously known as HailStorm, was described as a network of services controlled and managed by Microsoft and linked over the Internet that could be automatically accessed by enterprise consumers. As it has developed, it has included more than ten basic services such as calendaring, alerts, and an electronic wallet, all hosted by Microsoft's Internet service.

The only problem is that the firm's enterprise customers don't want to have their customer data stored with MSN. Microsoft has also gotten some heat from consumer groups and privacy advocates for its concept of having vast amounts of user data stored in a single warehouse. The enterprise customers interested in developing .Net My Services asked Microsoft to offer a packaged version of the technology that they could purchase to build and host services on their own. Even though they swore up and down that they would not make any of the information available to third parties, Microsoft caved under the pressure and changed direction.[11]

Admittedly, attitudes about privacy have changed a bit since 9/11. Some say the October 2001 signing of the USA Patriot Act into law, which gave government antiterrorism investigators more authority to collect information, meant privacy is dead. Consumers continue to fight back. Call-reject software to foil telemarketers is selling at a record pace, and the fact that consumers can delete unwanted e-mail doesn't lessen their annoyance with it and their insistence on not being bombarded by unwanted advertising.

Positive Steps

There is some good news. Online privacy practices and policies seem to be improving. A report released by The Progress & Freedom Foundation in March 2002 found that websites are collecting less information. Among the 100 most popular domains, the proportion collecting personal information fell from 96 percent to 84 percent, and the proportion using third-party cookies to track surfing behavior fell from 78 percent to 48 percent.

Privacy notices are also more prevalent, more prominent, and more complete and more sites offer choice, especially over whether information can be shared with third parties. The percentage of top 100 sites offering choice over third-party sharing jumped from 77 to 93, and the use of "opt in" as a method of choice more than doubled from 15 percent to 32 percent, according to the report. The report concludes, "The extent of online information collection has declined since May 20."[12]

Back in the early days of database marketing, my good friend

Don Schultz, professor of marketing at Northwestern University, remarked on the intended purpose of customer database information:

> For the database to have value for customers, it should simplify and improve their personal lives, not just complicate them with unwanted offers or ridiculous solicitations. Also, if the database was really working for the consumer—and not just the marketer—privacy would not be the issue it is.[13]

Substitute "CMR" for "the database" in Schultz's advice and it is as cogent today as it was eight years ago. This is not surprising since Schultz is one of the most forward-thinking guys I know. If the customer information were really working for the customer, as Schultz suggests, permission would not be a concern.

PERMISSION MARKETING

A late 2001 survey by direct marketing agency Brann Worldwide confirmed that marketers should get permission before sharing customer information. Of the 400 respondents polled, 92 percent felt positively toward companies that ask permission and 81 percent would be more willing to respond if permission were sought beforehand. Eighty-seven percent said being able to choose how they were contacted had a positive effect on their decision to grant permission and 42 percent felt strongly that they would give permission in exchange for timely news of holiday promotions.[14]

How much is too much when it comes to permission e-mails? James Rosenfeld gives us these statistics from FloNetwork, Inc. and NFO Interactive regarding how frequently Americans would accept permission e-mails:

- 12 percent, daily e-mails
- 18 percent, several times a week
- 31 percent, once a week
- 10 percent, every other week
- 18 percent, once a month
- 6 percent, less than once a month
- 5 percent, don't know

Although it appears that most companies and customers seem relatively comfortable with once a week, this preference may well change as the total volume of permission e-mail increases. In January 2002, 550 million e-mails were sent in the United Kingdom in comparison to 285 million domestic letters handled by Britain's postal service. Worldwide e-mail volume was projected to reach over a trillion messages annually in 2003.[15] E-mail advertising will be a big portion of this volume, with e-mail advertising revenue projected to have reached $1.26 billion in 2002. By 2005 revenue is expected to total $1.5 billion.[16]

Seth Godin, in his wonderful book *Permission Marketing—Turning Strangers into Friends and Friends into Customers* (Simon & Schuster, 1999), calls permission marketing "anticipated, personal and relevant": anticipated because people look forward to hearing from you; personal because the messages are directly related to the individual; and relevant because the message is about something the prospect is interested in. He equates permission marketing to farming: "Farming involves hoeing, planting, watering, and harvesting. It takes regular effort and focus. If you take a month off you might lose your whole crop. On the other hand, farming is scalable. Once you get good at it, you can plant ever more seeds and harvest ever more crops."

Trust Marketing

I keep an old editorial pinned to my wall. It was written in August 2000 by Nick Usborne of ClickZ. He confirms Godin's belief that permission marketing takes regular effort and focus. He says in part, "If you really want to practice permission marketing, change the name to 'trust marketing.' Call it trust marketing and everything changes. If you have to earn and maintain the trust of your customers, you have an ongoing task. You can't assume it. You can't hide behind it. You have to earn it, again and again. Tell everyone that they have to gain each customer's trust. Each day. Every day. With each visit. Every transaction. Every customer service call. Every outbound promotional e-mail. Because if you don't have your customer's trust, their permission is worthless."[17]

John Day, of ClickZ, says, "If a company takes time to ask for permission on an ongoing basis, they will retain the people who value their message and will gain a customer for life." He says, "Make it easy for those not interested in your message to opt out and concentrate on the people who look forward to your message."

Opting

Yes, but CMR must go beyond the opt-out option. In *Wireless Rules: New Strategies for Customer Relationship Management Anytime, Anywhere* (McGraw-Hill, 2001), my coauthor Professor Katherine Lemon and I take up the issue of "opting." We make the point that in the wireless world, we have the ability to invade the personal privacy of customers as never before, and customers don't want to be interrupted—unless they want to be interrupted.

We suggest that the new permission marketing is all about opting in, only it's not just about opting in. "It's also about opting *on*, opting *when*, opting *where*, opting *how*, and, most important, opting *now*." The six-step opting program goes like this:

- **Opting in:** Can I send you stuff? Making sure the customer wants to hear from you in the first place.
- **Opting on:** Will you agree to listen? It's not enough for customers to opt in. They have to listen to your message.
- **Opting when:** Will you tell me when you'd like to listen?
- **Opting where:** Will you tell me the locations in which you'd like to hear or not hear from me?
- **Opting how:** Will you tell me how (by what means) you'd like me to reach you?
- **Opting now:** Would you like me to be "always on" for you—whenever you need me?

Customers will pay attention to your communications only when, where, and how they want to. They have to tune in and turn on, on their terms.

It's Now the Customer's Turn

In customer managed relationships, customers will engage in new types of dialog with suppliers, often initiating the search for a solution. New concepts of self-service give the customer more control. There will still be a process of targeting, but now that process may include the customer's choosing the target firm.

From the earliest discussions of relationship marketing it has been said that the learning relationship the customer provides the company makes the company practically invulnerable to competition. The theory has been that once the customer has spent the time and energy teaching the company about his or her individual needs, this investment in the learning relationship creates a barrier that makes it more difficult for the customer to switch rather than remain loyal.

That may have been true when the company controlled the business relationship, but now the consumer has more freedom to let suppliers know he or she is open for bids. Any failure to respect a customer's privacy, any exploitation of the granted permission, any violation of trust will cast the customer loose.

Privacy and permission, therefore, can be taken off your list of constraints on doing business and added to the list of services you offer. With CRM companies so busy selling, they paid little regard to permission. In the process of helping customers to manage the relationship, you seek permission to serve. Will this be easy?

The answer lies in a story. If you are traveling in Kenya and ask about the distance to a destination, you are likely to be told, "Karibu, lakine, mbali," which translates to "It is near and it is far." The distance in Kenya is relative—to the humidity, to the rain, and to your physical condition. With CMR, the "distance" is relative to your commitment and the extent to which you have an enterprise-wide understanding of customer-centric principles within your company. It takes a lot of hoeing, planting, and watering and a dedication to serve to obtain a bountiful harvest through CMR, but some firms are using permission as an implement to cultivate strong customer relationships, as we'll see in the next chapter.

Permission in Action   6

The Internet as a permission-only zone

HAVING COMPLAINED ABOUT Neiman Marcus's intrusive e-mail in Chapter 1, it seems only fair that I start this discussion of permission in action by giving kudos to some of Neiman's offline activities. When my 2002 Neiman Marcus Gold Cards arrived in the mail, they were accompanied by a letter from Jeffrey Netzer, vice president of customer programs. In addition to thanking me for my past patronage and participation in the Gold Card Program, Mr. Netzer asked me to take a few minutes to complete and return an enclosed postage-paid reply form "so we may tailor this year's Neiman Marcus Gold Card program to your preferences."

The form asked for my preferred method of communication: telephone, postcard, or e-mail. It asked for several other preferences that would help them tailor messages to my interests, like my preferred leisure travel destinations abroad, and offered a gift reminder service, InCircle:

> InCircle would love to be of service to you in your gift shopping. Would you be interested in a gift reminder service that would help you fulfill your gift desires?
> ___Yes ___No

If yes, of what types of dates would you like to be reminded?
___Spouse's birthday ___Anniversary ___Family member's birthday
___Friend's birthday ___Other
What type of gifts would you like us to recommend?
___Apparel ___Accessories (Shoes, Handbags)
___Home decorative (Crystal, Furnishings) ___Jewelry
___Other

One could say this is a bit self-serving on Neiman's part as an obvious pitch for more of my business, but if the company can tailor their offers and services to me and begin to allow me to manage the relationship, they have earned my business. And, not so incidentally, my thanks.

That's the whole point: Permission marketing not only makes for a willing customer, but it can also drive business.

THE POWER OF PERMISSION

At the CREDO (Customer Relationship Excellence Dialogue One-to-One) Conference, "Integrating Seamless, Multi-Channel CRM & ECRM Strategies," in Paris in October 2001, David Brosse, marketing director of MYPOINTS Europe, the largest Internet rewards program in the world, gave a few cogent examples of the power of permission in action.

After deciding to embrace permission marketing techniques that put customers in charge of their preference details, Tower Records was able to conduct a series of e-mail campaigns during an eight-week period in which the last mailing pulled a response rate 10 times higher than the first. Another company had an increase in response to 29 percent from their average response rate of 18 percent, attributable to a permission approach. Another increased offer response from 20 percent to 37 percent, with conversion rates rising from 4 percent to 13 percent, all because of permission initiatives.

Brosse also reported that Whitbread, a U.K. restaurateur, is using permission-marketing techniques across its entire leisure and retail brand portfolio. TGI Friday's was the first Whitbread brand to be selected as part of the company's long-term move to permission marketing. Their goal is to use the strengths of permission marketing to move each of their brands closer to the customer. Other Whitbread brands to follow include Café Rouge, Bella Pasta, and David Lloyd Leisure.

Brosse called the Internet a permission-only zone and quoted a study that compared unsolicited solicitations to permission-based offers. In the study, customers responded to permission-based e-mail offers seven times more frequently than to those that were unsolicited. As people get used to the benefits of permission online they will expect the same opportunity offline. Permission reduces waste—waste of customers' time and waste of company's money. The largest savings will be gained in offline marketing where greater dollars are at stake.

None of this is surprising. When customers receive solicitations they have requested, the offers are anticipated and the recipients know that the offers will be relevant and personal.

Abbey National Bank

The stand-alone Internet bank, Abbey National's online bank, seeks customers' permission and then goes beyond that to offer personalized options that let customers tailor the relationship. To make it as easy as possible for customers to access their accounts and take care of their banking needs anytime, anywhere, Abbey National has given its best customers Siemens C351 WAP phones. They also include an in-car charger, a hands-free kit, and a free connection to the BT Cellnet network, all free.

e-Street

A test project, called e-Street in Sweden, grouped 2,500 volunteers in the northern city of Lulea who gave permission for businesses to send SMS (short message service) messages to their mobile phones for special offers from some 150 local companies. Mobile phone users could decide which messages they wanted to receive by changing their individual permission grants via the Internet. After McDonald's sent SMS messages to e-Street volunteers, 25 percent of their target group showed up in the restaurant and bought a hamburger. The McDonald's in Lulea became the most successful restaurant of its type in Sweden, breaking its own turnover records.[1]

Six Flags

Six Flags Inc. has found a new way to let customers manage the relationship at nine of its thirty-eight U.S. theme parks. Instead of having to wait in long queues, park visitors can rent a wireless "Q-bot" text pager that will notify them when they can return and get on a ride without having to wait. They simply point their Q-bot at a ride kiosk and wirelessly make reservations. When their time is near, they enter the ride through a special line. Customers love it because the devices allow them to eat meals, visit shops, and watch entertainment shows without having to wait hours at many rides. The company likes the idea because if customers aren't in ride lines, they are often spending money in other parts of the park. The devices, which look like round, colorful pagers, can also provide special offers to customers for park restaurants and other park vendors. The park started the test with just 80 pagers, had to increase that quickly to 800, and planned to have 1,200 available in summer 2002.[2]

MOBILE PERMISSION MARKETING

All kinds of businesses are finding ways to make customers' lives easier. With customers' permission, several travel booking agencies, such as Galileo.com, TheTrip.com, Travelocity.com, and some airlines are now using instant messaging to upgrade confirmations and to notify travelers of their flight status, departure gate assignment, and weather conditions in their destination city.

This kind of mobile permission marketing goes far beyond airlines and travel agencies. More than 800,000 people have given permission to two shopping malls outside London to send personal messages and special promotional offers. Customers choose which stores they want to hear from and then notify the service when they visit one of the malls. Messages are sent to their handheld devices only when the customer is in the mall.

Similarly customers of ICA Ahold, the Swedish retail chain, have given the supermarket permission to contact them when they are in the store. Using their WAP-enabled mobile phones, customers can check their account balance, be notified of the store's special offers—including personalized offers—and even pay for their purchases using their mobile.

Another interesting and fast-growing player in the permission marketing game is The Gator Corporation. Gator provides free software that automatically fills in online forms and remembers login IDs and passwords. In exchange for this service, users give permission to Gator software to display relevant and high-value pop-up advertising and promotions based on preferences of the individual user. These preferences are based on product or service choices the user made on previous Web visits. Gator is careful to respect consumers' privacy and does not collect individuals' names or any personal information. The service works like this: If a consumer uses the Web to research information about a product category, for example an SUV, Gator will offer special information about SUVs.

The Internet audience has voted and they prefer Gator to run-of-the-mill advertisers. As one writer said, "There are several million people out there who have decided that the normal advertisers out there, most of whom use advertising like a spray hose, aren't as useful or interesting as those who sign on to Gator, which uses advertising more like a valuable solution dispensed from an eye dropper."[3] The few million people the writer mentions actually amount to 20 million unique users. The power of relevant messages sent with permission of the users is demonstrated by click-through rates ranging from 6 percent to 26 percent depending on the product category. (For those not familiar with Web advertising, this compares to a typical 0.5 percent expected from a typical successful Internet banner campaign.) An October 2001 Greenfield Online survey established that 76 percent of Gator's active users are extremely satisfied or very satisfied with the software. The study also showed that an average user clicks on more than three Gator ads and offers a month. More than half said they saved money from Gator offers, with the average savings being $16.73.[4]

Gator is one of the first companies to achieve a mass scale of permission marketing and learning relationships using feedback, knowledge, and permission to individually customize offers. Gator's enterprise clients include the leading Fortune 500 advertisers in automotive, travel, financial services, entertainment, retail, and consumer packaged goods.

This new form of communication, with the customer giving permission to the company and the company responding with customized personal offers, is changing many of our long-accepted marketing beliefs. As customers begin to direct the course of communication, engage in more self-service activities, and offer opinions and advice, customer are helping to determine the marketing tactics of the company—an upside-down value chain revolution.

Type, Point, Click, and Send Now   7

Cheaper and faster than a letter, less intrusive than a phone call, less hassle than a fax

According to a survey of CEOs of several of the world's top technology companies, virtually everyone in the developed world will be in "constant connection" with the Internet by 2010.[1] The Internet doesn't change the fundamental rules of marketing, but it does give us the capability to get better results from the old rules.

What Does E-Mail Mean for CMR?

Since e-mail remains king of the Internet as the most commonly used function, it is worth stepping back to think about how e-mail can help us give customers greater power in the development of relationships. It's not just a matter of how much is too much or how much e-mail customers will accept. It's important to know the strengths and weaknesses of e-mail, how some companies are using it badly for CRM, how best to use it for CMR, and what cautions to take.

Anyone under thirty may find it hard to believe we haven't always had e-mail. Back in 1968 when the U.S. Defense Department developed ARPANET, the precursor to the Internet, programmers and researchers could use a program called SNDMSG which allowed them to leave messages for each other, but the program was designed to allow the exchange of messages only between users who shared the same machine. In 1971 a computer engineer named Ray Tomlinson started playing around with SNDMSG seeking a way to transfer files among linked computers at remote locations. He chose the @ symbol to distinguish between messages addressed to the mailbox in the local machine and messages that were headed out onto the network. "Adding the missing piece was a no-brainer," according to Tomlinson, "just a minor addition to the protocol. I used the @ sign to indicate that the user was 'at' some other host rather than being local." By 1973, a study found that 75 percent of all traffic on ARPANET was e-mail. Asked what inspired his invention, his response comes back as undramatic as the event itself, "Mostly because it seemed like a neat idea. There was no directive to go forth and invent e-mail."[2]

Now, thanks to Tomlinson's use of the @ sign we can send or receive personal and business related messages and, with the advent of Multipurpose Internet Mail Extension (MIME) and other encoding schemes, we can add attachments: pictures, formatted documents, even music and computer programs. When you send an e-mail message, your computer routes it to a Simple Mail Transfer Protocol (SMTP) server. The server looks at the e-mail address (similar to the address on a snail mail envelope), then forwards it to the recipient's mail server, storing it until the addressee retrieves it.[3] With the convenience of simplicity and speed, it's no wonder e-mail has become the most popular service on the Internet.

Benefits to CMR

E-mail offers a number of strengths for CMR customer communications. First, of course, it is inexpensive. And it's quick and easy to use—in seconds you can send messages across time zones—and, in many cases, e-mail is a good way to get a reply quickly. You never get a busy signal when you send an e-mail—well, almost never. There are times when your customer's mailbox may be full, but that's rather rare. You never end up playing telephone tag. The ability to contact large numbers of customers with a single act opens new opportunities for efficiency (while, at the same time, calling for cautions). Finally, e-mail can facilitate the dialog that is so vital to CMR as the customer and the firm become involved in discussion. In a Direct Marketing Association study of e-mail practices by direct marketers, almost two-thirds of respondent companies said e-mail was their most effective customer retention tool.[4]

Potential Disadvantages

On the downside, the participants in an e-mail discussion can be neither seen nor heard; social cues such as body language and tone of voice are absent, making it easy for people to make injudicious remarks. *The American Heritage Book of English Usage* gives this warning: "It's hard to remember what sort of audience you are addressing when all you can see is text on a screen. There is no one sitting around a table. You cannot see people's clothes. You miss their facial expressions and cannot tell what tone of voice they are using."[5] And this caution: "Because certain forms of e-mail are characterized by a rapid give-and-take that resembles conversation, they need to be more informal in tone than conventional print writing. As an insurance policy against a potential disaster, it seems a good practice to consider whether you would utter your remarks in a face-to-face meeting, and if not, why not. You must always do your best to ascertain who your audience is and to anticipate how your remarks may be taken."[6]

The rapid, conversational tone of e-mail correspondence has bred a raft of acronyms writers use to save keystrokes. Whereas things like BBL (Be Back Later), BTW (By The Way), and IMO (In My Opinion) are fine for conversation between close friends, it's best in business correspondence to steer clear of all except those that are already common in the English language, e.g., FYI. Just as unorthodox for business mail are the e-mail visual conventions known as "emoticons" or "smileys." It's best to save your happy :-) and sad :-(graphics for notes to friends.

For anyone over thirty this may not sound like very important advice, but as more and more teenagers socialize online, middle school and high school teachers are increasingly seeing the breezy form of Internet English move into students' formal written schoolwork. As one fifteen-year-old says, "You are so used to abbreviating things, you just start doing it unconsciously on school work and reports and other things."[7] Almost 60 percent of the online population under age seventeen use instant messaging, according to Nielsen/ NetRatings.

Simple Is Best

What you see when you are composing a message is not necessarily what your customer will see when opening your e-mail. The software and hardware you use for composing, downloading, and sending may be completely different from what your customer uses. There are still a large number of e-mail subscribers whose terminals do not have the word wrap feature to handle text lines longer than eighty characters, so it is advisable to be on the safe side and keep to 65–75 characters per line. Also, using HTML or Rich Text Format to add fancy fonts or colors can be risky. There are lots of folks who can't handle messages in these formats, and your message could come through as gibberish, or even cause a computer crash. The simpler you can keep your text message, the more assurance you will have that the reader will see it as you meant it to be seen.

As an example, Charles Schwab has 4.2 million active online accounts and nearly 1 million active e-mail products subscribers. Eighty-two percent of all of their trades are conducted online. Schwab learned that AOL subscribers, who represent 28 percent— nearly 300,000—of their total e-mail Alerts subscriber base, were receiving an inferior version of their e-mails. The messages were being received completely unformatted and lacked any interactivity with Schwab's website. Realizing the significant impact that this poor customer experience could have on their AOL users' satisfaction, the company created a new message template that dynamically adjusts AOL formatted code to replicate the appearance of a plain text formatted e-mail. Schwab's AOL e-mail users now receive e-mail alerts with top bar navigation, Schwab branding, clearly formatted layout, evenly spaced fonts and financial data tables, and hotlinked ticker symbols, improving the overall readability and interactivity of the e-mail alerts.[8]

Update Often

It is much more difficult to keep a list of e-mail addresses clean than it is with a postal address list. With Internet service providers constantly offering deals to get consumers to switch to their service (and some going out of business), the industry faces significant churn. Of the more than 100 million e-mail users in the United States, at least 20 million of those users change their e-mail addresses each year.[9] Even though the cost of sending electronic messages is significantly cheaper than print mail (one to twenty-five cents versus one or two dollars), it is easy to waste money. More importantly, you can fail to reach important customers.

Experts advise diligence in processing inbound e-mail, undelivered mail, and all customer contacts to capture changed addresses; and always make it easy for customers to update their personal profile. Of course, if you are truly involved in CMR, your customers will care enough to see to it that you have their latest information.

It is amazing to find that in this day and age, some companies have still not realized how important their e-mail communications are. If your company is able to deal professionally with e-mail, it will provide you with an all-important competitive edge.

And Keep in Mind

Bob Brand of the *Newtown Bee* in Newtown, Connecticut, offers additional e-mail advice that is important to keep in mind:

- **Use a heading and salutation:** "I may get a message that starts off something like: 'Juno has been sending out messages...' Is this directed to me personally? Is it from an e-list? Is it junk e-mail? I can't tell. When people send personal mail, I always like to see 'Hi, Bob' on the first line."
- **Keep messages to one page or less, and don't overquote:** "This happens when someone sends a long message (more than a full screen of text) that I have read before and tacks on just a short comment at the very end. When replying to a message, it's a good idea to carve out the major thoughts and insert your comments within these selected gems. By leaving the

original message totally intact, the reply insults the originator with the notion that they forgot the message he sent you."

- **Use correct spellings:** "The extra time it takes to run a message through a spell checker is trivial. If I personally don't know the sender of the message, frankly, I devalue the quality of messages containing misspellings."

- **Use a short signature block:** "Some subscribers to e-mail lists have large egos. They show little restraint when it comes to self-promotion. As a general rule, five lines should be considered an upper limit [for your personal information]."

- **Less is more.** "For those people who take the time to compose tightly crafted epistles, the quality shines through."

- **Avoid overusing HTML:** "Have you noticed the increasing amounts of HTML (hypertext markup language) showing up in e-mail? This e-mail has a mirror of the original message but also contains extra imbedded tags because it is intended to be read with a browser like Internet Explorer or Netscape Navigator. The sender is usually a raw beginner to the Internet and is using the browser for sending e-mail. I find that netsters using Microsoft Outlook are often the worst culprits. This problem is easy to fix. For Outlook users, click Tools\Options\Mail Format. Change the setting from HTML to Plain Text. Simple."[10]

A Quick Lesson in E-Mail Etiquette

By educating your employees as to what can and cannot be said in an e-mail, you can protect your company from awkward liability issues. A website called Emailreplies.com offers the following advice on how employers can ensure that they are implemented.

Why do you need e-mail etiquette? A company needs to implement etiquette rules for the following three reasons:

- **Professionalism:** By using proper e-mail language, your company will convey a professional image.

- **Efficiency:** E-mails that get to the point are much more effective than poorly worded e-mails.

▪ **Protection from liability:** Employee awareness of e-mail risks will protect your company from costly lawsuits.

How do you enforce e-mail etiquette?   The first step is to create a written e-mail policy. This e-mail policy should include all of the do's and don'ts concerning the use of the company's e-mail system and should be distributed to all employees. Secondly, employees must be trained to fully understand the importance of e-mail etiquette. Finally, implementation of the rules can be monitored by using e-mail management software and e-mail response tools.

The Emailreplies.com website also provides more details on the thirty-one tips that appear on the following page, as well as links to sample e-mail policy, e-mail management software, and response tools. It's worth a look.

BUSINESSES THAT PROFESS to be CRM marketers are violating these rules every day. Customers get tired of deleting irrelevant offers for books and flowers that clog their e-mail even though, in some cases, they have given firms permission to send them messages.

This brings us to the ugly subject of spam, or what some call "UCE," unsolicited commercial e-mail—any e-mail sent to a recipient who did not request it, and who has no prior relationship with the sender.

SPAM

Just how pervasive has spam become? E-mail traffic increased 14 percent between November 2001 and the end of January 2002, but in that period the amount of spam increased 46 percent, according to a survey by Brightmail, a company that develops spam-fighting technology for Internet service providers.[11] A 2001 European Union study estimated the worldwide cost of spam to be about $8 billion annually. Research firm Jupiter Media Metrix reported that Internet users each received an average of 1,470 junk messages in 2001 and can expect about 3,800 annually in 2006.[12] It's possible that instead of helping customers, we're going to cause them carpal tunnel syndrome from the repetitive motion of deleting spam.

E-Mail Etiquette Tips

1 Be concise and to the point.
2 Answer all questions and pre-empt further questions.
3 Use proper spelling, grammar, and punctuation.
4 Make it personal.
5 Use templates for frequently used responses.
6 Answer swiftly.
7 Do not attach unnecessary files.
8 Use proper structure and layout—short paragraphs and blank lines between paragraphs.
9 Do not overuse the high-priority option.
10 Do not write in CAPITALS.
11 Don't leave out the message thread.
12 Add disclaimers to your e-mails for legal protection.
13 Read the e-mail before you send it.
14 Do not overuse Reply to All.
15 For mailings to multiple addressees, use the bcc: field or do a mail merge.
16 Use abbreviations and emoticons sparingly.
17 Be careful with formatting to avoid awkward line breaks.
18 Be careful with rich text and HTML messages. RTF does not transfer well to all browsers so be aware of the recipient's capabilities.
19 Do not forward chain letters.
20 Do not request delivery and read receipts.
21 Do not copy a message or attachment without permission.
22 Do not use e-mail to discuss confidential information.
23 Use a meaningful word or phrase in the subject line.
24 Use active instead of passive verbs.
25 Avoid using URGENT and IMPORTANT.
26 Avoid long sentences.
27 Don't send or forward e-mails containing libelous, defamatory, offensive, racist, or obscene remarks.
28 Don't forward virus hoaxes.
29 Keep your language gender neutral.
30 Don't reply to spam.
31 Use the cc: field sparingly.

Spam might seem harmless. After all, a simple click on the delete key sends it away, but it is not without cost. Some users pay for the time they spend downloading e-mail. Business travelers are often paying phone fees by the minute to read their e-mail, incurring particularly onerous charges from overseas hotels. The bulk of spam is so great that $2 to $3 of every user's monthly e-mail bill goes to spam-fighting efforts and equipment upgrades by their Internet service providers.[13]

Not only is spam annoying to the vast majority of consumers; in some cases it's illegal. For example, it is now illegal to send spam with forged sending information or a misleading subject line to Washington State residences. A similar law that went into effect in California on January 1, 1999, requires senders of bulk e-mail to include a valid return e-mail address or toll-free number and specifies damage of $50 per message if a sender violates an ISP acceptable-use policy. A Nevada law lets residents sue spammers for $10 per unsolicited message.[14] In March 2002, lawmakers in the U.S. House Energy and Commerce Committee overwhelmingly approved landmark legislation that would allow consumers to refuse unwanted e-mail and would give Internet service providers the right to sue to block unsolicited e-mail from their networks. The legislation would allow ISPs to sue spammers for $500 per message in violation of the policy.

People who might have been receptive to marketing messages in the past are likely to delete all commercial e-mails—even those from companies they know—without reading them. It's not just the bad guys sending tens or even hundreds of thousands of e-mails an hour offering to clean up bad credit reports and making other dubious promises. It is, too often, reputable firms who claim to be using e-mail for CRM.

KEEP IT RELEVANT

The offer from a large, well-known department store for "looks you've got to get," "uplifting wedge sandals," and "flirty, sweet scarves" did not make my day. Nor did the offer of "The Power, the Passion, the Beauty of Art" at a 25 percent savings from American Express (even with its description of the "beautifully crafted masterpieces ready to hang in frames of impeccable museum quality"). Companies using e-mail in the wrong ways are spoiling it for the rest.

A most cogent argument for the use of e-mail for CMR comes from Gideon Sasson, executive vice president and enterprise president at Charles Schwab: "Until now, companies have viewed e-mail as merely an effective marketing tool. But, at Schwab, we've realized that it's one of the most powerful tools we have for building personal and deep relationships with our customers. And it can drive all sorts of behaviors—from building brand loyalty, to building brand identity, to building commitment. This, in turn, maximizes the value of customer relationships and transfers to increased profitability."[15]

Here are some things to keep in mind when sending e-mail to customers:

■ Be sure your mail will be readable the way you send it and limit yourself to 65–75 characters per line.
■ Let your customer tell you if his or her software can handle HTML or rich text format (RTF) before using it.
■ Keep your address lists clean and updated.
■ Keep it simple. One page is best.
■ Don't be a spammer.
■ Above all, be sure your message is timely and relevant for your customer.

E-mail *is* cheaper and faster than a letter. It *is* less intrusive than a phone call. It *is* less hassle than a fax. But if your e-mail message is not relevant to your customer, it's not an effective marketing tool. Irrelevant e-mail, even to your best and most loyal customer, is no better than spam.

Who's Minding the Store? **8**

CMR is not about how you look at customers— it's about how customers look at you

A s discussed in Chapter 1, CMR means switching from a product-centered strategy to an experiential-based strategy—creating value by making customers' lives easier. This must include the in-store shopping experience. Research by Jay Scansaroli, global managing partner of Anderson's Retail Industry services, and David Szymanski, director of the Center for Retailing Studies at Texas A&M University, supports the belief that customers want to be able to do their own customization, not have retailers and others do it for them.

They make the point that a major benefit touted in the days of the dot-com euphoria was the future ability of online retailers to customize the retailing experience to each customer when they logged on. It was personalization that was going to make the Internet the channel of choice for consumers. Online customization never materialized in the form that had been promised to shoppers, and the authors suggest that no one really cared.

> Our trend research offers insight into why customization by the online retailer (or the traditional retailer) was not a desired benefit. Customers do not necessarily want any retailer to define the experience for them. Offering customers the opportunity to tailor their

own experience through easy, simple, and multi-optioned navigation, however, would be valued. Customers want to exercise power and they want to define their own spaces and experiences. Therefore, enabling shoppers to customize the experience to their needs and wants, easily and efficiently, are competitive mandates. It is rare to find surveys of online shoppers reporting complaints of sites not being sufficiently customized to the individual shopper. Complaints of navigational difficulties, however, are commonplace.

What does this mean for retailers of all forms? It means that retailers have to provide an infrastructure that enables shoppers to customize the retailing experience to the degree and in the form they want. The retailer should not be the customizer, rather retailers of the future should be the enablers of customization. The retailer should provide customers with shopping and experiential options so that the customers can: 1) control the experience, 2) define the retail space in their own terms, 3) create stimulation and sanctuary from the same general retail space, 4) find unique meaning that fits unique attitudes and interests, and 5) even pursue the formation of communities by connecting with outside organizations or connecting with other customers.

As individuality and experiences of 'one' are sought by customers, retailers must create modular, multi-purpose and multi-interpretational environments for consumers. The store of the future will be filled with contradictions—personal service (sales associates), with no service (self-checkout), wide arrays of merchandise (to customers who shop the whole store) with narrow assortments (to destination-oriented customers), simple (straightforward) yet memorable (different enough to be compelling) experiences, and so on. Future success will be grounded in the possibilities for retail customization among diverse consumers. The shopping experience is what the consumer interprets and tailors it to be. The opportunity for multiple consumer groups to have unique interpretation is where value will be.[1]

Letting the Customer Choose

Borders Group Inc. is certainly a multichannel retailer, with 360 domestic and 22 international brick-and-mortar Borders locations; about 850 Waldenbooks retail stores; 36 Books Etc. locations in the U.K.;

Borders.com, a joint venture with Amazon.com; BordersStores.com, devoted to Borders retail stores; and PreferredReader.com. They don't try to customize the shopping experience for their customers. They provide the infrastructure to enable shoppers to customize their unique retail experience. Mary Campbell, senior manager of customer relationship marketing, says, "We don't push one branch over the other. What I like to stress is the customer first. Our e-mails have a link to Borders.com and the BordersStores site, and we say, 'you choose.' It's really up to the customers, and I think they appreciate that."

Using the links Campbell describes, customers have the ability to check store inventory; to buy a Borders gift card that can be used at Borders.com or Borders retail stores; to sign up for the stores' cobranded FirstUSA credit card; to request any of the special topic newsletters; and to read an online version of the company's in-store magazine, *Inside Borders*, to check on store events.

Campbell explains how customers do the customizing: "If customers say go ahead and customize offers for me based on my purchase transactions and what you think I'll like, we'll do that. But we like to let people decide what they want to receive versus us just pulling it out of transaction history."[2]

Some years ago the Dillard's department store chain found a way to empower customers and give them greater control of the shopping experience. In the chain's three major catalogs one holiday season, customers received colorful, pressure-sensitive red Santa hat stickers. Customers were asked to "play Santa" to the 51,000 Dillard's store associates and to reward exceptional service with the red hats to be worn on the employees' name badges. The idea came from college football coaches' adding stars to players' helmets. At Dillard's associates who earned the most stickers received valuable awards. I visited the stores at the time and talked with customers. They loved the power they felt as they withheld or awarded the stickers. Sometimes little things can lead to CMR.

PROVIDING CUSTOMERS WITH OPTIONS

What can you do to create multipurpose and multi-interpretational shopping environments?

Customer Segments

Begin by considering how different customer segments think and how they shop, giving consideration to those who shop the whole store as well as destination-oriented customers. What do your different customer segments really want from your store? Are there products and services you should add or discard? Benchmark your delivery of customer needs against the rest of the shopping possibilities in your area.

Businesses have very detailed information on what customers do online. They know what areas of the site customers visit. They know how often customers don't check out their shopping carts. But within the four walls of a store, they have had very little insight into how customers shop. Enter technology.

In January 2002, Brickstream, an Arlington, Virginia–based company, launched its Brickstream System, which links a company's software to computer hardware and in-store cameras that provide a view of in-store browsing and buying behaviors. Through software algorithms, the company's applications analyze factors including the busiest parts of a store, paths through the store, what customers are doing after interacting with a display, how long customers wait in line, and how many customers abandon a line. The solution is transparent to the customer yet yields a wealth of information and customer insight for the retailer.

Starting Small

Another source for learning how customers think and how they shop is a company called Envirosell. Envirosell's Paco Underhill has been called the Sherlock Holmes for retailers based on hard data he has developed in thousands of hours of field research in shopping malls, department stores, and supermarkets. In his entertaining book, *Why We Buy: The Science of Shopping* (Touchstone Books, 2000), Underhill describes the process,

> Trackers are the field researchers of the science of shopping, the scholars of shopping, or, more precisely, of *shoppers*. Essentially, trackers stealthily make their way through stores following shoppers and noting

everything they do. Usually a tracker begins by loitering inconspicuously near a store's entrance, waiting for a shopper to enter, at which point the 'track' starts. The tracker will stick with the unsuspecting individual (or individuals) as long as the shopper is in the store (excluding trips to the dressing room or the restroom) and will record on a track sheet virtually everything he or she does. Sometimes, when the store is large, trackers will work in teams in order to be less intrusive.

Underhill gives us a perfect example of how this kind of sleuthing can help a retailer allow customers to shape the shopping experience. In a study Envirosell conducted for a dog food manufacturer, they noticed that whereas adults bought the dog food, the dog treats—liver-flavored biscuits and such—were often being picked out by children or senior citizens. Because no one had ever noticed who exactly was buying (or lobbying for the purchase of) pet treats, they were typically stocked near the top of supermarket shelves. Trackers saw children climbing the shelving to reach the treats, and even noticed an elderly woman using a box of aluminum foil to knock down her brand of dog biscuits. When Envirosell's client moved the treats to where kids and older individuals could more easily reach them, in effect letting customers customize the shopping experience, sales went up overnight.[3]

Remind yourself that customers are not all alike. Think about what you are doing now. Does it make sense to the customer? Start small. Pick an area of your business to re-think. Make sure it's important to the customer and relevant to your business. Start by correcting deficiencies at opportunity stores. Compare current store layout with what your customers are telling you they want. Develop action plans to correct deficiencies in selection, adjacencies, and placement within schematics. In many cases categories can be reset to reflect what the customer comes to the store for. Look for opportunities to create narrow assortment areas for destination-oriented shoppers.

One of our client stores is trying to do this. Our reward came in a letter from a customer who said, "Your store is my family's favorite place to shop because you have a way of meeting our needs before we know there is a need."

It's not enough just to make changes. To make the changes work it is critical to communicate the reasons for your changes to your people on the firing line in the stores and provide the customer data they need to understand the changes.

Redesigning the Store

One of the more aggressive examples of a company redesigning a store and its services based on how customers think and how they shop is the Prada Epicenter that opened at the corner of Prince Street and Broadway in New York in January 2002. Prada calls it a laboratory where the company can experiment with new forms of customer interaction. It is worth a detailed study.

The store carries Prada's current collections for men and women in ready-to-wear, sportswear, handbags, shoes, accessories, and beauty items. Limited edition vintage pieces from the collections of the 1980s and early 1990s, including women's clothing, handbags, and shoes are also exclusive to this store. The store provides locations of concentrated creativity, spanning a spectrum from the public to the ultra-private, allowing these boundaries to constantly shift.

The space is designed to support new forms of customer service, merchandising, and programming. It is a space that enables change: change in the configuration of the store itself, its surfaces, its function, the content on the display devices, and the way customers are serviced. It is a place, ultimately, where Prada can experiment with new conditions and constantly reinvent itself.

The merchandise throughout the ground floor is displayed in moveable volumes. This "hanging city" consists of a series of aluminum-mesh cages suspended from the ceiling which are configured to include hanging bars, shelving, and space for mannequins and other displays. The units are mounted on motorized tracks that allow them to be positioned differently throughout the store.

The cylindrical glass elevator that provides access to the lower floor contains a display of Prada handbags, allowing customers to shop as they descend to the lounge and accessory area downstairs. In the lounge, customers can browse bags and leather goods while seated on banquettes covered with gel pads. The lower level also includes a cosmetic display area, more shoe displays, and a series of rooms formed by customized compact shelving units of the type used in libraries. These units can be combined or separated to create different special conditions depending on the volume of merchandise. They provide the sense that the customer is shopping behind-the-scenes in an environment that is part storage, part display.

At the start of the design, a number of key concepts were established: be unobtrusive, integrated, and functional; support, rather than change, existing ways of working; help provide better service the way the customer wants it; and build on interactions and relationships in the real world.

At the center of the technology-based service scenario is the hand-held wireless store database terminal giving the sales associate up-to-date access to inventory and customer information. In addition, the sales associate's service device serves as an interface for other elements of service—reading radio frequency identification (RFID) tags that identify products, staff, and customers via a personalized customer card. The device also controls video displays throughout the store.

Information from the staff device can be displayed on any of the various screens in the store and so shared with the customer. When not employed as service terminals, those screens (called ubiquitous displays) exhibit other content—video, graphic material, computational information—and can be placed with merchandise on hang bars, on table tops, or in display furniture—creating changing contexts for the products, supporting and challenging them. A unique database system allows such content to be extremely diverse, easily changed or reprogrammed.

In the dressing rooms service information is directly accessible to the customer. Any article the customer places into the closet is registered automatically and displayed on the closet touch screen. From that screen, the customer can access product specifications, and alternative and complimentary items that then may be stored in a personal Web account.

The dressing rooms also contain a video-based "magic mirror" that not only shows the customer's back but also displays a delayed playback when the customer turns, a mirror that works in time as well as in space. In addition, multiple lighting scenarios allow the customer to change the atmosphere of the dressing room and consider choices in several light environments. Dressing room doors even transform from translucent to transparent with a simple switch, to afford waiting companions a quick look.

Prada's Web presence is the first phase of the service section of a larger website aimed at extending the relationships formed in the store into the virtual. To maintain an exclusive and personal relationship, only products that have been tried on in the store or recommended by a sales associate can be investigated on the Web. Personalized customer care that is provided by sales associates in-store can continue online with the store having its own small fulfillment center and customer care center.

Wow! How far can you go in reinventing a store to make the shopping experience what the customer wants? We'll watch this with interest.

What Can You Do?

Not all companies are ready to go as far as Prada has. You don't have to have motorized tracks, cylindrical glass elevators, handheld wireless database terminals, or magic mirrors. There are smaller steps you can take to redesign your store and its services to empower customers by giving them more control of their shopping experience.

Sears, for example, has taken steps to make customers' lives easier by allowing them to search for items and order them directly through in-store kiosks. They also allow customers to pick up or return purchases to their nearest Sears store, regardless of the channel that was used to purchase the item. With forty-five contact centers and 3,000 retail locations, such integration and changes to the pre-existing workflow involved enormous amounts of logistical technology and culture change, but Sears is putting the customer first.

Because they are listening to customers, Sears is giving them the power to go to Sears.com and plug in their zip code to find the nearest store, even to find out what is on sale this week at their local store. No need for a newspaper circular—a customer can use a computer to virtually leaf through the retailer's product offerings and click through to order on the spot. In the company's 2001 annual report, CEO Alan J. Lacy talked of four corporate-wide priorities. The company becoming "truly customer-centric" was one of them.[4]

There are lots of options. You can use Brickstream. You can use Envirosell. You can take the big plunge like Prada, or start with the basics like Sears. The important thing is to find the best way to empower your customers and let them define the shopping experience.

Personalization Technology—Boon or Bust?

9

Empowering the customer requires more than just personalization

PERSONALIZATION IS NOTHING NEW. The best retail sales associates have always kept what they called "black books" to keep track of clients' preferences and buying habits, helping them to personalize future visits. For years direct marketing pros have been using personalization—targeting customers for special offers based on customer lifestyle or life stage, or customers' past transactions. These savvy sales and marketing people weren't thinking about helping customers to manage a relationship, they were simply trying to get a larger share of each customer's wallet.

Personalization is one of the hottest buzzwords in marketing and, as used today, it is most often associated with technology. With the swift advance of technological solutions, personalization has moved from the selling floor and the envelope to the Web, to e-mail, to voice messaging, and to multimedia. But what does personalization mean to CMR? Before we can answer that question we have to define personalization and customization and understand the difference.

PERSONALIZATION AND CUSTOMIZATION ARE NOT THE SAME

Personalization and customization mean vastly different things to different people. Some say personalization is the ability to call a customer by name and make offers based on the customer's profile. Others add the capability of predictive modeling to formulate offers based on a customer's past transactions. Personalization is not including headline features of general appeal in your e-mail. It's not announcing sale items of the day, even if they are targeted offers. It's not achieved in what one expert called "no-brainer cross-sell:" You bought the handheld video camera, here's an offer for a carrying case. Personalization is a process of reorienting each transaction around a customer's implicit preferences, rather than simply pushing out canned offers that seem relevant.

The Personalization Consortium, an international advocacy group (www.personalization.org) defines personalization in this way:

> Personalization is the combined use of technology and customer information to tailor electronic commerce interactions between a business and each individual customer. Using information either previously obtained or provided in real-time about the customer and other customers, the exchange between the parties is altered to fit that customer's stated needs so that the transaction requires less time and delivers a product best suited to that customer.[1]

For the purposes of CMR we would expand the definition well beyond electronic commerce to include all interactions between a company and its customers. Nevertheless, in simplest terms, personalization is driven by the computer, which serves up individualized offers based on a coding of algorithms derived from statistical models. It is a passive process for the user, a process one writer compared to a delightful experience like walking into a restaurant and being called by name or having your favorite bookseller pull out a copy of a book he just knew you would really like.

By contrast, customization at it's best is under direct control of the user. The user explicitly selects between certain options. In talking about customization on the Web, Michael Rosenberg, a contributing writer for ITworld.com, offers this description:

> Customization involves end users telling us exactly what they want, such as what color of fonts they like, the cities for which they want to know the weather report, or the sports teams for which they want the latest scores and information. With customization, the end user is actively engaged in telling the content-serving platform what to do.[2]

On the Web, customization occurs when the user can configure the interface and create a profile manually, adding and removing elements. Everyone equates customization with the Web, but customization goes far beyond the Web.

In a relationship with a retailer, customers might indicate their preferences to help the retailer tailor messages to their interests. The Neiman Marcus story in Chapter 6 is an example. In a business-to-business relationship, customers might specify only the specific product categories they will find of interest. Customers should also be able to choose the level of service that best fits their needs.

Customization is a dialog in which the user is actively involved and begins to control certain elements of the relationship. Both personalization and customization offer benefits for the customer and the company, and these benefits are worth reviewing.

BENEFITS OF PERSONALIZATION AND CUSTOMIZATION

The benefits of personalization and customization are substantial for a company, but customization seems to produce the most results. A March 2001 study sponsored by the Personalization Consortium found more than 50 percent of the study's respondents more likely to make a purchase at an e-commerce site that offers some sort of personalization features. Sixty-three percent said they would be more likely to register at a site in exchange for personalization or content customization features. And 82 percent said they would be willing to provide information like gender, age, and ethnicity, in return for the site's remembering their user preferences.

There are reports of simple name-slug personalization lifting response rates by 30 percent and true content personalization lifting customer response rates to offers by as much as 300 percent. All of this is great, and some of it addresses the issue of helping customers to manage the relationship, but only when it empowers the customer— or as Scott Martin says, allows the customer to gain control—does it deliver CMR.

Truly empowering the customer requires more than just personalization; it demands customization. Even with the best artificial intelligence, a computer can't guess a customer's needs at any point in time. And, consumers who customize are more likely to spend more money online. The Personalization Consortium study found that 28 percent of consumers who used customized websites spent $2,000 more on purchases during a twelve-month period than the 17 percent of users who did not use a site's option of customization features.[3] What a customer wants on one visit may be very different from what he or she wants on the next. Reacting to the wrong need of the moment would be like your favorite waiter at the restaurant calling you by the wrong name, or refilling your cup of coffee when you asked for the bill.

When we allow the computer to try to be smarter than it really is and second-guess customers' needs, we create an inconvenience, forcing the customer to take the time to correct the information. That's a long way from letting the customer manage the relationship.

Office supplies retailer Staples knows it is not enough to let the computer personalize the site or to try to second-guess the customer's needs. They allow customers to customize the Staples.com site to create multiple lists, for example, one for items the customer buys once a month, and another for items purchased only when needed. In addition to individual lists, companies can set up group lists for employee use. Customers can also request e-mail reminders. Staples is making it easier for customers to buy by using customization to let their customers manage the relationship.

Most credit card issuers have online account management offerings, but few have found ways to structure them for CMR. One credit card marketer, Metris Companies Inc. in Minnesota, has started to use its online account management offerings to allow the customer to take more control of the relationship. Hundreds of thousands of Metris's 4.6 million cardholders have registered at the site,

Let Your Customers Know What You Are Doing

Letting the computer loose for personalization can have dangerous consequences. Jack Aaronson, an expert on personalization, tells a story about creating the personalization practice for barnesandnoble.com.

"A customer had bought a book for his sister. The book was about lesbianism, and he bought it as a gift. At the time, the B&N home page had a drop-down box containing fifty different subjects, including history, fiction, adventure, sports, and gay & lesbian. When this guy returned to the site a week later, 'Gay & Lesbian' was pre-selected in the box. From a company perspective, this level of personalization might seem reasonable, but *there was no personalization on the home page*. The list box was powered by a random generator. Whenever the home page loaded, the box displayed a different subject as the 'default' selection. One person would see 'Fiction' highlighted, another would see 'History,' and so on. On *this* day on *this* page, on *this* particular refresh, the highlighted subject was 'Gay & Lesbian.' The odds were about one in fifty any particular subject would be highlighted. That day, the odds were not in B&N's favor."

The customer may not have noticed if any other default had been selected, as it would have been the week before. The coincidence of the selected default matching his recent purchase had the customer thinking that B&N made an assumption about his reading preferences based on a single purchase. Aaronson reports that the customer's complaint went through customer service all the way up to the CEO. He learned this lesson and gives this advice:

"The home page had no personalization. But it had a sense of *perceived personalization*. There was dynamic content that looked different to different users and could conceivably have been personalized. The two principles of perceived personalization are:

1 People think you are personalizing their experiences, especially if your site has dynamic content.

2 If you collect information that could be used for personalization but don't actually personalize anything, your users will think you are doing a bad job and get frustrated. If you have dynamic content that isn't personalized, make it clear you aren't selecting content only for that user."[4]

and each of them can create a brand experience that is unique. Metris has expanded statement history, added personalized financial reports, and allowed customers to search for specific transactions and request e-mail alerts.

Patrick Fox, executive vice president, says greater interactivity will be added to the site—if cardholders want it. He says card marketers need to redefine the value proposition on a personal, even emotional, level. The customized website is one way to do that. "Traditionally you never heard from your issuer, except once a month when you went to your mailbox to get your statement. The Internet provides a cheap communication channel for more frequent dialog. Our goal has always been to make our customers' lives easier and more satisfying. We think this channel gives us a great opportunity to do so."[5]

Mall operator Taubman Centers, Inc. has attracted 350,000 registered users at the twenty-nine websites it operates for the thirty malls it owns and operates in the United States. These consumers have signed up to receive personalized weekly news of sales and other events at their favorite mall stores. Visitors are asked to register for an online bulletin, but to receive that e-mail they have to choose up to twenty of their favorite stores at the mall. They can sign up for a gift-giving reminder e-mail service and a personal wish list. Taubman is responding to consumer feedback from thirty-six focus groups nationwide that said time-pressed shoppers wanted to check their local mall's site before heading over. The responses also indicated that customers preferred online information over e-commerce functionality.[6]

THE EMPOWERMENT ASPECT

Personalization and customization are not just about enriching the online experience; they offer opportunities to empower customers and strengthen relationships with every interaction. A highly respected Connecticut retailer, with big-ticket clothing stores in Westport and Greenwich, is a leader in personalizing the customer experience. Andrew Mitchell, the company's vice president of marketing, says, "Let's face it, we're in the suburbs and our affluent customers can travel anywhere in the world they wish to go. We have to give our customers something different; something they're not going to find elsewhere. We know we have the kind of merchandise they want. But that's not enough. We also know that we have to continually build on our relationships with our customers which requires a deep-rooted understanding of their every need, want and desire."

In addition to continuing personalized communications, the stores offer free alterations, local delivery, and special gift wrapping services. They will send clothing and a tailor, if necessary, to any customer anywhere in their metro region. They even offer VIP fitting rooms complete with all the clothing and accessories laid out for a specific customer's needs, with complimentary cappuccino and imported water.

Closet consultations are routinely offered free of charge. At the customer's request, a sales associate goes to the home to help inventory, organize, and add onto the closet's contents. The client receives suggestions on how to creatively mix and match the existing wardrobe, as well as ideas on how to add new pieces from the store's seasonal merchandise offerings. Free maintenance and a company tailor

---

Why Personalize?

Scott Martin, vice president of CRM and Alliances at Critical Mass, a website developer: "The benefits to the customer can be extraordinary if strategically approached personalization allows the customer to gain control, so the underlying statement is all about empowerment."[7]

Rachael McCarthy, Unica general counsel and chief privacy officer: "Personalization can save consumers time and money. Rather than wasting time and clicks wading through Web pages and promotions that are not of interest, the customer is presented with product and service options, information and promotions that are relevant."[8]

Jamie Fiorda, senior product marketing manager at E.piphany: "Real time personalization can prevent customer churn, enable cross-channel consistency and encourage the use of value-added services."[9]

Bruce Kasanoff, one of the original partners of Peppers and Rogers Group and author of *Making It Personal: How to Profit from Personalization Without Invading Privacy* (Perseus Books, 2001): "You can save people time by eliminating repetitive tasks or remembering transactional details. You can save people money by preventing redundant work, eliminating service components unnecessary to a person or identifying lower cost solutions that meet all other specifications. You can deliver better information. Usually this means providing less, but more relevant information that's tailored to a person's needs or expertise. You can address ongoing needs, challenges or opportunities by providing one-stop services, accommodating unique personal preferences and recognizing and rewarding achievement with special treatment."[10]

to handle alterations are readily available. Outfit combinations are photographed, and discarded items are brought to the customer's designated charity by the sales associate. These folks really understand today's overloaded customer and they're finding innovative ways to empower her.[11]

Because so much of the hype about personalization and customization is about Web companies, one might conclude that businesses not actually selling on the Internet have little need of the two features. But how many brick-and-mortar customers are also using their Web services? Sixty-six percent of multichannel shoppers browse in one channel but purchase in another.

And multichannel shoppers spend more. Consumers that either browsed or purchased in all three channels—on the Internet, through catalogs, and in retail stores—spent $995 on holiday shopping in 2001, compared with shoppers who browsed or purchased in two channels ($894) and consumers who used only one channel ($591). Despite all the excitement about online purchasing for holiday 2001, retail stores continue to be the most popular channel for purchasing among multichannel shoppers. Out of the average $894 spent by multichannel consumers, $572, or 64 percent, was spent in retail stores; $233, or 26 percent, was spent on the Internet; and $89, or 10 percent, was spent through catalogs. Fifty-four percent of customers purchased through both retail stores and on the Internet, and 22 percent made purchases through all three channels.[12]

So personalization and customization are not just for the Web. They can let customers have more control of the relationship, wherever and whenever—on the store's selling floor, on a sales call, and in the call center.

TECHNOLOGY

Personalizing communications is not easy. Most companies do not have the expertise or the technology to do it well on their own. There are personalization vendors that specialize in this process, providing turnkey solutions for businesses. Steve Van Tassel, senior vice president of products for personalization at NetPerceptions, says: "If a company's top business priority has nothing to do with a website it may be in luck, since personalization vendors are looking for new outlets for their software anyway. The pure dot-coms went away, so our primary emphasis is on the contact center more than it is on the website, by far. Although the Web's instant and accurate flow of data made it an ideal early channel for real-time personalization efforts, pragmatism is dictating a new direction. The business volume that flows through the contact center is much higher than that on the website, so it's easy to quantify short-term benefits of personalization."[13]

Clothing retailer Norm Thompson takes this to heart by applying personalization technology to its outbound customer service phone calls. The company can trigger voice messages to its customers either confirming shipment of their orders or letting them know that a certain item wasn't in stock and will be delayed. These are not stilted artificial speech messages. The Norm Thompson application uses pieces of natural human speech that have been recorded and electronically spliced together for a natural sounding message.

A customer can automatically receive a phone call saying, for example, that two of three ordered items were shipped, but that the third item is back-ordered until next Monday. This is especially effective for the large number of customers who either don't have Internet access or have requested that the company not contact them through the Web or by e-mail. Norm Thompson is empowering the customer to make the choice of communication channel. Steve Jones, Norm Thompson's marketing vice president, says, "In the past back-order notification could take days and if the customer had ordered an item for Christmas or for someone's birthday, we might not have left them time to buy something else. Now we can alert customers to a potential back-order within hours and the customer can be given the opportunity to cancel the order, leave it as is or select something else."[14]

Customization to put the customer in charge of the relationship can't be based just on transaction history and demographics. It cannot be just a computer function. It requires dialog with customers to let them tell you how they want the relationship to grow. My favorite comment on this comes from Sandeep Krishnamurthy, a contributing writer for *Digitrends:*

... individuals are not their past behavior. Rather, they are hedonistic agents passing through life making idiosyncratic choices as they go along. No single choice defines them nor does it satisfactorily predict their future behavior.

Personalization will work in the future. But this will occur, not because firms will arrive at better predictors of human behavior or better models. Rather, personalization will work in the future because firms will learn to place consumers in charge of this process.[15]

Personalization and customization will work only when a company can gain an in-depth understanding of its customers: What are their individual needs? What do they like? What do they dislike? How do they want to be contacted for different interactions? Are they more concerned with quality and value or are they price shoppers? Do they want high-touch, personal service? If so, are there times when that is not required?

Good customization should serve those who want sophisticated options as well as those who do not. Some customers won't go to the effort of using all the personal features you provide. Some won't need them. Some will surprise you and use the customization in unexpected ways that you can develop for use by others.

A few tips from an expert:

- Don't make your customizable site too hard to fine-tune.
- Don't make users go through a long process over and over again to teach the system what they like.
- Don't limit the customization to users' requests. People also need recommendations, surprises, and new ideas.
- Use "creeping customization" or "progressive customization." Start people off with a generic version. Let them customize it gradually as they see fit. Then watch what users are doing and actively recommend personalization ideas.[16]

There is one cardinal rule that must be obeyed. Once you have asked for information from the customer, don't ask for the same thing again. The study quoted earlier, sponsored by the Personalization Consortium, found 87 percent of people surveyed were annoyed when a company asked for the same information more than once.[17]

CREATING A BALANCE

Some customers will not want to give you information even though they realize they will be giving up some potential benefits. As Bruce Kasanoff says in his book, *Making It Personal: How to Profit from Personalization Without Invading Privacy* (Perseus Books, 2001), "Some people are simply private, and prefer to mind their own business and let you mind yours. Others recognize the growing infringements on private space and choose to take the cautious route."

So the need to balance privacy with personalization is still a concern. As another writer said, just because technology allows you to know your customers right down to their vacation destinations, their reading habits, their prescription drugs, and the roots of their hair doesn't mean you should know all these things. If you visit the Levi website and use the Style Finder, the questions you are asked include items such as your preferred type of music and the kind of movies you like to watch. As one scribe comments, "The best technology is not the most advanced technology but the one that best solves your marketing problems. If you want to help your website visitors find styles, then simply ask them what styles they like."[18]

It is worth giving a lot of attention to what information is captured, how it is gathered, how customers can access and control the information, and how your company can safeguard it from others that might want it but shouldn't have it. Personalization is critical to CMR, but more isn't always better. Before capturing or using personal information it's always wise to ask the question, "Will our use of this information make our customer's life easier?"

If you decide to pursue a personalization strategy, consider these ten commandments of personalization from Susan Cohen, columnist for *SAS Com Magazine*.[19]

1 **Personalize for customer reasons:** You should personalize if it will make your company's products and services more convenient for your customers.

2 **It's not about technology:** Technology isn't the place to start—nor is it the most important success factor in personalization efforts.

3 It's a corporate culture shift: Are customers at the core of your culture or is your company organized around products and services? Personalization is not an add-on. To succeed, it must be a fundamental element of every aspect of your business.

4 Preparation is hard—and critical: Understand your customers, refine your business process, and prepare your employees.

5 Analyze before you personalize: You need to understand your customers before you initiate a personalization strategy.

6 It's about people: Personalization is all about people. To be truly personal, you need to use personal language with a personal voice. Remember to treat your customers like individual people during every customer interaction.

7 Enough is enough: Find what level is right for your customers and your company. More isn't always better.

8 Privacy is paramount: No matter what your personalization strategy, do not compromise customer privacy and security.

9 Customer data is cash: You should treat your data about customers as if they were money. Each time you analyze your customer data you create value for your company.

10 Measure success: There are many ways to measure: improved return on marketing campaigns; increased overall revenues and profits; increased lifetime value of customers; increases in the number of multiproduct sales; and increased loyalty, which can be measured by an increase in the duration or frequency of customer interactions.

Scott Martin was right, the benefits of personalization and customization can be extraordinary if your strategy allows the customer to gain control.

But What About the Loyalty Card? 10

Does CMR mean the end of traditional loyalty marketing?

S OME YEARS AGO, advertisers would sarcastically say that the value of a radio station's advertising rate card was that it provided the station's address and phone number so that you could contact them to negotiate the price for a time buy. Similarly, it can be said the greatest value (to the firm) of a customer loyalty card is that it allows us to capture data to help us better understand customer behavior. The information generated by use of the loyalty card increases our customer knowledge, allowing us to make better decisions across many areas of the company—not just marketing—resulting in improved sales and profits. But, does a loyalty card program necessarily assure customer loyalty?

Brian Woolf, a global leader in loyalty marketing and author of *Customer Specific Marketing* (Teal Books, 1996) and *Loyalty Marketing: The Second Act* (Teal Books, 2002), gives a definitive answer: "A loyalty card is not a replacement for any of the basic loyalty drivers but is a supplement to them. Just as a hammer doesn't build a house, a loyalty card doesn't build customer loyalty. Both the hammer and the card are tools that, when properly and appropriately used, help bring the architect's blueprint to life."[1]

Jim Barnes, author of *Secrets of Customer Relationship Management*

(McGraw-Hill Trade, 2000), says, "Loyalty schemes must be seen for what they are—not 'loyalty' programs at all but rather programs to drive repeat business. As the latter they are generally successful, in that they tend to bring people back again and again, but not because they are emotionally loyal, but because they want the rewards. So, they are more accurately termed 'rewards' programs."[2]

Michael Lowenstein, coauthor of *Customer WinBack: How to Recapture Lost Customers—and Keep Them Loyal* (Jossey-Bass, 2001), adds "Loyalty schemes, also known as frequency marketing programs, only have value when they create—and the sponsor uses—information and insight which enables a company to improve value in all areas a customer considers important. The primary role of a retailer loyalty card is to gather data about customers."[3]

THE VALUE OF LOYALTY PROGRAMS

The customer's use of a loyalty card gives us the data required to identify our biggest spenders. Yet some years ago the president of one of our client companies refused to use customer data to segment most valuable customers, telling me in no uncertain terms, "I want our people to treat all of our customers equally." Of course, all customers should be treated with respect, but treating them all equally can lead to missed profit opportunities.

Profit Opportunity

How important is this? There is more to it than Pareto's Law (20 percent of the buyers account for 80 percent of sales volume). Garth Hallberg in his excellent book, *All Consumers Are Not Created Equal* (John Wiley & Sons, 1995), points out that for twelve of the twenty-seven packaged goods brands analyzed by MCRA Information Services, leaders in consumer behavior research, high-profit category buyers who bought the brand numbered less than 10 percent of households. In soft goods, heavy category buyers of sixteen of the eighteen apparel and footwear brands totaled less than 5 percent of households; the average below 2 percent. Five percent of households buy 85 percent of Levi's blue jeans and three percent buy 82 percent of L'eggs pantyhose.[4] It's not just U.S. packaged goods brands. In our global work with companies of every size in most major industries we see the same pattern. The biggest spenders always represent a small share of the customer universe—so small in fact that company management is always shocked by the fact. One small retailer with a database of 70,000 customers found that just 456 customers—less than one percent—accounted for 10 percent of total sales. How much is too much to invest to makes these customers' lives easier?

Biggest spenders and most frequent shoppers are generally the most profitable. In Seklemian/Newell's work with banks, supermarkets, and other businesses, we have consistently found that top spenders often generate more profit than the firm makes in total. Low spenders and occasional shoppers are often a drain on profits.

Garth Hallberg gives us another example of this with a packaged goods firm he disguises with the name YopleX. YopleX's annual net profit from its high and medium profit customers totaled $13.1 million; its low- and no-profit customers produced a net loss of $3.9 million, reducing the firm's total net profit to only $9.2 million.[5]

Value to the Customer

In many businesses the real value is in the customer information that loyalty card customers provide voluntarily. Voluntarily is the critical word. When customers volunteer personal information in return for expected benefits, the question of privacy goes away.

Some years ago Richard Barlow, founder and CEO of the loyalty marketing advertising services company, Frequency Marketing, Inc. (FMI), and publisher of Colloquy.com, established this definition of *relationship* to be used by the teams at FMI in their work with clients: "The voluntary exchange of information and value between the buyer and the seller, with the mutual expectation of gain."

He says that as consumer privacy concerns enlarge, and formal and informal mechanisms are put in place to secure privacy, relationships in which customers volunteer to be known will be essential, since without such volunteered information, customers will become increasingly invisible and difficult to reach. He says,

Loyalty programs demonstrate daily that customers gladly trade information for value. Aside from actively assuring that all their purchase activity is tracked, loyalty program members respond to surveys enthusiastically. Response rates are routinely above 20 percent, and sometimes exceed 50 percent. That's because members have learned over the years that program sponsors turn information into value for members—more points or miles, which convert into more free rewards and special treatment.[6]

Value to the Retailer

Point-based loyalty programs offer other advantages for the retailer. Brian Woolf lists more than a dozen of these advantages in *Customer Specific Marketing*:

- **Creating simplicity:** Points are a very simple way to skew rewards in favor of best customers.
- **Targeting groups:** Points permit easy targeting of groups for short-term promotions.
- **Targeting departments or categories:** Extra point offers can spur sales of specific items or from selected departments.
- **Strengthening price image:** Bonus points can replace price reductions as incentives.
- **Avoiding price wars:** Points can become the tie-breaker when you do no more than meet a competitor's price.
- **Encouraging multiple purchases:** Points can be used to encourage multiple purchases of items: extra points for three or more, and so forth.
- **Building incremental sales:** Points can be used to build incremental sales by offering bonus points for cumulative sales in a given time period.
- **Enhancing school-funds programs:** A points reward scheme is more flexible than the typical tapes-for-schools program, which assures a percentage of each customer's total spending for the schools.
- **Offering special rewards:** Points can be used as rewards for customers who attend special store functions.

- **Promoting quality control:** Some stores award points to customers who discover quality control problems. Woolf gives the example of an Irish supermarket that gives customers 100 program points if they encounter one of fifteen quality problems, such as finding an outdated item on the shelves or discovering a squeaky wheel on their shopping cart.
- **Generating employee rewards:** Besides being very well received, these point awards benefit the company because the employees' experience makes them very knowledgeable when answering customers' questions about the program.
- **Building partnerships:** Building partnerships with other companies allows cardholders to accumulate points at a faster rate.
- **Preventing defection:** As customers build up points balances, approaching even more attractive rewards, they are less likely to abandon the program.
- **Differentiating:** Given price parity, points can be a very powerful differentiator for a retailer.
- **Encouraging card carrying:** An incentive for the customer to show the card with every purchase.

There is no question that point-based loyalty programs do have value. The question is have they become so commoditized that they have lost some of their earlier punch? Barlow, a recognized expert on loyalty programs, has developed data that show more than 60 million Americans belong to frequent flyer programs. In one major market, three out of four households belong to at least one grocery frequent-shopper program, with half of those households belonging to two.

McKinsey research found that about half of the ten largest U.S. retailers in each of seven sectors have loyalty card programs, with a similar rate in the U.K. The research also found that 53 percent of U.S. grocery customers and 21 percent of the customers of casual apparel retailers are enrolled in card programs.[7]

Credit cards with reward components are the fastest growing segment of the credit card business, and reward programs increasingly are attached to debit cards. Barlow points out, "Consumers can earn miles while they eat, with their mortgage payment and on their phone bill."[8]

With all these opportunities to earn benefits, card reward programs create greater value for customers, but do they really build loyalty?

THE DOWNSIDE

Peter Leech, managing partner, Equilum Consulting and publisher of the *Know Thy Customer* newsletter, notes the downside to the overabundance of loyalty cards. "Many retailers today have launched loyalty cards and points programs to find that almost all of their shoppers have picked up a card and are gaining points or discounts. This is initially good news until shoppers pick up their competitor's card as well ... and begin to gain points in several programs simultaneously. The problem is simple ... these programs require no spend increase or loyalty commitment from the shopper in return for increasing value."[9] As many as half of all members of loyalty programs are free riders, enjoying benefits without spending more at the business that provides them. Is this widespread acceptance of loyalty cards a deterrent?

Richard Barlow expresses his concern for the current state of both hard and soft benefit loyalty card programs:

> Traditional recognition tactics like special access to reservations, customer service and product information, and special deals and discounts are so widespread that their impact and execution are diluted.
>
> Likewise, traditional hard benefits like miles and points for free flights, free nights and retail gift certificates saturate the membership environment as significant deterrents. First, it's harder than ever to redeem miles and points for flights and nights. Too much promotional currency is chasing too little available inventory. Second, the one percent to two percent standing funding rate [points per dollar spent] for rewards offerings in retail and credit card programs becomes more plainly inadequate as consumers play in more programs and experience multiple instances of low return on their loyalty investments. The antidote to parity is innovation, and regardless how skillfully we manage to deliver our messages to the customer, customers are becoming choosier as a result of the barrage of 'relationship' offers. Sooner or later, it all boils down to what's in it for the individual customer.[10]

CMR will address what's in it for the customer. Firms will have to use the information gained from the loyalty card program to serve customer needs, rather than company needs.

LOYALTY AND CMR

Ralph Harrison, managing director of The Harrison Company, whose business is providing industry-specific proprietary advertising and marketing products and services to the community banking industry, thinks most banks are going about loyalty marketing all wrong:

> Frequent Buying Programs by definition reward a customer for frequent buying. But in banking, customers do not frequently buy a bank's most important products and services; i.e., a home loan every five years, an auto loan every three years, and a CD perhaps every two years, etc. And when the concept is not frequently used by the customer, its perceived value is frequently forgotten. These programs commonly favor the more affluent customer who spends more and earns more rewards in the process. The less monied customer may never be motivated to participate and be recognized for his valued lifetime contributions to the bank.

In 1992 working with the handicap of very limited supporting software and data processing technology, Harrison developed a pilot loyalty project for a community bank that helped the bank to increase banking relationships per customer from 3.62 to 5.51 and increased the bank's return on assets from 1.17 percent to 1.40 percent. The concept, based on a customer-managed methodology, recognized the banking industry as "marketing handicapped and deficient." Harrison decided to reverse an age-old marketing concept and instead "teach the customers to buy" by rewarding them for their behavior. Harrison's theories were sound, but the limited technology in 1992 prevented Harrison from rolling out the program on a broader scale.

Now Harrison says he is ready to take advantage of the enhanced support of a new, patented Web-enabled software system and is about to launch a Loyalty Banking system based on CMR. He believes the new program will allow banks to grow and retain the financial services relationship portfolio of every customer—for a lifetime— by focusing on customer need rather than bank need. Harrison's loyalty banking is based on the customer-driven marketing principles that have been employed for frequent flyer programs. The loyalty card has now come to represent a customer profile, which the customer controls through marketing incentives provided by the bank.

All of this suggests that, although loyalty cards still have value as an incentive for the customer, thus assuring data capture, they, as Brian Woolf said, are not a replacement for any of the basic loyalty drivers but are a supplement to them.

CMR does not suggest the end of traditional loyalty marketing. Loyalty cards will continue to have great value as one element in the mix that encourages customers to volunteer information. Customers showing their cards with every purchase will still enable complete data capture. Bonus points will still offer valuable opportunities for firms to reward customers while avoiding deep discounts, and will be helpful for targeting departments, categories, or items for limited time promotions. Because loyalty programs provide such a rich, effective mechanism for allowing companies to reach beyond their own products and services to create compelling added value for their customers, they will survive and prosper.

The differentiator that makes the customer's relationship with your firm more valuable than your competitor's loyalty card will be your empowerment of her through your CMR initiative—your ability not just to give her conditional discounts but also to make her life easier. The innovation that will answer Richard Forsyth's question—"what's in it for the customer"—will be the enrichment of customers' lives as you turn more power for managing the relationship over to them.

All said and done, the primary role of a loyalty card is to enable a company to gather customer data. For CRM that customer information allowed companies to drive repeat business by rewarding customers for frequent buying. They also provided opportunities for businesses to target individual customers and customer segments for special offers to cross-sell and up-sell—all company-centric activities.

The customer information is just as critical for CMR, but firms must use it to develop innovative ways that empower customers and make their lives easier, creating emotional loyalty to the business relationship as opposed to reward loyalty to the card.

Use of Customer Information from Loyalty Cards

CRM	CMR
Recognize customers' spending	Recognize customers' needs
Target individual customers for products and services the company wants to sell	Find products and services individual customers want
Increase customers' purchases	Make customers' lives easier
Reward customers for purchases	Provide customers with a relationship experience
Develop loyalty to the card	Develop loyalty to the business

No Card? No Problem! 11

Customers tell us a lot without volunteering personal information

YOU DON'T HAVE TO HAVE a loyalty card program to find ways to empower your customers and make their lives easier. Electronic stores, furniture retailers, auto dealers, and, of course, online retailers have enough customer information to track customers' purchases and interactions with the firm. By gaining contact information early in the sales process they are able to create a continuing dialog. Then there is the television industry. Most network executives wish they could accurately track viewer interactions. Some broadcasters are finding new ways to do so.

For example, British Sky Broadcasting (BSkyB), the U.K. satellite broadcaster, has learned how to use its viewer information to empower customers and reduce churn (customers canceling the satellite service). BSkyB, based in West London, has 5.5 million customers. The company launched its digital service in October 1998 and gradually migrated the entire customer base to digital, discontinuing analog service in 2001. In the quest to reduce churn they previously focused on customers who cancelled the service, trying to get them to change their minds. The company realized that effort and resources were being wasted on the least loyal customers and changed their focus to predicting which customers might churn, enabling action before a customer cancelled.

Even without a loyalty program, Ian Shepherd, customer marketing director at BSkyB, could see opportunities to react to what his customers were telling him. Using algorithms applied to a broad selection of data on preferences and attitudes, BSkyB embarked on what Shepherd calls a "personalization theme." He says, "If you know customers well and they know that you know them well, they are less likely to cancel. They feel good." When BSkyB saw that a customer was buying five pay-per-view movies in a month instead of subscribing to the movie channel, the firm took action to move that customer to a movie channel subscription. The subscription offers a better value to the customer and tends to develop longer-term customer relationships.

Based on this monitoring of customer activity, rules are now in place to personalize messages and prevent overcommunication. BSkyB combines careful research on preferences and attitudes with customer interactions to learn what is important to each individual. The company is careful to respect the customer's time and attention, making sure they receive no more than one mailing a month, and that no two consecutive mailings contain sales messages.

By learning what is important to each client. BSkyB is succeeding in empowering customers. As a result, BSkyB's churn rates are the lowest of any broadcaster in the world, while growth in average revenue per subscriber reflects that more of their customers are choosing profitable premium channels.[1]

INCENTIVES CAN DELIVER INFORMATION

In Uruguay I found one of the most interesting programs for capturing customer information without having a loyalty card. Héctor Bajac, marketing director for Johnny Walker in Montevideo, and his team have developed a very successful customer relationship program for the Johnny Walker brands. Customers can purchase a bottle of Red Label or Black Label at their local pub and register with their national identification number. The distiller has provided pubs with special shelving for the customers to store their bottles between visits. Information about bottle purchases is collected weekly from the pubs and entered into a database. By tracking customer purchases, the firm is able to segment customers by monetary value and use the information to reward steady purchasers with complimentary upgrades from Red Label to Black Label. Señor Bajac told me the complimentary upgrade often results in a conversion of the customer to the premium label. He is capturing customers' e-mail addresses, developing dialogs, and learning more about their interests. In addition to the benefits accruing to Johnny Walker, the pub owners love the program because it keeps their patrons coming back—an added distributor loyalty factor for the firm.

CUSTOMER-CENTRIC MARKETING RESEARCH

Many retailers (and manufacturers) without loyalty card programs and with very little customer data owned at the household level can empower customers. Some are finding it a profitable exercise. I knew very little about a firm called Spectra until the company invited me to speak to its annual conference themed "Innovative Consumer-Centric Marketing Solutions." Spectra Marketing Systems, Inc., headquartered in Chicago, Illinois, serves the fast-moving consumer goods industry with consumer-centric marketing solutions. I was amazed to learn the many ways they can and do help packaged goods brand manufacturers and retailers learn enough about their customers to engage in customer-centric initiatives.

Spectra provides customer data that includes TV viewing by respondents every fifteen minutes, Internet clickstream data, loyalty card data, and very sophisticated syndicated purchase tracking. Clients can use these data sources to create a multifaceted picture of their customers that goes far beyond spending and shopping frequency. The insight allows companies without proprietary loyalty card programs to define customers by their true value to the firm. More than that, Spectra's customer knowledge helps retail chains to understand the consumers who are most involved with the chain. Spectra helps the chains learn enough about customers' special needs to enrich their shopping experiences while increasing sales and profitability.

A Case Study

A grocery chain enjoyed a strong market share but was experiencing negative comp sales (sales in stores open for more than one year) in several key grocery categories. A new competitor was spending heavily to acquire market share. The chain responded initially by maintaining uncompetitive shelf prices and reducing promotional spending to protect margin. They then decided to learn more about the shoppers who cared the most about the chain and to find ways to empower these customers by reacting to their individual needs. The following details of the case study provide a good example of what meeting the specific needs of best customers can do for any business.

With help from Spectra, the chain selected customers that were at least 33 percent loyal (as defined by share of wallet) to the chain. These customers represented 29 percent of all customers and 78 percent of chain dollars; they spent nine times as much as all other chain customers and were six times as loyal. Within this target of chain-centric top loyals, the chain found customer differences. It identified seven groups of customers, each with distinctive shopping patterns. The marketers' goal was to tailor promotion and in-store presentation to specific customer groups to react to what each customer group was "telling" them.

The end goal was to understand the customers who are most involved with the firm, and funnel marketing dollars to these customers at the expense of many others. They would also use the customer knowledge to market to different customers differently.

For the test phase, the chain chose two segments, which accounted for 50 percent of top shopper dollars, yet still offered substantial opportunity for sales growth. By studying lifestyle and life-stage data, the chain defined segment A as "The Cleavers Loyal Shoppers," traditional family households with kids, and segment B as "The Bunkers Loyal Shoppers," urban, mid-urban melting pot, and downscale urban, without kids.

Defined as	**Segment A** *The Cleavers* *Loyal Shoppers*	**Segment B** *The Bunkers* *Loyal Shoppers*
Average annual spending at chain	$5,274	$3,783
Spending at competitor	$1,666	$1,951
Trips per year to chain	89	90
Share of wallet	76%	66%

Since both Cleaver and Bunker shoppers devoted more of their total basket sales to cereal than did other shoppers, the chain chose to work first with the cereal category. Cleavers spent more on cereal, bought more units per shopper, and bought a wider variety of UPCs (Universal Product Codes) in cereal. The chain defined the cereal category as having seven subcategories:

- Adult Indulgent
- Adult Nutritional
- All Family
- Kids Sweet
- Kids Better
- Bagged Cereals
- Variety Packs

Adult Nutritional was the largest subcategory for both customer groups. Bunker's adult share, particularly Adult Nutritional, was higher. Cleaver consumers devoted most of their cereal dollars to Kids subcategories, particularly Kids Sweet. Adult Indulgent Bunker buyers spent nearly one-third of their cereal dollars on Adult Nutritional. Among Cleaver buyers of Kids Sweet, Kids Sweet accounted for one-quarter of their total cereal dollars.

This sounds complicated, but think about it for your business. Every business should be able to identify those customers who are more involved than others, and should be able to find opportunities like this for growing share of wallet. All it requires is insight to these customers' special needs and the marketing discipline to execute the targeting strategy.

Two opportunity stores were then selected for the test phase because of the large concentration of Cleavers in one store and Bunkers in the other. Demographics of each store's trading area were analyzed in more detail to validate the match against the targets, verifying that Store 107 had a high percentage of Cleavers shopping and Store 33 had a high percentage of Bunkers shopping. The demographics were not surprising:

Store Number	107	33
Customers	Higher percentage of Cleavers	Higher percentage of Bunkers
Age	55% are 35 to 54	57% are over 45
Income	72% earn more than $50,000	32% earn more than $50,000
Children	48% have children	28% have children
Ethnicity	87% white	50% white

The chain created two programs targeted to Cleaver and Bunker households through a Spectra grid customized for each store to measure category volume, overall basket size, and share of wallet. Targeting at the household level, the chain created direct mail campaigns with segment-specific offers for appropriate cereal subcategories and items: Adult Nutritional to the Bunkers in Store 33, and Kids Sweet to the Cleavers in Store 107.

For Cleavers, category dollars increased significantly for one program in Store 107 while basket size and share of wallet increased for the other program. For Bunkers, category dollars increased significantly for both programs while basket size and share of wallet actually declined.

The chain proved that it could reverse the declining trend in a key category, even in the face of the new competition. Since meeting the needs of best customers was the primary objective, the chain considered the effort positive enough (despite the small decrease in basket size in Store 33) to roll the initiative out to other opportunity stores with high concentrations of each customer segment.

What can you learn and apply to your own business? Using loyalty data to segment customers based solely on spending or frequency of shopping is not enough. These measures do not provide insight on *how* these customers care about the chain, or their potential opportunity. Companies without loyalty card programs and with little proprietary customer data owned at the household level can empower customers and gain share of wallet by using third party data. It's a matter of finding the real issues, and using the data to find real solutions, all in the name of consumer-centric marketing. Finding ways to understand customers' special needs and exercising marketing discipline to respond can work for any business.

It's Not Just for Retailers

Mass advertising sometimes brings in the wrong customers. Targeting profitable customers is an important initiative for supermarkets since 45 percent of customers in a supermarket at any given time are value shoppers. This requires customer knowledge, but doesn't necessarily require a loyalty card.

Packaged goods brand manufacturers have a similar need. More and more purchase decisions are becoming routine and low-involvement for consumers. In today's world of overload, people don't take time to think about what brand of cereal or cookies or laundry soap to buy. They just want to get what they need, get out of the store, and get on with their lives. As a result, top-line growth is slow for packaged goods manufacturers. Marketing spending has been increasing, but manufacturers are seeing diminishing return on those expenditures. Add to that the facts that they have little opportunity to market—to talk directly—to their millions of end users; they have very little individual customer data owned at the household level; and with annual brand revenue per household typically under $25, direct media is becoming less and less affordable. With access to product purchase behavior, consumer response to marketing stimuli, consumer attitudes toward category, and lifestyle/lifestage data, companies can become customer-centric marketers without loyalty cards. They can become more relevant to their customers in near-CMR fashion by discovering the differences that matter to customers and developing programs that are more productive.

There are other kinds of hammers, beside the loyalty card, that will allow companies to capture customer behavior data to identify biggest spenders and increase customer knowledge. If you don't have a loyalty card program there are third party sources, like Spectra, that can help you get at the data that will identify the real issues. As traditional customer recognition tactics become even more widespread, as it gets harder and harder to redeem miles and points for free flights and free nights, and as the impact of loyalty card rewards become more diluted, more companies will be turning to external sources of customer knowledge.

The critical point is not how you gain the customer information, it's how you use it. It has to be more than just targeting customers to sell more of what you want to sell. Your success will require using your customer knowledge to provide more of what the customer tells you she wants, giving the customer greater control of the relationship.

All Cows Look Alike **12**

Brand building—it begins and ends with the customer

I<small>T'S HARD TO TELL THE DIFFERENCE</small> between cows. So it was in the Old West, and so it is even still today; it's a brand that makes a cow different. And now with 40,000 products in a supermarket, more than 200 brands of conference room chairs, 225 models of mobile phone handsets, and more than 100 brands of computers, it's hard to tell what makes each brand different.

Branding is one of the most important marketing developments of the last century. It's not just ranch cattle; virtually everything is branded—from personalities to puddings, from sneakers to sports teams, and from cars to corporations.

But the spotlight on branding has been dimming as companies concentrate on short-term sales. When the economy falters, too many businesses put aside their long-term strategic planning process in favor of short-term goals—perhaps one of the reasons why weak companies often abandon brand marketing efforts in hard times.

Brand building is not just advertising; you can't build a brand through advertising alone. Many of the dot-coms proved that. Pets.com spent more than $30 million in advertising, including $2 million on a Super Bowl spot, and now they're gone.

With today's acceleration syndrome—where customers are constantly intensifying the need for speed—you can't build loyal brand advocates with push advertising alone. Brand loyalty comes from the customer experience, and CMR can enhance that experience. To understand that declaration, you have to step back and think a bit about what really constitutes a brand.

WHAT IS A BRAND?

A brand is not a name or a logo or a color scheme or a design layout or a tag line or an advertising theme. A brand lives in the customer's perception. A brand is not what the marketer says it is; it's what the customer thinks it is. A brand begins and ends with the customer, and most important to the customer's perception is the customer experience. Customers will believe their own experience before they believe the advertising. Advertising works only when it is supported by the customer experience, and strong brands are built one customer experience at a time.

Branding, like an iceberg, exists mostly below the surface. The visible brand messaging accounts for what we see above sea level. The invisible brand—the company culture, the customer experience—adds the mass below the surface. One of the best explanations I have seen of this came from David Wolfe and Richard Frazier of the Wolfe Resources Group, a Virginia-based company that offers a workshop series on building bridges to consumers' minds:

> Customers, not companies, control most markets. They do so by zapping commercials, walking away from company incompetence, taking leave of stores that give poor service, hanging up phones, and freely choosing what they will buy and from whom they will buy it.
>
> Our brands are not ours to do with as we wish. We are but the trustee of our brands on behalf of their real owners—our customers. Our brand value is based on what customers are willing to put into it, not on what we can expect to get out of it. Brands are personalities. Customers only invest themselves in brands whose personalities they like. The only brand positioning that makes sense is one that allows customers to see themselves when beholding the brand.[1]

Companies thought CRM would build brands. That hasn't happened. Wolfe and Frazier are right: The best brand positioning is one that allows customers to see themselves when beholding the brand. The company must know its customers and the brand must represent part of how customers want to see themselves. They may want to be more stylish or more athletic. Proper brand positioning allows the customer to see himself a certain way with the help of a brand.

This is a great argument for CMR. When we put the customers in charge we, in effect, let them see themselves when looking at the brand. A serious customer-centric business model creates empathetic links with customers. As Wolfe and Frazier say,

> It promotes dialogs in which empathy flows back and forth between company and customer. It allows both company and customer to be more vulnerable, a requisite for unguarded communications that inform both parties for mutual benefits. These are conditions on which healthy personal relationships depend. Healthy company-customer relationships depend on these same conditions.

CUSTOMER DIALOG

Most CRM initiatives have failed to involve the customer enough for the customers to see themselves when beholding the brand. They haven't given power to the customer in ways that would allow both company and customer to be more vulnerable. CMR changes the game. It builds what Lois Geller, in her book *Customers for Keeps* (Adams Media Corporation, 2001), calls "friendship marketing." She says, "Turns out the very attributes I look for in friends are the same ones I look for in brands. Friendship branding is a method of creating a warm, emotional bond between buyers and sellers—between businesses doing business with each other—in short, between any two parties in a transaction." This type of bond requires the mutual respect of friendship that can best be achieved with CMR.

As Ray Jutkins, a noted direct mail consultant and speaker, says, "The idea is to treat customers the way you treat your best friends; in the very best way. First, as people. And then with first class service; a top quality product. You reach out and touch—hold their hand—be their teddy bear."

The trick is to get customers to invest themselves in your brand, to reach out to you in friendship, which requires sharing. This will happen only when you let the customers manage the relationship. When customers can talk to you and define their needs, they begin to insert themselves in your brand. This calls for questions, not just about the customer's needs, but about his or her interests, lifestyle, and current life stage. Customers will share this information if they see added value coming back to them from the relationship. One way to create this closeness is to involve customers in your business activities.

CUSTOMER INVOLVEMENT

Procter & Gamble uses the Web to give consumers an inside look at products that haven't been formally launched yet. Consumers have an opportunity to try these new products and comment on them. The consumer then has some "ownership" of the product when it comes to market.

Not to keep picking on the now defunct Pets.com, but theirs is a good example of a failed attempt at brand building. They, and a great many other pure play e-retailers, never got close enough to customers to allow customers to see themselves when beholding the brand. Pets.com spent their marketing dollars exposing their charming puppet to a mass audience and not on connecting with individuals. Amazon, on the other hand, spent little, if anything, on TV and chose instead to concentrate on understanding their customer: "We know the books you have purchased in the past. Here are some like those we think you will like." Amazon built their great brand by understanding the customer.

The Web must be used with a different understanding of the consumer's interaction. The strength of the Web for CMR is not about selling more products but connecting with the customer. Michael Bayler and David Stoughton in their book, *Promiscuous Customers: Invisible Brands* (Capstone Publishing, 2002), make the point that when customers go online, their behavior often switches, like the swapping of left and right in a mirror image. They write,

Somehow, in digital markets, the expectations of our most valuable customers are almost absurdly heightened and accelerated. They are inclined to shoot first—assassinating the brand with remarkable callousness—and not bothering to ask any questions at all. The Internet changes everything. It commoditises everything it touches, with a reverse Midas touch that strips not only cost, but value, from almost every process.[2]

There are some who would quarrel with that thinking because they have found ways to involve customers in unguarded communication and build brand relationships on the Web. Budweiser's now famous "Whassup?!" campaign was hugely successful across the world, exceeding expectations and embedding itself in the vernacular of many languages. People took the characters to heart and felt they were part of the brand.

Audience interaction with the Budweiser brand was achieved by introducing interactive elements on the website including screensavers, phone icons via SMS (short message service) mobile messaging, wallpaper, TV ads, and sounds. The screensavers had a message function that could be personalized, and the site enabled people to send a variety of icons to their phones. The ability to e-mail characters from the ads was most popular within the site.

Integration with Budweiser's TV advertising campaign kept people talking about the site. Yet-to-be-broadcast ads were hidden on the site for viewers to find. Budweiser film crews visited bars around the country auditioning people to act out their own version of Whassup?! The prize was the chance to appear in ads to be screened on both TV and the website. Whassup?! was the fourth most-talked-about-website of the year. People became involved spontaneously in what was essentially a cultural virus, infecting the lingo wherever it went.[3]

The Whassup?! campaign offers evidence that there is a lot more to brand building on the Web than click-through. It's still about involving customers, empowering customers, and building brand value based on what customers are willing to put into it, not on what companies can expect to get out of it. Consumers were empowered to share in the Whassup?! campaign, sometimes even adding to it. Budweiser offered e-invitations to the bar events, allowing friends to invite each other.

Budweiser's "Whassup?!" became the first catchword of the new millennium, as a result of the discussions it generated among its target customers—its "talk value." Budweiser also enjoyed its best sales trends in seven years.

THE BRAND PROMISE

Your brand is the promise you keep with your customers, and part of that promise is simplicity. As you give the customer more power to manage the relationship—as you learn more and more about what they want from you—you will make their lives simpler by eliminating choices you know they don't want.

I often use the example of Hilton Hotels. They have made it their business to know enough about what I want and what I don't want that they don't bother me with things of no interest to me, while keeping their promise on things I consider important. For example, they know I want a smoking room near the elevator with a king-sized bed; I don't have to tell them these details each time. I call the Hilton, "My Hotel." When your customer calls your brand "My Brand" you have won the branding game.

When you have reached this kind of close relationship, you have built a strong defense of forgivability. There will always be a time when something goes wrong with a product, a service, or your customer communication. The customer who considers your brand "My Brand" will be more forgiving. The folks at the Bridgestone/Firestone retail stores learned this when they had to deal with the manufacturer's massive, high-profile tire recall in 2001. Jim Stahulak, manager of database/Internet marketing for the retail and commercial operations division, said, "We learned that as long as the relationship between the customer and the store was good, the news wasn't going to change the customers' impression of our brand or their loyalty to our products. Customers actually thought we handled the recall very well."[4]

It's not just product, service, or communication goofs that can hurt a brand. Sometimes it's the corporate leader. William Arruda, founder of Reach, a global branding company, writes,

In this day of celebrity brands, it is becoming essential for senior executives to build and communicate their personal brands to expand both individual and corporate success. An executive's brand is his/her promise of value. It separates executives from their peers and allows them to expand their personal success while building greater success for their organizations. Executive branding is not about building a special image for the outside world; it is about understanding an executive's unique combination of rational and emotional attributes—his/her strengths, skills, values and passions—and using these attributes to stand out.[5]

We don't have to dredge up former Enron Corp. CEO Ken Lay; there are less egregious examples of harmful executive branding. Hewlett-Packard Company, Compaq Computer Corporation, and Cisco Systems, Inc. were the three technology companies that did the worst job of maintaining brand value in 2001, according to the Liquid Agency Inc. "Bruised and Battered Brands" survey. According to this report released in early 2002, HP CEO Carly Fiorina was the technology executive perceived to have harmed her company's brand most in 2001, followed by Oracle Corporation CEO Larry Ellison and Microsoft Corporation CEO Bill Gates. Fiorina's aggressive push for a merger with Compaq had a negative impact on the HP brand according to poll respondents, as did Microsoft's battle with the federal government and the states.

The survey also identified public relations as the most effective way to market and create demand for technology brands in a tight economy, followed by customer relationship management and brand advertising.[6]

How could CMR have helped these executives? Listening to customers—the dialog part of CMR—would have told these executives they were miscommunicating with their constituents. With the kind of sharing friendship Lois Geller describes combined with empowered customers and employees helping to define their strategy, they would have had a better feel of the public pulse. CMR could have helped Carly Fiorina sell her HP/Compaq merger more positively and perhaps gotten even more of the industry on her side. It's impossible to say whether or not Bill Gates could have turned around the case against Microsoft, but strong CMR initiatives would certainly have brought more folks to his side of the argument.

THE EXPERTS WEIGH IN

Many experts agree that the process of brand building has changed. Their thoughts support the concept of CMR.

Scott Bradbury, CEO—Brandstream "We often underestimate how long brands can hold on to a negative association, even if it's just water cooler talk about a car that continuously breaks down. The Web has increased the consuming public's ability to rant and rave about a company or a service. Smart companies now recognize the necessity of being responsive in real time. Lots of consumers are looking for information and brand cues. Companies that fail to deliver these will lose the sale to someone else who does. Price is not everything."[7]

Richard Rosen, president and CEO—AlloyRed, Rosen/Brown "Prospect interaction with an ad or marketing campaign is the key to satisfying the information needs of prospects while meeting the marketing objectives of the company. Interaction serves as a bridge between brand awareness and involvement, increasing a prospect's awareness and favorable consideration of the brand. It also increases involvement by motivating the prospect to make a purchase or take the next step in the sales dialog."[8]

Regis McKenna, chairman—McKenna Group "If you look at the top 50 companies of the Fortune 500 in 1989, you'll see that ten years later, 39 had dropped from the Fortune 500. These are the companies that spend the most money advertising and promoting their brands." McKenna sights Starbucks taking over traditional coffee brand positions not by advertising, but by building service centers (customer relationships) in our communities. He makes the point that, "The Internet has certainly changed the way in which you brand products, but not in the way most marketers think. The Internet is not a broadcast medium like television. It is much more of a service medium in which you allow people to interact and exchange information with you."[9]

Al Ries, chairman—Ries & Ries "The Web has caused problems for many brands because most companies think of the Web as just another advertising medium like radio, television, newspapers and magazines. I am strongly opposed to that view. True the Web is a mass communications medium. The difference between the Web and any other mass medium is that the Web is interactive. The user of the message is in charge, not the sender."[10]

John Hagel, chief strategy officer—Twelve Entrepreneuring "Historically a brand has been a promise that says, 'If you buy this product or buy from my company, you can rely on me because of the attributes attached to the brand.' We're going to see a new kind of branding emerge, a much more customer-centric branding where the promise is, 'I know you as an individual customer better than anyone else, and you can trust me to assemble the right products or services to meet your individual needs.'" Hagel says it's not a matter of one vendor dealing with one customer at a time, "What customers really want are many vendors to one customer. They want to leverage the full capability of the network to access whatever resources they need from wherever they are."[11]

NEW CHALLENGES

With the proliferation of products and brands and the swift acceleration of consumers' lives, branding brings new challenges. Are the doomsayers right?

In *No Logo* (Picador USA, 2002), Naomi Klein talks about what she calls the "unsavory dominance" of big brands and predicts a "brand boomerang."[12] Websites such as Cluetrain.com protest the corporate marketing-speak of modern brands, claiming that most corporations only know how to talk in what they call the soothing, humorless monotone of the mission statement, the marketing brochure, and the "your call is important to us busy signal."

Brands that engage their stakeholders not only live longer but are worth more. Paul Twivey, founding partner of Circus, a London agency, gives us hope and makes a strong case for the kind of customer engagement CMR can deliver:

Great brands are about great stories, brilliantly told and acted out every day, engaging all the stakeholders in their community.

Brand engagement is the process of forging ties between a brand and all the people who have an interest in it, including employees, consumers, shareholders, partners and suppliers. Why is it important? Because brands that engage their stakeholders through a passionate integrity not only live longer, but are worth more and improve the quality of peoples' lives.

Brands that engage people make them feel good as well as delivering higher shareholder value and higher return on investment. They score highly on most financial measures you care to apply.[13]

Successful brands of the future will be those that empower customers and tailor their interactions with them in ways that enrich customers' lives and relieve stress. These will be the brands that will allow customers to see themselves in the brand.

Key Points

- CMR is not a substitute for building brand; your brand is still your difference.
- Your brand is your promise to recognize what your customer considers important.
- Listening to customers and understanding their needs will build your brand.
- Unless there is a real closeness between the customer and the brand, personal communications will not be accepted.
- The customer experience means more for brand building than the advertising.
- Putting customers in charge and getting them to invest in the brand is one part of brand building.
- The Internet is not a broadcast medium. The user of the message is in charge, not the sender.
- The CEO is an important part of the brand.
- Brands that engage their stakeholders live longer, are worth more, and improve the quality of people's lives.

PART THREE

How to Change

Before You Build a Better Mousetrap 13

Is CMR for everyone?

H OW CAN YOU KNOW whether or not CMR is important, or even right, for your business? You might start by thinking like Yogi Berra, who once said, "Before you build a better mousetrap, it would help to know if there are any mice out there." There are some cases where a firm's customers don't fit the CMR "trap," and you won't find any mice waiting.

One of the measures of potential CMR value to a company is the frequency of its customers' purchases. Without frequent interaction, it is difficult to maintain the dialog to empower customers. Donald Libey, president of Libey, Inc. and renowned direct marketing and e-commerce prognosticator, gave me some of my earliest lessons in database marketing. He made the importance of frequency clear to me with the example of the builder of bridges across the Mississippi, whose customers contract for bridges about every 100 years. This bridge builder would have little opportunity for CMR.

What else should you consider before embarking on the CMR journey? As is often the case, the answer to this question leads to more questions:

- Are you prepared to move CMR to the center of your corporate strategy as a process of learning to understand the values that are important to your individual customers?
- Will CMR fit with your business strategy—can it serve your financial and business goals?
- Can you get everyone in your company to agree on a common definition of CMR and understand that CMR is not just an advanced stage of database marketing?
- Are you willing to give away power to the customer? Can your corporate culture support this change?
- What will be the cost of deploying CMR? What will be the cost of not deploying some degree of CMR?
- Can your competitors put you at a disadvantage if they empower their customers before you do?
- Will you be able to integrate your customer data so that all of the data sources can be used to create a single view of the customer? Can you afford to do it?
- Will your IT team be willing and able to find new ways to manage the customer data and make it available on an enterprise-wide basis?
- Can you identify the kind of customers that are right for your business?
- Will some of your best customers want to be empowered? Will that empowerment add value to their customer experience? Will it add value for your firm?
- Will your sales managers, product managers, sales personnel, and others be able to develop customer service strategies and product offerings based on customer needs?
- Can you identify what return on investment will be expected from the CMR initiative?
- Do you have total commitment from most senior management?
- And, finally, will you and your company—and that means everyone in the firm—have the belief in the durability of this customer-centric process and have the patience to see the project through?

If you can't answer yes to all of these questions, it's time to close this book and look for a new challenge somewhere else. But, if you've responded with an enthusiastic "yes!" to each of these questions, it is worth examining them more closely.

GETTING BEYOND THE DREAM

Are you prepared to move CMR to the center of your corporate strategy? Everything we see suggests that most companies want this to happen. The Gartner study, mentioned in Chapter 1, showed 52 percent of surveyed companies rated customer relations their highest priority. But that study was asking about CRM initiatives—there are no statistics developed yet to measure commitment to CMR. Empowering customers is a great dream, but be realistic.

Will CMR fit with your business strategy and serve your company's financial and business goals? If your business strategy dedicates your firm to be the low-price leader (period!), there is not much chance that CMR is important or even right for your company. That is not to say a low-price leader shouldn't or can't find ways to empower its customers. Wal-Mart, as a low-price leader, has never taken the position that they are a "low-price leader, period!" In *loyalty.com* I quoted Paul Higham, then senior vice president, marketing and customer communications of Wal-Mart. His comments are particularly appropriate for this discussion:

> If there ever was a retailer who had built their reputation on the attribute of low pricing, it certainly is Wal-Mart. But, how well we know that low prices are only half the process. Only when it is counterbalanced by a commitment to the lives, needs and wants of customers does it all make sense. Price deals with the fact of the matter. But the human factor, like customer care and service, leads us to another thing, every bit as important—the heart of the matter.[1]

The question of whether or not CMR will fit with your business strategy has little to do with your pricing policy and everything to do with your people policy—how much you care about the human factor and how much you are willing to empower your customer. If you can commit to the lives, needs, and wants of customers you can find the way to make CMR serve your financial and business goals.

Does Your Mousetrap Have a Market?

A good starting point in deciding if CMR is right for your business is asking if you're up for the challenge of getting everyone in your company to agree on a common definition of what CMR is. This should be addressed with the understanding that there are different levels of CMR, and that the right level for each business is based on the long-term economic model of that company. Defining these key concepts is not something that should be left to the marketing department, the IT team, or the bean counters. Your definition should be carefully crafted by an interdisciplinary team: marketing, operations, product specialists, IT, financial, associates on the firing line, and senior management.

Only after you have reached agreement on your definition can you address the next questions: Are you willing to give away power to your customers and does the way you manage the business support this change?

In making this decision it is time to explore the opportunity cost of not deploying some degree of CMR—not an easy calculation. Referring to earlier CRM implementations, Dennis Pombriant, research director at the Aberdeen Group, made this observation, "Opportunity cost is hard to measure because you are measuring something that is not there. Some would say the opportunity cost the company is missing is the equivalent to the return on investment (ROI) that they would have gotten post implementation. However, looking at the loss of ROI can be too simplistic. Opportunity cost affects a company's growth and development far out into the future, and because of that, it is so hard to measure."[2]

The fact is that the customer does have new power. If a company is not prepared to recognize that element of the business equation, then, sooner or later, that company will be losing customers and revenues, and few companies can afford to see their customer base diminished today.

Louis Columbus, senior analyst at AMR Research, says, "In the present economic environment, many companies are surviving only because they are holding onto their current customers. We still aren't into positive economic growth yet. Given the fact that so many companies are relying on their customers for sustaining revenue streams, they can't afford not to have information captured. Simply put, with as much as 75 percent of a typical company's revenue coming from current customers, the opportunity cost of not deploying CRM is lost sales."[3]

Competition

How can your competitors put you at a disadvantage if they empower their customers before you do? In their dealings with companies of all kinds, across all industries, customers are seeking empowerment. If they don't find it in their relationship with one firm they will be quick to look for it with another. It's a strong bet that some of your competitors will understand and act.

Cost

CMR will require you to have a 360-degree view of your customer across all channels, and this integration will have a cost. It has been reported that General Motors invested $20 million to put its CRM project in place.[4] Many smaller companies have accomplished data integration with five-figure budgets. The good out-of-the-box solutions available today mean you don't have to be the size of GM to get into the game. But you will need good tools, so the investment in these assets will have to be factored into your decision.

Working with client companies, I have found the simple technology solutions are often the best. Big dollars don't always buy big wins. There are other costs of course: people to manage and maintain the database, analysts to turn the data into information, and supportive hardware costs.

The greater question is whether or not you can count on solid support from your IT team to make your customer knowledge available, in real time, enterprise-wide. You will need their buy-in from day one because, in the end, they are the ones who must supply the customer data that will drive the CMR engine.

Can you identify a return on your CMR investment? This gets us back to the discussion of the cost of not deploying CMR. There are metrics that can be applied. Starting with benchmarks of share-of-wallet and customer retention, it is a simple matter of calculating the profit potential of a set amount of improvement for a defined segment of the customer base. This becomes your goal for the program. Those incremental profit dollars, less the cost of your implementation, begin to define the potential ROI. This is discussed further in Chapter 17.

Customer Selection

We have talked before about identifying the customers who are right and most profitable for your business. Now you have to decide if your best customers will want to be empowered and to what degree. Chances are you will find that empowerment adds great value to some but not all of your customers. That presents no problem, since you can't start by providing a total CMR experience for all of your customers. We have found that word spreads swiftly. You may find that as some of your more reluctant customers begin to see the results your CMR initiatives are delivering for others, they will ask to join the program.

Sometimes it's difficult to predict whether or not it will be worth it for a company to empower its customers. You might never expect CMR could have value for a baker of cheesecakes. Yet Chicago-based Eli's Cheesecake has proved the value of empowering its customers. Since giving customers the option of custom designing their purchases, the firm has experienced a big payoff in sales and repeat business. After the addition of the customization feature, sales increased 65 percent. A spokesperson says, "We're driving more repeat business from existing customers because they like the fact they can create their own message and medium."[5] This is more than just offering a new service; it empowers customers by letting them design their own customized product.

Employee Commitment

You can deliver customer empowerment only if everyone in the firm can contribute. Of course that starts with all customer-facing personnel, but it goes far beyond to include back-office systems associates and even those responsible for the product. At the end of the line, the value of the customer experience depends on the delivery of the right product at the time the customer needs it. If you can't deliver on the promise, don't get in the game. When Kmart began fighting for its life, having filed for Chapter 11 bankruptcy protection in January 2002, one of their immediate challenges was to build relationships with best customers to try to keep them loyal to the firm. The biggest problem in doing that, they told me, was that they couldn't be certain they would have the merchandise the customer wanted on the shelves. They were afraid to promise something they couldn't deliver.

The question of total commitment from most senior management should really have been first on the list. Without that backing, your plan will have no chance of success. And, that commitment must carry with it the understanding that the process of customer empowerment is not just another short-term campaign, but the life blood of the company's growth and development far out into the future.

AN EVOLVING PROCESS

The important thing to remember as CMR evolves—and it will evolve—is that it will be less of a cost-cutting tool and more of a way to listen to the voice of the customer and to enrich the customer's relationship with your firm. The long-term cost of missing this opportunity will be significant.

But before you make the commitment to CMR, you need to know more than just how many mice are out there. You need to know whether or not empowering customers is important for your business and whether or not you can deliver on the promise. Ask the questions and get the answers before you start building the mousetrap.

Customer Service— Who Cares? 14

CMR doesn't mean "best customer service" for everyone

ACCORDING TO A GARTNERG2 REPORT, online retailers looking to solidify their business amid difficult economic conditions must deliver convenience to customers above price. The survey reports that 79 percent of online customers value convenience when making a purchase, more than twice as many as the 32 percent of respondents who say lower prices are their main concern.[1] Erin Kinikin, vice president of the research and advisory firm Giga Information Group, says surveys of ISP businesses show that consumers consider good service equivalent to competitive pricing—both are top reasons for subscribing. Kinikin rates strong service at EarthLink as the reason for an attrition rate about half that of EarthLink's similarly priced competitors.[2]

We read every day that customer expectations of service are on the rise. Like Moore's Law of computing, customer expectations seem to be doubling every eighteen months. And, that's not just for online retailers and ISPs. Service is important for every business. But is it everything? Is its importance the same in all industries, for all companies and, more importantly, for all customers?

CUSTOMER EXPECTATIONS

Companies have always believed that "best customer service" for everyone is a hallmark of CRM. Unfortunately, trying to serve everyone equally well usually means serving everyone equally poorly—an expensive, inefficient effort. The concept of CMR changes that. Letting the customer manage the relationship means delivering the service level the individual customer wants, with a trade-off on price. Some retail chains have been founded on this principle. For example, Wal-Mart knows it's not Nordstrom and offers less expensive items without the consistently outstanding customer service. IKEA says, "We do our bit. You do yours. It's easier to save money when we all lend a hand." They ask customers to assemble their own furniture and manage their own delivery. IKEA also does not accept special orders and has limited service in their stores. So even though Wal-Mart and IKEA don't customize service levels for individual customers, both are examples of CMR in action— delivering only the service level customers want which, in turn, allows them to offer lower prices.

No More, No Less

Trying to provide "best customer service" to everyone is one more reason for CRM failure. Customers look for different levels of service from different businesses. The same customer who is annoyed at having to wait thirty seconds for a sales associate at Saks will wait patiently in the long checkout lines at Kmart and Wal-Mart. The contrast in customer expectations is not just different for different companies in the same industry. Customers' service expectations also vary by industry. They have learned not to expect the same level of service from their utility or phone company that they do from their bank or broker. The more personal the business relationship, the higher the expected level of service.

None of this should be new. What's new is the need to realize that both expectation of and desire for service vary by each individual customer—even within a company. So the fact that customer expectations of service are on the rise does not mean you should try to provide "best customer service" for every one of your customers—only the level of service each individual customer desires and expects Providing more leaves you overgiving for no benefit; providing less means you are going to lose a customer.

Allowing the customer to manage the relationship in this way not only deepens the relationship between the customer and the company, but also it can save the company money. This is not a matter of cutting corners to see how little service you can get away with for a customer. Finding the right balance requires that the company create the kind of dialog with customers that will teach the firm each individual's service requirements. When companies get this kind of feedback they are often surprised at how much money they were wasting by providing services some customers found to be of no value.

A Good Example

Xiameter, an online arm of Michigan-based Dow Corning that sells silicone products directly to industrial buyers, understands this. They instituted a "no service" approach for some of their best customers who didn't really require follow-up customer service and tech support. Michael Lanaham, commercial director of Xiameter, says, "A lot of customers were saying to us, 'We buy a lot of silicone, we know how to use it, and we don't need the technical expertise you are known for.'" For these customers, Xiameter has set up a less expensive real-time ordering and inventory system that offers no technical support. Sales communications are handled primarily by e-mail, with responses normally given within one business day.[3] This is the ideal win-win situation. Customers don't have to pay for tech support they don't want or need, and the company is able to reduce the size of the service staff to save money.

E-SERVICE AND SELF SERVICE

An early 2002 Gartner report on e-service cites studies that show 70 percent of corporations believe they have a well-run contact center that provides their customers with good customer service. Yet only 46 percent of their clients report being satisfied with the service. Gartner proposes that world-class e-service requires enterprises to adapt to users' needs and requirements, saying, "Customers are demanding more information, easier and expanded access, and support through newer channels. Through year-end 2002, enterprises that properly implement e-service solutions that enable their customers to get better, easier access to information through more channels will increase customer satisfaction by between 5 and 10 percent."[4]

A 2002 study of 500 business-to-business marketers by Performark, Inc. found that 60 percent of the marketers did not respond to customer inquiries within sixty days. The study measured responses to over 1,000 inquiries made via the Web, business response cards, and toll-free telephone calls. Clearly, it will take more than the Internet to improve companies' responsiveness. Many companies say that their websites serve important marketing purposes; however, companies are not using their websites as cost-effective customer relation tools.[5] Moreover, as customer inquiries continue to rise, most contact centers are not making proportional increases in staffing and in many cases are even being forced to reduce the number of customer service representatives (CSRs). The growth of online customer interaction and the increased performance pressures on conventional call centers will force companies to implement the kind of e-service solutions that Gartner proposes. Giving customers better, easier access to information is more than just cost effective, it is the start of empowering customers through CMR.

Not all companies understand this. In an Insight Interactive survey, 52 percent of companies did not consider automated customer access relevant to their CRM strategy.

I am indebted to Richard Forsyth, founder and editor of the CRM-Forum, for this perfect example of bad and good customer service. If you need online support for a Sony Vaio PC you need to register with the Sony Club Vaio Site where you are asked to provide:

- An eight-digit product code (pre-completed)
- An eight-digit serial number (pre-completed)
- A user ID and password
- A significant amount of personal data

You are then given a sixteen-digit customer ID which you are never asked for again but are afraid to lose. Beyond all that, the product codes in the website are often different from the ones on your PC or in the marketing literature, making it difficult to buy the right memory for your PC. (This was the case at the time this was written. A later visit to the site showed an update that eliminated some of Forsyth's horrors, but the site was still difficult to navigate.)

Forsyth contrasts this with a similar service from Dell, in which you are asked to provide only a six-digit service tag number or a nine-digit express service code, both printed on the bottom of your PC. He gives a banana peel to Sony and a gold star to Dell.[6]

Measuring Your Success

Elaine Cascio, self-service practice manager of Vanguard Communications offers three strategies for learning how well you are doing with your e-mail and self service:

- **Talk to your customers:** Ask not only about customers' use of your current applications, but also about the experiences they have had with self service overall, and the applications they'd like to see you offer.
- **Talk to your CSRs:** CSRs know customers and the inquiries and transactions they need better than anyone else in the company. Ask what interactions could be automated, and what they hear from customers. (And show them the value of self service in off-loading routine tasks.)
- **Benchmark:** Find out the types of applications and interfaces offered by others in your market, both over the phone and on the Web.[7]

If Sony had listened to Cascio's advice, they could have earned a gold star from Forsyth.

The Importance of Self Service

Web-based companies seem to be quick to understand that online customer service is crucial to their success—a Direct Marketing

Association (DMA) report released in March 2002 found that 75 percent of online companies now integrate their customer service functions fully into telephone, fax, and Internet-based systems.[8] H. Robert Wientzen, president and CEO of the DMA explains, "Traditional direct marketers who built their reputations on customer service were early adopters of real time technologies. As a result, they are applying their existing customer service fulfillment technology to realize economies of scale when conducting Web business."[9] The direct marketers' service technologies that worked so well for telephone requests have been translated to the Web and have been accepted by customers.

The importance of these kinds of self-service offerings was further documented in consumer research conducted by the Future Foundation for a consortium entitled "The Self Service Society." The research found that nearly two-thirds of customers in the banking and mobile phone sector consider the ability to self-serve important in their choice of supplier.[10]

When CFO Research Services queried senior finance executives in the United States and Europe in August 2001 to explore the changing role of information and communications technology (ICT) they found improved customer service was the highest priority for ICT investments. Eighty percent of CFOs said their investments to improve customer service were absolutely crucial or very important, the highest percentage of any ICT investment category.[11]

Investing in Self Service

Some companies are heeding Gartner's advice and gearing up their service activities with big investments. For example, in January 2002 AT&T announced a plan to pay $2.6 billion over five years to the consulting firm Accenture to bolster its customer service, assigning 4,300 of AT&T Consumer's 13,000 employees to the new operation. At the same time, Nextel, with partner IBM, inked an eight-year $1.2 billion deal with CRM outsourcer Tele-Tech Corporation to improve its customer care capabilities. Tele-Tech will manage Nextel's six customer relationship centers, which staff 4,500 customer service personnel.[12]

Turning to Web-based service strategies seems to be a necessary alternative. No matter how much money a company pumps into its contact center, there will be only a fixed number of calls that can be handled efficiently in one day based on the number of employees in the facility. Companies have not found the perfect way to predict spikes in service demand resulting from promotions, new products, or seasonality. This leaves them with one of two results: too many employees working or too few. They either upset customers with long waits at peak times or spend too much for excess capacity on the slower days. Self service on the Web solves some of this dilemma by reducing the number of inquiries that require human interaction. This points out the real value of self service to a firm and its customers: it frees up service representatives to give personal attention to those customers who actually need human interaction.

Ping, a leading manufacturer of golf equipment, implemented a Web-based self-service solution to better manage customer e-mail. Prior to its installation, customer support representatives were personally responding to 1,500 to 4,000 e-mails a month. Many of the inquiries dealt with the same questions, which meant human and financial resources were not being used cost-effectively. Once customers were able to find the right answer 24/7 through self service, inbound e-mail dropped by about 50 percent. With traditional e-mail management costing about $10 per incident and self service only about $1, Ping immediately realized a return on its CRM investment.

Perhaps a word of caution is in order here. Although a drop in inbound e-mail is economically sound, a company loses some opportunity for dialog. It is important as you move customers to self service to monitor the questions your customers are asking.

When another golf equipment maker, TaylorMade-adidas Golf, installed KANA Response, an automated, Web-based e-mail response application, they cut the time required to respond to an e-mail query from 5.5 minutes to 2.7 minutes per message. Due to the improved service, the number of e-mails TaylorMade receives annually actually increased, a result that doesn't bother the company. Rob McClellan, global e-marketing manager, says, "When a customer receives a 'good' response, customers often send a 'thank you' message which counts as another inbound e-mail. Sometimes it's like they're testing us, and when they get a good response, they come back with follow-up questions and continue the dialog. The cost of additional messages isn't a concern, since the efficiencies of the operation more than compensate, and it makes us look like a high-quality company." The savings the company has realized from reduced headcount has already covered the costs of the e-mail initiative, and the applications have virtually paid for themselves.[13]

Another company, network provider 3Com, saved $16.8 million in 2000 by encouraging customers to switch from its support center to its website and learned that some customers actually prefer self service when it is done well.[14] "When it's done well" is the key. Joe Lethert, Performark founder and chairman, says, "Even companies that are responding to inquiries are not doing a good job. They are saying to their prospects and customers: 'everything you want is on the website. Go find it yourself.'" Lethert makes the point that customers enter the sales pipeline at different levels of readiness and need to be nurtured differently.[15]

According to a study by RightNow Technologies there are four adjectives to describe what customers want in e-service: fast, meaningful, compelling, and customer-driven:

- **Fast:** Customers expect to be able to find the right information and content immediately. They have little patience for intro screens or repeated clicks on menus.
- **Meaningful:** Customers expect the information they find on the Web will be timely, up-to-date, and relevant to their immediate needs. If it isn't, they will develop a bad impression of the company.
- **Compelling:** Customers expect content will be presented in a way that's interesting, interactive, and focused. These expectations are a result of their other online experiences.
- **Customer-driven:** Customers don't want to have to wade through marketing-oriented propaganda to find what they're looking for. Companies must, therefore, ensure that their e-service content is driven by the most frequent customer questions—not by what company staffers think customers might be most interested in.[16] CMR will change the customer-driven objective to demand that e-service content be driven

not by the questions the *average* customer asks most, but by the known interests of the individual customers the company is trying to empower.

One of the problems with companies doing self service well is that too many of them consider it a cost reduction program instead of an advantage for the customer. In a 2002 study from KANA, almost half of consumers surveyed said that the most negative aspects of dealing with a company are having to repeat their orders, questions, mailing address, and payment method, due to the company's failure to track their interaction history. On the positive side, 45 percent of those polled said that having a personalized account set up, either in a call center, on the Web, or via e-mail, made their interaction "more beneficial."[17]

The ability to get it right for each customer is becoming critical as consumers continually raise their standards as the result of experience. Unsatisfied customers are quick to spread the bad word. A year-long study of online customer experience and expectations conducted by the Future Foundation for First Direct confirms this. The study shows that the proportion of respondents that actually warned other people against using websites at which they had experienced bad service had nearly tripled in one quarter, and they had told more people than previously.[18]

Time

Web requests, just like contact center interactions, require immediate responses. The record for swift response has not been good. In a December 2001 study tracking online retailers, for example, Jupiter Media Metrix learned that only 33 percent resolved basic customer service requests within six hours. Forty percent took more than three days to respond or didn't respond at all. This hurts more than just the online business: The Jupiter report concludes that 53 percent of consumers polled say they would not be likely to buy from a retailer's offline store if they had a negative experience in the online channel.[19]

One writer commenting on this dismal report makes a good case for customer empowerment: "If so few retailers answer our e-mails in

It's More than Good Service: It's About ROI

Beyond delivering the obvious benefits that come from making customers happier, Web-based self service can deliver return on investment by leveraging a company's Internet infrastructure, legacy systems, content repositories, and other existing technologies. Guarav Verma and Todd Hollowell at Doculabs, a research and consulting firm, document the key components required at a technical level:

The portal interface. The portal extends the capabilities of service reps to customers. The product should provide a browser interface that lets customers modify their profiles. It should also provide case-management capabilities to let users view, create, or edit trouble tickets or service requests. In addition, it should let them run reports, such as summaries of all outstanding trouble tickets, and provide a Web-accessible search engine for customers' use.

Collaboration tools. These features let customers interact in real time with service representatives or other customers to share information such as simple fixes for problems, via Web chat or e-mail discussions. Many products allow these group discussions to be posted in a threaded manner and let representatives moderate the discussion groups. Access control is a critical capability, because CRM products must automatically authenticate and govern discussion-group access and limit it to authorized users.

A comprehensive knowledge base. This component provides an extensive repository of content and includes a search engine that lets users locate all documents and information related to their queries or requests for service. Customers can use the knowledge base to manage product or company information and invoices, bills, transaction records, and histories of service inquiries. The knowledge base should support various search methods, such as full-text and Boolean searches, and the use of index fields or parameters associated with information managed in the knowledge base. It also may be able to automatically "learn" from a customer's previous knowledge-base sessions, and to use this information when determining the relevance of information to the customer's search request.

a timely fashion, the next best person I can trust to fix things is myself. Allowing me to go online and look on my own can solve so many problems. Did my order go through? When did it ship? Is it in transit? Where do I send returns? What do I do if the widget is missing a part? When are the repair people coming? Offering customers access to the same data your customer service personnel have can help stem phone calls and e-mails. Just think of it as less you have to ignore."[20] This is a great argument for CMR, which means giving

Self Service In CRM Suites

Vendor	Product	Web self-service functionality
Avaya	Interaction Center	Allows indexing of content Lacks full-featured knowledge base
eGain	eService Enterprise	Includes full-featured knowledge base Available either licensed or hosted
E.piphany	E.5	Lets users access data within E.5 or back-office systems Can provide access to transaction information and general content
Kana	Kana iCare	Includes full-featured knowledge base Offers integrated knowledge base and e-mail response
PeopleSoft	PeopleSoft 8	Links to enterprise applications Provides portal that lets customers obtain product, account, and service information
RightNow Technologies	RightNow Web	Offers robust reporting Includes full-featured knowledge base Available either licensed or hosted
Siebel Systems	Siebel 7	Integrates with third-party knowledge-base products Provides prebuilt personalized portal for self service
Talisma	Talisma Service 4.2	Includes self-help query engine Has limited knowledge-base functionality

DATA: DOCULABS; SOURCE: GUARAV VERMA AND TODD HOLLOWELL, "CRM MAKES STRIDES IN SELF SERVICE," INFORMATIONWEEK.COM, FEBRUARY 18, 2002, PP. 1–3.

your customers direct access to all of the information and application functions they need to make doing business with you easier.

There are some stars. Federal Express's website lets the customer explore services, shipping, and packaging options, as well as opening accounts, tracking, and getting proof of delivery—all in a convenient friendly format that allows the customer to control every aspect of a transaction. The company confirms incoming messages and responds to them within five business hours in one of eight languages. Frederick

Smith, chairman, president, and CEO of FedEx, has been finding ways to empower customers since he founded the business. He was the first to provide software to his corporate customers, empowering them to fill out their own shipping forms and do their own tracking of shipments. The goal at FedEx is 100 percent accuracy, quality, and customer satisfaction on all transactions. Every part of a transaction has some measurable quality to it. The system identifies failures from the customer's point of view and then looks for ways to correct its mistakes. (The employee-centric culture at FedEx helps assure this customer care. A spokeswoman for the company says, "If we take care of the needs of our people, then they'll provide the service our customers expect."[21])

Wendy Close, CRM research director at Gartner, has studied companies that she says are getting cross-channel customer service right. She reports Compaq's global e-business applications group bolstering it's "one face to the consumer" strategy by providing its partners with one user profile, allowing one entry point for security and one simple log-in, and consolidating various business groups within the company to present a single image to customers. Close says, "Compaq projects that these partner and customer management efforts will contribute $100 million to earnings during the next three years."

Close cites Harrah's Entertainment, one the world's largest gaming companies, as having done an especially good job of taking the multichannel approach to a new level by combining a single-view philosophy with loyalty programs and CRM analytics. "Its emphasis on multichannel contacts," she says, "allows it to create a holistic view of its customers."

Close's third winner is Boise Cascade Office Products. "Not only has Boise Cascade moved to create a consistent customer experience across its website, call center, and other touch-points," she reports, "it has involved its customers in the process, exposing customers to its programs during design, implementation and testing."[22]

And things seem to be improving. The research firm Answerthink tracked a major improvement in Web retail experience during the 2001 holiday shopping period, thanks largely to the implementation of customer service tools: storing frequently used shipping addresses and billing data, offering express checkout, providing the ability to access product availability, and featuring gift registry and wish lists. The study surveyed 200 online retailers in November and December 2001; participants included pure-play online stores, catalog-based companies, and brick-and-mortar retailers.[23]

Loyalty and satisfaction depend more than ever on the quality of the experience associated with goods and services. Christmas 2001 had its share of customer experience horror stories from some of America's finest companies. For example, hundreds of people who bought Microsoft's hot new XBox received defective systems and some said they had to wait weeks and endure shoddy customer service before their systems were repaired. One man said his $300 system stopped working the day he received it, and it took a month of aggravation with XBox customer service before he got a replacement. One woman said she had taken down her Christmas decorations and her son hadn't gotten to play with his Christmas toy yet, after nine calls to customer service. Fewer than 1 percent of the Microsoft units were faulty, but the response to those customers who do have problems is more important than how many units actually break.[24]

I didn't have to go to the press or the airwaves to find stories of poor service problems. In 2001 I had planned to leave on Christmas day for a week in Cancun. Since I have such little time to read anything but industry news, I looked forward to a week out of the office to catch up on a couple of new books. On December 16 I logged on to the Barnes & Noble website to place an order. Since the delivery promises on the books I wanted were unclear, I clicked on the AOL Shop Direct Customer Support Chat Service icon to inquire about delivery by December 24. The service was kind enough to send me a transcript of the discussion:

Thank you for using AOL Shop Direct Customer Support Chat service. We are happy to help you at any time.

For your reference and records, we have attached a transcript of the chat session below.

Topic: Christmas delivery

Fred. Newell I have just ordered 2 books. Before confirming to ship I need to know if they will arrive before Christmas.

Carol Hello Fred and welcome to AOL Shop Direct. I am Carol, your Customer Care Consultant.

Fred. Newell Can you answer my question?

Carol I understand your concern regarding the question.

Carol Please let me know when this order was placed.

Fred. Newell It is on my screen now but I won't place it until I know.

    [Long pause]

Fred. Newell Hello?

Carol I'm sorry for the delay.

Carol Fred, it normally takes 7-10 business days for the product to reach you.

Fred. Newell "Normally" doesn't help. Can I have these by Christmas?

Carol Fred, I cannot give you the exact date but as to ensure our customers get their orders quickly, we process online orders immediately after receiving your request.

Fred. Newell Are these books in stock for immediate shipment?

Carol Please let me know the item numbers of the books.

Fred. Newell The Final Days by Barbara Olson and When Character Was King by Peggy Noonan.

    [Long pause]

Fred. Newell Are you still there?

Carol Fred, please wait a moment.

Carol Fred, since it was advertised on our site, the books are available with us.

Fred. Newell For immediate shipment?

Carol Yes, Fred, as informed earlier, we ship the product immediately as soon as we receive the request.

Fred. Newell Many thanks.

Carol You are welcome.

Carol Thank you for visiting AOL Shop Direct. A copy of this chat will be e-mailed to you shortly. Good-bye and thanks again.

I placed the order and within minutes an e-mail confirmed my order number. Later, on December 20, I received the following not very helpful notice:

Package Progress

Date	Time	Location	Activity
Dec. 20, 2001	2:02 A.M.	US	Billing Information Received

Given only that vague confirmation that my books were somewhere in the United States, I e-mailed the company asking again for confirmation that this order would be shipped to arrive before Christmas, asking them to change shipping details as necessary. Four days later, on the afternoon of December 24 I received the following:

> Dear Fred Newell
>
> We are pleased to inform you that your order has been shipped.
>
> I show that you should have received the first part of your order. Yet the last half, When Character Was King, did not ship out until 12/18/01. I show that the delivery is scheduled to arrive on 12/27/01. Since the order has shipped out I cannot change the shipping method. We are very sorry for the inconvenience, and have a good day.
>
> We look forward to your next visit.
>
> Sincerely,
>
> John

Sure! And have a good day. It doesn't help a customer to say visit our website and click on the icons in the upper right-hand corner if the product isn't delivered as promised. It helps even less to say have a good day if the customer is having a bad day. What could Barnes & Noble and AOL Shop Direct have done better?

At the time of the original order on December 16, the customer service representative should have specified the ship date and the expected date of delivery instead of saying, "We ship the product as soon as we get the request." On the December 20 progress notice, instead of indicating that the package was in the United States at 2:02 A.M., the company should have specified a delivery date. This would still have allowed time for the customer to call and cancel the order. Better yet, knowing from a prior conversation that the books were needed for Christmas, someone at Barnes & Noble should have suggested faster express delivery rather than let the order go through with a nine-day shipping process. This personal experience is an example of several things having gone wrong: a meaningful dialog was not created and the information learned from the customer was not put to good use.

Time Accelerated

The whole issue of customer service becomes more critical in this age of acceleration where the faster we go the faster we want to go. Marianne Lewis, assistant professor of management at the University of Cincinnati, calls this the Acceleration Syndrome. "The more we supposedly save time, the more we intensify the need for speed. We're constantly intensifying."[25] Hers is a perfect description of our customer in the new millennium where the speed of computer chips doubles every eighteen months; time saved is measured in minutes, seconds, even milliseconds; and customers click off websites that don't load in four seconds.[26]

In what the Future Foundation calls "The 24-Hour Society" consumers expect instant gratification. More and more stores are open 24/7. Books can be ordered in the middle of the night and on holidays. Internet banks are open 365 days a year. In this I-want-it-now age, companies that don't help make customers' lives easier are perceived as customer-hostile.

A recent example helps make the point. I have been a regular customer of my local pharmacy for twenty-five years. When the kindly owner retired and sold his business, the first thing the new owner did was to remodel the store. No problem in that—except I have always gone to the back of the store to the pharmacy counter to wait my turn to pick up a prescription. I would sign for the insurance as the store associate rang up the sale. I was in and out in just a few minutes. Now, in the remodeled store, I wait my turn at a bright new pharmacy counter where I sign for the insurance. Then I am told to take the prescription to the register at the front of the store to have the sale rung up.

When I questioned the new process and explained that waiting in a second line up front is a waste of my time I was told the new process is "more efficient." More efficient for them, perhaps, but certainly not for the customer. The new system goes a long way from making customers' lives easier. This storeowner has not thought about letting customers manage the relationship and hasn't taken into account the customer's point of view in this age of acceleration.

The Acceleration Syndrome is a compelling argument for working to let the customer manage the relationship—for finding ways to make customers' lives easier as they race breathlessly to make every second count. But turning a company into a customer-centric business is not easy. Delivering customer service on the customer's terms can be expensive. You can't do it for everyone, yet I was surprised to learn that only 19 percent of companies have a separate contact strategy for high-value customers.

This is not to suggest you should limit your CMR efforts to the biggest spenders or just the obvious segments of profitable customers. The process of learning the specific level of service that customers want will unearth some customers who can be made profitable. This will occur with changes in service functions that will please the customer while saving company expense.

THE COMPETITION

It's important to remember how easy it is for customers to switch to competitors today. It used to be that if you had a customer's business for a few years, chances were that customer wouldn't jump ship over a small problem. Today if you make a customer unhappy, even over a little thing, he or she can and will find a new supplier in an instant.

A company called RightNow Technologies has some answers that help businesses let customers manage relationships. RightNow's Web-based self-service solution creates a knowledge base that allows customers to shape the service in ways to make it most relevant to them. Because customers typically repeat the same questions, the RightNow solution can draw from a central repository of information they call the "knowledgebase" to provide immediate answers. This allows the system to answer thousands of inquiries at the same time. The knowledge base is "self-learning" and "self-maintaining." Each individual customer manages his or her relationship, shaping and adding value to the knowledge base by determining what is most relevant to him or to her. The information individual customers find most useful and most timely becomes the most easily accessible.

As we've said, the need to seek help from a customer representative dramatically increases call center and e-mail loads, which in turn threatens the quality of service. Customer inquiries can jump as much as 300 percent after a company adds an online element to its business, and even offline companies are learning that customers expect to find help twenty-four hours a day. This was happening at easyRentaCar, whose customer service staff of twenty was being snowed under with e-mail inquiries. Because the company had to write an individual reply to each inquiry, it was taking as long as a week for customers to receive a reply. Within one month of the RightNow Web solution, 95 percent of the inquiries were being resolved within twenty-four hours, and a full 80 percent of all inquiries were being answered through self service.

When customers sign onto the easyRentaCar site, they're presented with a choice of languages and taken to a welcome page where the basics of the company's offerings are listed. Links on everything from booking online and locations to prices and policies are presented, including a link to the customer service site. At the customer service site visitors can search the knowledge base or immediately send a request for assistance.

Phil Jones, chief technology officer for easyRentaCar, says, "We are now in a situation where we are proactively managing the customer support process, empowering the customers to find the answers to their questions, and when they do need assistance from us, scheduling and prioritizing requests and providing a more consistent answer."[27]

The customer management of relationships can be approached through a variety of traditional channels including telephone calls, e-mails, and website interaction. Complete, multichannel, integrated, robust solutions are critical. When considering the cost of each method, many businesses are finding that applications, which include Web-based self service, are what one industry expert calls the "sweet spot" in the customer relationship marketplace. Forrester

Research reports the average cost per interaction is $32.74 by telephone, $9.99 by e-mail, $7.80 by online chat service, and $1.17 by knowledge-based self service, making the RightNow solution a big bargain.[28]

TRAINING

Wouldn't it be wonderful if someone could design a digital knowledge base that would assure consistency of employee motivation and understanding of the company's CMR commitment? It's still true that a high percentage of customer service inquiries come at the store level. Martha Rogers, Ph.D., a founding partner of strategy consulting firm Peppers and Rogers Group, says, "You strive for the customer-focused company, but your face to the customer is manned by individuals who just don't 'get it'."[29] Sometimes the breakdown comes from lack of motivation, which means you have to give employees the opportunity to understand what's in it for them, and you have to build commitment to the CMR program, not just compliance. This is part of driving the vision down to the level of execution.

Sports Authority, the number-one sporting goods retailer, understands this. In 2000, it created the new position of director of training and customer service. Rob Van Craenbroeck, who holds the new director position, says, "We wanted to maximize synergies from feedback we were getting from customer service, so that [learning] could help shape our training program." His task was to develop a training program for employees that emphasized scouting out customers' needs. The company mined its resources to find out what the customer really wanted from the store. Management learned they had an obligation to educate consumers around the products they offered. "That's what they wanted when they walked into our stores," Craenbroeck says. "In other words, if someone is really interested in fitness, and thinks a treadmill will help them achieve their goals, is that the product they should be using in the first place?"[30]

He makes a point that sums up CMR: "It's not about selling the most expensive product; it's about selling the right product to the right consumer. In the end, that builds relationships, and hopefully they will be comfortable enough to recommend us to a friend. We think that's a solid way of doing business."[31]

Training is part of the process, but after that you also have to give the employees the tools to serve each customer knowledgeably. Radio Shack is a good example of how to implement this philosophy. In consumer electronics there are so many products and so much change that training itself could be a full-time job. The retailer has developed a high-speed Internet tool for its stores. The high-speed retrieval-based system gives the sales associate a tool that finds the information he needs to answer customer questions. The Internet site gives any sales associate instant access to all Radio Shack product information with just a few keystrokes. Radio Shack intended to equip 95 percent of its 5,000 stores with the online tool in 2002.[32]

Segmented Levels of Service

As mentioned earlier, the fact that customer expectations are on the rise does not mean you should try to provide best customer service for every one of your customers. Alan Crowther, managing officer of CRM consulting firm Adjoined Technologies, confirms our case: "Most of the focus [today] is on segmenting the level of service based on the value of the customer. Companies are looking to spend more on their better customers and less on lower value customers. As a result, these companies save on the cost of customer service because they are only delivering a high level of service to the customers who provide most of the profits. Differentiating service based on customer profitability also is an effective way to define which customers are most valuable, which have the most potential for growth, and which might best be politely ushered to a competitor."[33]

Even computers can't make everyone feel special. This leaves us with two rules of service for the new CMR:

1 Don't try to offer the same service benefits to all customers. Learn what individual customers want. Invest in the ones who can be profitable for you.

2 Let your profitable and potentially profitable customers manage the relationship on their terms by learning the level of service each individual customer wants and delivering no more and no less.

A Few Reminders

- Customized services not only deepen customer relationships, they also can save expense.
- Customers are demanding more information, easier and expanded access, and support through newer channels.
- Enterprises that enable their customers to get better, easier access to information through more channels will increase customer satisfaction by between 5 percent and 10 percent.
- Web-based services will be a necessary alternative with e-service that is fast, meaningful, compelling, and customer-driven.
- Find the link between customer segmentation and investments in service.
- Involve customers in the process.
- Give employees the tools they need to service each customer knowledgeably.
- Above all, look at your business from the customer's viewpoint. Find ways to empower the customer to make his or her life easier.

Which Customers and Why *15*

You can't make everyone happy

A S MUCH AS WE LIKE TO TALK about one-to-one marketing, it will never be possible to allow *every* customer to manage the relationship with your firm. Even companies trying CRM had to narrow down the selection of customers they could try to manage based on specific characteristics. In earlier work helping companies to establish CRM initiatives, the team from Seklemian/Newell would create a list of criteria by first asking clients how well they knew their customers. We would typically ask questions like these:

- Who are your best customers who contribute the majority of your revenues?
- Do you know how many are shopping your store more or less frequently than a year ago, or spending more or less per visit?
- How much of their spending is done in your store versus in a competitor's?
- How satisfied are they with your current offers, including the non-product aspects of your offers?
- How vulnerable are you to competing offers?
- Do you know why your customers might be dissatisfied with you or with your competitors?
- Are you their store of choice?

These are all good questions from a company-centric standpoint, but not enough to set a course for CMR. Beyond identifying your best customers and charting their visits and spending patterns, CMR requires knowing more about their potential. To find the customers you can best turn into assets, and to learn the things you will have to change as you re-engineer your business processes to allow the customer to manage the relationship, the questions are a bit different. Here are some questions to help start your thought process:

- Can you describe, in great detail, the type of customers that hold the greatest growth potential for your business? Why do they need you, what is their greatest need, and what parts of your business process limit their ability to help themselves to information and transactions?

- Out of all the customer types you think are already doing business with you, can you pick the type you are most likely to be wasting your money on this very minute? Can you learn anything about their interests and needs that would enable you to turn more of the relationship-building power over to them, thus reducing your expense and making them more profitable customers?

- Do you know how to reach the types of customers that are happiest with your business relationship but exist only in small numbers? Chances are these customers have already discovered ways to participate in the management of the relationship. What can you learn from them that will translate to a broader market?

- Can you describe in detail the type of customer who is most likely to recommend you highly to a friend? Can you identify the elements of this business relationship that are most responsible for this strong tie?

- Can you identify the type of consumer who is most likely to spend money with you once and then never again? Are there things you can change in the business relationship that, through empowerment, would keep this type of consumer as a loyal customer?

- Would you recognize your best prospect type if you were sitting next to him on an airplane, and would you know how to have a meaningful conversation with that person?

Within any one of these customer segmentations there will be customers you can count on to continue to give you their business, and there will be customers at risk. There are some important issues that can make the difference. The next step is to find those issues as they relate to each of the customer segments.

THIS IS A WAY

In this process of evaluating customers and trying to learn more about them we often turn to a research company called Message Factors. In hundreds of Value Analysis studies in fields including B-to-B, B-to-C, financial, food service, and health care, their research shows that the average company has customers who can be defined in one of three ways:

- **Loyalists** (31 percent),
- **Content** (21 percent), or
- **At risk** (48 percent)

The Message Factors's Value Analysis has identified four types of issues that make the difference between loyal customers and those at risk.

1 **Basics:** A set of standards expected of every company in the category; things you must do satisfactorily. For example, a bank must be safe; a restaurant must be clean.

2 **Value issues:** Where the company goes beyond the basics and gives their customers something more that they value. Value issues may be financial or nonfinancial in nature. Value is what leads to differentiation and customer loyalty, and is based on customers' perceptions of what is given up for what is received. There are three drivers of value:

—*Quality* includes quality of products, merchandise selection, quality of staff, physical environment, and additional services.

—*Price* includes everyday pricing and sales prices.

—*Convenience* includes overall convenience, the ease of shopping, and location.

3 Irritations: Issues on which customers are dissatisfied, but aren't very important; these things won't drive them away. Certainly one of the greatest aggravations for customers is having to punch in a long series of numbers on the phone to get served by interactive voice response systems. Federal Express built a business by eliminating customers' irritation: Mailers could never know when a package sent through the U.S. Postal Service would arrive at its destination; FedEx guarantees a set time for delivery and offers a tracking service for delivery confirmation.

4 Unimportant issues: Things companies do that their customers don't care about. In many cases, customers are not even aware of these issues. For example, one supermarket doubled its budget for floor cleaning so they could claim the cleanest floors only to learn that customers didn't care; they expected the floors to be clean.

For CRM it was enough to concentrate on only the value issues. These issues are still vital for CMR, but the irritations are also just as important to focus on. Even though these dissatisfactions may not be driving customers away, they still offer giant opportunities. The Great Indoors used their early conversations with the customer to understand exactly what frustrates her about shopping for home décor, and then built their business around removing those annoyances.

Even the unimportant issues need to be examined. If a company is spending money on services or other activities that customers don't care about, the opportunity is there to transfer funds to changes that will make customers' lives easier.

The Message Factors's three-part segmentation of loyalists, those who are content, and those who are at risk is a good place to start, but within those groups it will pay to probe more deeply into the kind of questions discussed earlier. We need to know which customer segments offer the greatest chance to change customer behavior, and then how best to influence and empower the individual customers in each group.

▪ *Who are the occasional shoppers with whom we can increase frequency?* That was enough to ask when we were just using the information to target cross-sell offers. To gain the benefits of empowering the customer we have to drill down to learn why these customers are only occasional shoppers. What can you change in the relationship process to make these customers' lives so much easier by shopping with you that they will become regular shoppers?

▪ *Who are the best customers and what are the methods of communication that will enhance relationships with them?* This question is still valid for CMR but you must go beyond the question of what communications are best and ask what actions can we add (or subtract) to give these customers more power.

▪ *What are typical cross-category shopping tendencies and how can you maximize these opportunities?* Just because you are trying to turn power over to the customer doesn't mean you don't want to sell more. The new question is how can you make cross-sell and up-sell of more value to the customer.

▪ *Who are the cherry-pickers who buy from you only on promotion?* It's probable that you can't turn too many of them into great assets for the company, but what can you do about reducing the frequency and range of communications to them to reinvest these expenses into relationships with higher value customers?

▪ *Can you use customer information to improve merchandise assortments?* One-to-one experts think of this as customization, but it can be more than that. Often in our work with clients we see them eliminating slow-turn or low-margin products or categories without checking to see who is buying them and what else those customers are buying on the same shopping trip. At one time a major department store decided to close its fur department in a suburban branch because women were buying furs in the downtown store and returning them to the suburban branch resulting in an unprofitable branch department. The branch manager was wise enough to check his customer database to learn that these customers were not only some of his best but were, in fact, spending large sums in other departments each time they came in to return the fur they had purchased downtown. The store made the wise decision to retain the fur department in the suburban branch and avoided what might have been lost sales.

As this is written, Sears has made the decision to drop its cosmetic category completely. If they are wise, they have already checked the shopping habits of the customers who counted on them for cosmetics—they won't be making those customers' lives easier.

PERMISSION INTENSITY

CMR involves getting consumers to be interested in your firm and to participate with you in building a relationship. In an excellent paper, "A Comprehensive Analysis of Permission Marketing," Sandeep Krishnamurthy, assistant professor in the Business Administration Program at the University of Washington, defines some useful terms:

Consumer interest An individual's overall judgment of the effectiveness of the program in adding value to his or her life. If an individual receives promotional messages that are not well targeted or if the promotional messages are for disliked brands, he or she may well conclude that the program [relationship] is uninteresting. On the other hand if the messages closely map the needs of the consumer, there will be interest.

Consumer participation The extent to which an individual is willing to engage actively in a two-way exchange with the marketer. The lowest level of consumer participation is exit. The highest level of consumer participation is active engagement where consumers make every effort to provide accurate and timely information to the marketer, and attend to the messages, responding to the relevant ones appropriately.[1]

Permission intensity Consumers define the boundaries of their relationship with firms. In some cases they give the business tremendous leeway and in others the firms are held on a tight leash. Formally, permission intensity is defined as the degree to which a consumer empowers a marketer in the context of a communicative relationship. High permission intensity is characterized by three factors: high information quantity, high information quality, and information usage flexibility."[2]

It was difficult to attain high intensity permission with past customer relationship management programs. Consumers receive an excessive volume of proposals for relationships with firms. When they do not perceive control over the terms of the relationship and do not see much value added, they have little interest in engaging actively in a two-way exchange. CMR is aimed at developing high intensity permission and active engagement. The only way to develop high intensity permission is to give customers the power to manage the relationship in ways that will make their lives easier and the relationship more rewarding.

You can't make that happen for all of your customers and, in reality, some customers will never be worth the effort. Every business has cherry pickers who will always be switching suppliers, looking only for the lowest price. Every firm has customers who are impossible to satisfy. It makes no sense to overinvest in customers with little or no potential for growth.

GROWING YOUR BUSINESS

Research carried out by Forrester shows that 49 percent of companies cannot identify customers at risk. They do not know what customers think of the products or services offered and whether they plan to stay or to go.[3]

Start with those customers that hold the greatest growth potential for your business based on their existing relationship, not just the ones who currently contribute the majority of your revenues but those, as well, who have the greatest potential. Learn what your best customers value most about their relationship, ask the right questions, and look for the biggest opportunities: the largest sales, the best margins, the fastest results, the longest lasting results and, finally and most importantly, the biggest benefits to the customer.

Implementation

None of that information gathering will help you build relationships if you don't empower your front-line customer representatives with real-time information to differentiate customers and to enable the representatives to interact in ways that will make your customers' lives easier. BancoRio, a forward-looking bank in Latin America, understands this. Despite the overwhelming economic turmoil in Argentina in early 2002, when all banks were closed for days at a time by government decree and most bank offices had to cover their entrances with corrugated steel to protect them from angry crowds, the BancoRio team worked tirelessly. Even in these chaotic conditions, they continued to develop empowerment for their customer representatives.

Over several years the bank had developed sophisticated customer information systems. The systems made it possible to create effective and very profitable campaigns from the central office, but the customer information was not accessible by the customer representatives in the branch offices. Moreover, there was no way for the individual customer knowledge the representatives gained from personal interaction with their customers to be added to the central database.

Federico Tapper, vice president of the bank's commercial division, moved BancoRio ahead of its rivals with the earlier customer information system. He wanted to be sure when some economic normalcy returned to the country that his bank would be the first financial institution ready with the most powerful tools to rebuild customer relationships. His plan called for six stages of implementation:

1 Segment the customer base.
2 Assign individual customer portfolios to individual customer representatives.
3 Define different service levels for the different customer segments.
4 Develop real-time customer information tools to enable the representatives to interact with their customers to improve the customer experience.
5 Create goals and budgets by customer portfolio instead of by product.
6 Communicate the strategy to the enterprise.

The BancoRio team—comprised of senior members of the marketing and IT departments, plus regional managers and branch managers—started with an in-depth analysis of the 1.2 million customer base to learn which customers offered the greatest potential for the bank, what share of business the bank was getting from each of these individual customers, and the specific needs of individual customers that would offer opportunities to make those customers' lives better, while growing profits for the bank.

The customer segmentation grid ranked customers vertically by their potential value to the bank, based on income and other available measures: A for best, B for good, C for moderate, and D for poor. Each segment was ranked horizontally representing share of their financial services business these customers were giving to BancoRio.

A Big Change for the Bank

After its analysis, the bank made a profound change in the role of their customer representatives. Customer rep responsibilities had always been defined by product. In the new CMR plan each customer rep handles all products and has responsibilities for specific customer segments. The reps were changed, in effect, from product managers to customer portfolio managers. Each A representative became responsible for a segment of the A customer list, every B representative, for a segment of the B customer list, and so on.

A representatives are responsible for "gold" quality attention to their customers, giving very personal attention and catering to them with the level of communications and dialog each customer desires. B representatives are responsible for pro-active catering and personal attention, but with fewer communications. C representatives are responsible only for reactive attention and communications. D representatives are little more than greeters. Although D customer portfolios represent mostly unprofitable customers, these reps are responsible for capturing information from their customer segments to identify customers that develop the potential to upgrade.

An important element of the plan was not just making the customers' lives easier, but also making the representatives' lives easier by giving them the real-time information they would need to provide these personal services. The new system gives reps access to complete information of all customer interactions with the bank in real-time.

The first forty-five minutes each morning, before the bank opens, each representative opens a "sign-in" screen on his PC. The screen starts off with "alerts" for the day that will require specific customer communications. For example, if a customer's deposit has not cleared, the rep is to notify the customer; or if an investment certificate is about to mature, the rep is to help with the reinvestment. Next on the screen is a section called "My Portfolio," which digests highlights of the rep's individual customer information, including notations of any current campaign offerings that have been made to each customer. Additional views of the customer data are available to give the representative in-depth detail of each customer's interactions with the bank.

Goals and budgets for each representative are set based on each customer's potential and each customer's special needs. Even the C representatives have goals and budgets that are important to the bank and to the customers. With about 400,000 customers in the C customer segment, if the C reps can gain just one dollar a month in bank income from members in this group, that means a substantial gain.

Another important element of the plan was that the development team involved branch bank representatives in the planning at the outset. As a result the concept and the tools were accepted enthusiastically by the ultimate users. The new structure and systems were tested for ninety days in just three branches. Response from both customers and bank employees was so positive that the project is being rolled out to the other 267 branches as this is written.

This is a great example of a firm moving from a product-centric culture to a true customer-centric enterprise. BancoRio has found the way to identify the customers who hold the greatest growth potential for their business. They are learning what customers value about their relationship with the bank, and they are investing in the appropriate level of service for each customer. Hopefully, by the time this story is published, Argentina will have solved its economic woes and BancoRio will have developed high-intensity engagement with its customers and will earn its rewards for this outstanding restructuring.

Final Reminders

- Understand it will never be possible to work one-on-one to allow every customer to manage the relationship with your business.
- Find the customers you can best, and most easily, turn into assets.
- Work with the customers that can provide the greatest growth for your business.
- Don't waste time and money on customers that may never be profitable.
- Find different CMR solutions for your loyalists, those that are content, and those at risk.
- Use information from your customers to find the right CMR actions.
- Encourage customer participation, and develop permission intensity.

Crossing the Chasm—
What Will You Need
to Change? **16**

Eight steps to CMR success

C HANCES ARE YOU ALREADY HAVE in place a CRM initiative of some dimension. If you've gotten this far, you passed the test in Chapter 13 and are ready to implement CMR. To do that, what must change? What can you keep, and what will you have to throw away? How do you make the transition?

Just about everyone in the business offers steps to successful customer intelligence systems, and the steps are almost always about the same. With CMR you'll find similar steps for improving customer service, retaining customers, increasing the lifetime value, and treating different customers differently, but they will require going further. Here are the eight steps for successful CMR:

1 Think differently
2 Establish a benchmark
3 Define measurable goals and objectives
4 Create the strategy
5 Reengineer the processes
6 Get ready for change
7 Keep technology in its place
8 Select the right tools

Step 1: Think Differently

The first, and perhaps the most difficult, concept to cast overboard is that the benefits of your CMR efforts would accrue to the company, not to the customer. Most CRM programs are driven by the desire of the company to improve the efficiency of the business process and reduce cost while increasing sales. In many cases, the inward focus on company benefits ignores or avoids required changes within the company, not realizing that, for all the firm's talk about customer centricity, the customer can still have a less than delightful experience and receive less than expected value from the relationship.

In most CRM practices companies are not asking customers what they need, what they want, or what bothers them. As you transition to the CMR philosophy, you will have to ask customers these question to find out which processes matter to them and what you can change to make their lives easier.

For example, the telecom industry claims to recognize the value of implementing CRM applications and has been investing huge sums in infrastructure and related applications to build customer relationships. But one look at their sky-high churn rate shows that customer service is still not a core competency. They have failed to learn what the customer cares about most. The biggest complaint customers have about their relationship with their telecom providers is inaccurate billing. But most telecom's customer databases are not integrated, and many billing systems are based on old and outdated applications.[1] This goes back to the basic tenet that in many cases, business processes themselves must change to enable a company to practice CMR to its advantage.

For CMR we have to get down to the basics, and that simply means what the *customer* wants. Failure to adapt to customers' needs can be costly such as a mortgage company that turned away high-value mortgage applications because it was not geared to deal with customers whose needs were outside the norm; or a telecom company whose in-bound call center left sales enquiry call-backs until quiet periods that never came, leading to a three-month buildup of potential business worth six figures.

Step 2: Establish a Benchmark

You usually set your benchmark by determining how many customers your company currently has, defining the current usage of your products and services, and evaluating your existing customer intelligence infrastructure that helps you to serve these customers. This step always leads to the question, "How do I capture more of them?"

Establishing the benchmark for a CMR initiative involves determining the best potential customers for your business and learning what it means to have them manage a relationship that is rewarding for them and profitable for your company. Only after establishing these requirements is it time to set your benchmark based on how many of these customers your company currently has and the degree to which you are making their lives easier.

The benchmark process also includes a thorough study of current processes and costs, so that cost/benefit comparisons can be made in the future. (More about this in Chapter 17.) Balance is needed to meet both the requirements of the customer and the requirements of the company. CMR must also deliver value to the shareholders and stakeholders by turning customers into assets.

Step 3: Define Measurable Goals and Objectives

Most advice in this area suggests that pitching senior management on cost savings is a much easier sell than talking about revenue increases, which is why the benefits of most CRM initiatives are structured to accrue to the company and not the customer. The truth is, the things you should measure to turn customers into assets are economic, not operational. Ultimately increased revenue and customer equity are two of the greatest long-term values of CMR, and profit should still be the number one goal.

ROI Metrics   It is necessary to establish new ROI metrics to measure the success of your CMR activities and to know how they are effecting the customer base. These new metrics must be established in the setting of goals and objectives. It is important right at the start to find agreement on what will constitute success and to set the parameters for measurement. Metrics and financial analysis are concrete and will always win over vision and possibilities.

A serious weakness of too many of the old CRM programs has been the failure to consider the issue of metrics a top priority. Adrian Payne, professor of services and relationship marketing at Cranfield School of Management in the U.K., says, "Our research shows that only a small percentage of people have done proper measurement of acquisition and retention economics, and therefore have a view about what the lifetime value of a customer is—and so how much to invest and where to invest resources."[2]

CMR can be an expensive exercise, especially if a company cannot define what it wants to accomplish with the initiative and measure progress against that objective. Yet, only one-third of companies in a recent survey could provide any estimate of their expected return on CRM investments.[3] A big part of defining your goals is defining what should be measured and planning measurement as a repeated exercise to prove you are turning customers into assets.

There are various schools of thought about what to measure. Some opt for measure of increased lifetime value. Others look for increased sales, increased margin, or greater retention of customers. When a company is able to define the metrics for return on its CMR investment, the process is straightforward.

One Seklemian/Newell retail client set as their objective an increase in sales from a targeted group of customers. They created a test that would measure the ROI for implementing CMR. Customers in the third decile of spending represented the segment most likely to grow, so they selected a random sampling of these customers for a CMR pilot. From the same decile, they selected a control group that perfectly matched the target group in spending habits and demographics. They implemented a carefully planned progression of personalized services—a private toll free number, free coffee during visits to the store, advance notice of store events, and surprise gifts—for the CMR test customers and continued their traditional target marketing offers for the control group.

At the end of twelve months they found a 14 percent increase in sales from the CMR group versus a 2 percent increase in sales from the control group. After converting the sales dollar increase to margin dollars and subtracting the difference in marketing costs between their CRM efforts and their target marketing efforts for the control group, they showed a return in margin dollars seven times the additional cost of CMR. Based on this success, they rolled out the pilot to all stores and began to test efforts to upgrade customers from even lower levels of spending.

Call Center Metrics   Looking at call center metrics is only going to confuse the issue. Bermuda's 1-800-BERMUDA call center, profiled in Chapter 3, could never have been transformed into a customer-oriented service center if the call center manager had to defend the relationship-building investment on the basis of shorter calls and reduced contact center costs.

When setting goals and objectives for your call center, it is simply not enough to set service level performance standards based on calls per hour. As Brad Cleveland of *Call Center Magazine* points out, "You can achieve a service level objective while also creating waste, extra work and low quality even though your agents: misunderstand customer requests; enter data incorrectly; relay the wrong information to callers; make callers mad; miss opportunities to capture valuable feedback; and unnecessarily cause repeat calls. Average call time cannot measure whether the callers and your organization achieved the call's purpose."[4]

Economic Metrics   To deliver value to the shareholders and stakeholders by turning customers into more valuable assets, even with a CMR initiative, many of the old CRM economic metrics that measure the movement of customers into assets still apply:

- Average order size will increase as you make it easier for customers to find more of the things they need on your website, or gain access to their sales rep on their terms.
- Campaign response will improve as your offerings become more relevant to your customers' needs.
- Cross-selling and up-selling during sales and service interactions will prosper as your customers give you more and more information about their needs and interests.
- Customer profitability will improve as your new knowledge

earns a greater share of each customer's wallet and you are able to migrate customers from mid to high activity levels.

▪ Customer retention and customer lifetime value, the strongest measures of your customers as corporate assets, will increase as you strengthen the bond between your company and your customers.

But CMR demands some new metrics. That starts with the measurement of the strength of your customer dialog and the quality of the information gained. We have always said no contact at all from a customer can be a defection warning signal. Now we must say that if the share of communications initiated by the customer is not growing, you are not making CMR work. If your customers are not finding it easier to communicate with you and get the information they need, you are not empowering them to manage the relationship.

Much of this is moving from product measures to customer measures that involve the breadth, depth, and length of the customer's relationship with you, and some of these new metrics must go beyond the economic and measure the emotional connection of the relationship. This emotional loyalty cannot be measured simply through retention figures; it must be found by examining what motivates and retains a company's loyal customers.

Jim Barnes, author of *Secrets of Customer Relationship Management* (McGraw-Hill Trade, 2000), says, "A relationship involves emotions. We need to understand the emotional connection. We need to ask why, and get at the true customer viewpoint. Beyond functional loyalty lives emotional loyalty, and this should be the goal."[5]

Step 4: Create the Strategy

In the "Eight Building Blocks of CRM," Gartner talks about strategy: "A CRM strategy is not an implementation plan or road map. A real CRM strategy takes the direction and financial goals of the business strategy and sets out how the enterprise is going to build customer loyalty. The objectives of a CRM strategy are to target, acquire, develop and retain valuable customers to achieve corporate goals."[6]

The objectives are the same for CMR but the business strategy itself must change. CMR is not a snap-on tool. It is not a technology that can be purchased. Taking existing methodologies and management processes and applying them to CMR will create an initiative that addresses the wrong issues.

A CMR strategy must develop a seamless integration of every area of the business that touches the customer through the integration of people, processes, and technology. Truly empowering the customer is new and uncharted territory for most businesses.

To be successful, your strategy will require well-developed, integrated programs that will facilitate relationship building. This will raise new questions such as how to deliver new empowerment to your customers, and how to deal with the many new ways to reach customers and for customers to reach you. Your strategy must provide for new training for all personnel to understand where the company is going and to understand the new objective.

One element of this relationship building is allowing your customers to choose the communication channel they prefer and training all personnel to respect the customer's choice. As hard as it may be to believe, I still see many marketing executives defending their personal kingdoms at the expense of the customer and the company—executives responsible for e-commerce at brick and mortar companies actually discouraging customers from shopping in the company's stores.

Beyond that, strategy must include providing the right tools and developing guidelines to ensure that the entire workforce can use the CMR tools effectively. The right tools are not always the most expensive ones. Business writer David Simms quotes Doug McRae, president of Vancouver-based Governor Consulting, Inc., "Ask the people who really do the work what tools they need to really do the work. A lot of executives who make the dollar decisions get drunk on the toys. They see this weird and wonderful stuff and don't understand the pain and frustration it takes to get there—they go from nothing to exotic technology without any middle steps." Simms has a great way of expressing this. "Plucking a soccer mom out of her hunter green minivan and sticking her in a Formula One race car doesn't qualify her as a Formula One Driver."[7]

Finally, the strategy must take into account how all these new efforts will create increased profits and shareholder value. If CMR strategy is not closely aligned with the company's profitable growth objectives, failure is certain.

Step 5: Reengineer the Processes

It's one thing to talk about the reengineering of processes to move from the goal of improving efficiencies and reducing costs to the goal of transferring power to the customer, and quite another to make it happen within the enterprise. All companies have cultures, whether they know it or not, and embedded culture is resistant to change. It leads to the old argument against change, "We've always done it this way."

Internal Culture   In talking about this challenge I use the old story of the woman who always cut off the end of a ham before putting it in the roasting pan. When her husband asked her why she did that, she told him her mother always did it when she cooked a ham. Finally the husband had an opportunity to ask his mother-in-law why she did it. The mother-in-law's answer was "My roasting pan was too small."

I have now found another good story to explain the creation of a group culture.

Start with a cage containing five monkeys. Inside the cage, hang a banana on a string and place a set of stairs underneath it. Before long, a monkey will go to the stairs and start to climb toward the banana. As soon as he touches the stairs, spray all of the other monkeys with cold water. After a while, another monkey makes an attempt with the same result: all the other monkeys are sprayed with cold water. Pretty soon, when a monkey tries to climb the stairs, the other monkeys will try to prevent it.

Now, put away the cold water. Remove one monkey from the cage and replace it with a new one. The new monkey sees the banana and wants to climb the stairs. To his surprise and horror, all of the other monkeys attack him. After another attempt and attack, he knows that if he tries to climb the stairs, he will be assaulted.

Next, remove another of the original five monkeys and replace it with a new one. The newcomer goes to the stairs and is attacked. The previous newcomer takes part in the punishment with enthusiasm! Likewise, replace a third original monkey with a new one, then a fourth, and then the fifth. Every time the newest monkey takes to the stairs, he is attacked. Most of the monkeys that are beating him have no idea why they were not permitted to climb the stairs or why they are participating in the beating of the newest monkey. After replacing all the original monkeys, none of the remaining monkeys have ever been sprayed with cold water. Nevertheless, no monkey ever again approaches the stairs to try for the banana. Why not? Because as far as they know that's the way it's always been done around here.[8]

The point is that with anything new you can expect resistance. Some will resist because they have always done it another way and others will be too concerned with protecting their own territory to appreciate the new corporate goals. We must respect tradition but we should also respect the words of Somerset Maugham: "Tradition is a guide, not a jailer."

Internal CMR The reengineering will require an internal CMR approach. For external CMR ask your customers to take the lead in telling you how you can help them manage the relationship. For internal CMR, enlist associates at all levels into the reengineering process, bringing front- and back-office staff in early. This will allow employees to learn about the project from first-hand involvement while, at the same time, giving you a valuable understanding of the things required for your team members to perform their jobs. Involved personnel will be more inclined to work hard to make the project succeed. If employees are not involved in the design and development, and if they don't believe they are a driving force behind the project, it won't be successful. People always run more enthusiastically on a track they helped to design and build.

My friend Barton Goldenburg, president and founder of ISM, a leading CRM consultancy, tells a story about a large publishing organization that integrated three companies under a new umbrella. Its vice president of sales realized the new conglomerate needed a common perspective on its customers. Recognizing that users would ultimately drive the success of the project, he brought together fourteen people within the company to form a super user group—those who would be most affected by the new program.

Comprised of salespeople, managers, and representatives from editorial and distribution, the team held brainstorming sessions and came up with a list of business functions that would benefit the entire company. Then a survey went out to all customer-facing personnel asking them to prioritize the list. Based on that response, the user group and management reached an agreement on which functions would be implemented in which phase of their project. Carefully chosen super users became ambassadors for the project. They were excited about the initiative and shared their enthusiasm with coworkers throughout the process. They lit a fire inside the company.

Sandra Gudat, president and CEO of CRM consulting agency Customer Communications Group, stresses that buy-in comes from a healthy mix of motivation, education, tools, and training, and its importance should not be underestimated. She advises,

> Assemble a change-management team, an enthusiastic group of leaders, handpicked to represent every department in the company. The team's mission is to identify how each department will be affected by the new initiatives, create action plans for implementing those initiatives, and communicate the message to others in their individual departments. This process will also help the team identify some ways to get 'quick wins'—small victories that will help prove to skeptics that the new business strategy really does have legs. These steps give employees a measure of control and ownership, and help the team leader tailor the company's plan to meet departmental goals.[9]

Gudat lists these questions employees will need answered:
- How is each division, department, and employee affected?
- What new skills will they need to learn?
- What will their daily tasks look like?
- What are they doing today that will support this new-world vision?

- How will their efforts be measured?
- What will change, both initially and as the program takes shape?
- What are the things that won't change?[10]

She then suggests, once you have answered these key questions, to commit it all to paper in a manual or training guide as a way to foster a common understanding and cohesive mission.

It appears this kind of collaboration is taking root in U.S. companies. An *Information Week* 2002 research survey of 100 business technology professionals shows 84 percent of companies are in the process of improving collaborative practices with employees. Fifty-nine percent of respondents also said that they expect collaborative initiatives with employees to increase within the next twelve months. Supporting the caveat that change will not be easy to accomplish, one in three responding to the survey said they are grappling with developing a comprehensive collaboration strategy and they are finding resistance to change by employees.[11]

Employee Empowerment   It is important to remember that experienced employees, as well as customers, are the company's most valuable assets. Employees should be treated as valued assets just as customers should be. Companies don't always treat employees that way. When one company established a telecommuting program to allow some employees to work from home, they learned they had to set realistic goals and expectations for teleworkers and managers, and establish a regular and frequent schedule for communication. They ended up realizing that they didn't even have that in place for any of their other workers.

This is what reengineering the process means. You can't expect employees to work effectively without a process of regular and frequent communication. It doesn't matter whether they telecommute or work side by side, they can't collaborate if they can't communicate, and good communication may require some new processes.

Jonathan Copulsky, partner in the CRM practice of Deloitte Consulting, says his firm's research and client experience point to a strong correlation between employee satisfaction and customer satisfaction and, in turn, between employee loyalty and customer loyalty. He says,

> Companies appearing on the lists of the most popular places to work are those that not only clearly communicate expectations to employees, but also link reward systems to how well workers measure up to those expectations. Companies with loyal employees also excel at helping workers understand how their performance against expectations contributes to shareholder value and, ultimately, to the company's future.[12]

Copulsky stresses that top companies do a number of concrete things to reinforce both worker and customer loyalty. The best, he says, communicate ways in which expectations can be carried out with specific behaviors. He gives the example of Ritz-Carlton, which not only tells employees precisely when they should look customers in the eye and greet them, but has also set up some ground rules to help their employees. The Ritz-Carlton credo lists twenty "basics." Two relate directly to the hotel's emphasis on empowering staff to provide genuine care and comfort to guests: Number 8 is that any employee who receives a customer complaint, "owns" the complaint; and number 9 is that instant guest pacification will be ensured by all. React quickly to correct the problem immediately. Follow up with a telephone call within twenty minutes to verify the problem has been resolved to the customer's satisfaction. Do everything you possibly can never to lose a guest.

Three basic tenets support these rules:

- Move heaven and earth to satisfy a customer.
- Every employee has spending authority of $2,000 to solve a customer's need.
- Everyone has the authority to call in a coworker for help.

Every day, all members of the staff have a "daily quality line-up meeting" with their boss and discuss one of the twenty basics. Perhaps this is why the JD Powers survey shows 94 percent of Ritz-Carlton customers are satisfied, when the closest competitor can only achieve a 57 percent satisfaction rating.[13]

Other hospitality chains seem to be following the Ritz-Carlton example. Recently, through a miscommunication at the front desk, I had to wait at the Lexington, Kentucky, airport forty-five minutes for the Hyatt Regency van to pick me up. When I complained to the driver, he was quick to call the front desk on his cell phone and tell them to upgrade me to a suite to make up for the inconvenience. Just a few minutes after I had arrived in the suite, the driver appeared at my door with certificates for complimentary breakfasts during my two-day stay—a wonderful example of employee empowerment.

The thought that value assets can be created by a mutually beneficial exchange between the firm and its employees suggests a move from employee relationship management (ERM) to relationships managed by employees (EMR). Empowered employees, just like empowered customers, will find their own incentives to contribute and receive value from your business system.

Step 6: Get Ready for Change

As we move from customer relationship management to turning the power over to customers to manage the relationship, a lot of things will have to change. Trying to let customers manage the relationship means no longer using your customer information to see what products or services you can push to customers. You will be using this information to learn what products and services customers want. This will require changes in the management of the customer knowledge base. All that most companies required for their CRM activities was transaction processing. Producing segmentations from a multimillion-name customer file is essentially a batch process dependent only on processing power. CMR activities demand the total integration of customer information gathered from all interactions and delivered with speed and precision. That will require more than horsepower. The IT team will have to find new ways to manage the customer data and facilitate the sharing process on an enterprise-wide basis. All of those in any way involved with customer contact will want their customer information complete and easily accessible, and they will want it now!

Step 7: Keep Technology in Its Place

As mentioned in Chapter 2, too many guidelines for CRM start with technology. Technology applications are essential enablers for your CMR strategy, but the technology must be secondary. Too many CRM initiatives have failed because of one of two technology issues. The first one is what some have called automated chaos—leaping into automation of existing business practices. Determining the business functions to automate should be a simple step, but automating a flawed business process leads to disaster. In *A Paradigm Shift for Customer Care*, Marion Howard-Healy says, "A poor process that is automated remains just that—a poor process."[14] Rule one is get the CMR business process right before trying to absorb the technology, and then don't try to automate too many things at once. Jerry Sparger, Global Business Solutions, Inc., makes this case solidly in his "Eight Steps to Success:"

> Companies often try to roll out new business processes and technology all at the same time. This can create more work for the employees, with less benefit. We have seen cases where employees just did their job the old way, while keeping separate information to satisfy the new way. This is extra work, and often not effective. You should gradually implement processes and technology, either by time phasing the implementation, or by implementing small isolated groups. This will keep users involved and motivated, yet minimize the shock to your organization.[15]

Rule two is don't allow your new CMR program to be seen as an IT project. Enlist associates at all levels into the reengineering process. When developing new customer-centric programs employees at all levels will wonder what is happening, why the program is needed, and what it will mean to them individually. When they see it as a technology project they lose interest quickly, sometimes even sabotaging the program. They need to see it as a customer service project heralding a fundamental change in the quality of customer interaction leading to deeper relationships, designed to make customer interactions more effective, better for the customer and more profitable for the company. Beth Eisenfeld, research director, Gartner, confirms this second rule with two case studies:

- **BMC Software** made two failed attempts at implementing a CRM system. The first time the IT department took the lead. Lack of adoption killed this first effort. Only 50 percent of end users (employees) began using the system at all, with use dropping to 30 percent after a few months. Two years later, the IT management software firm tried again with the IT group in charge. The team did not perform an analysis of user work flows; instead, the group made assumptions. Once again, the end users resisted. The company's third try stressed executive sponsorship and involvement of the people who were going to use the system. Business processes were well documented and the project team included members from all stakeholder groups. This concentration on change management and user involvement resulted in a 97 percent usage rate.

- **AMF Bowling's** CRM implementation failed on its first two tries. These attempts also failed because of lack of involvement of end users. A company spokesperson said, "Typically, what happened was that the IT department would come up with a sales application and go to the sales team and say, 'This is what you've got, and now you've got to use it.'" On the third try, the company involved the sales force in every stage of the project and held a review every two weeks. When the application was rolled out they chose a salesperson to make the presentation at the annual sales conference. The final implementation made it to the Aberdeen Group's top ten CRM projects for 2001, which is based on a product's ability to achieve measurable ROI and meet its business objectives.

Eisenfeld suggests the primary lesson learned by both BMC and AMF is "Be certain to involve all stakeholders—including customers and end users—from the project's outset."[16] In other words, CMR needs to be thought of as a new way of doing business rather than an IT project. And that must be made clear at the very start to everyone involved.

Step 8: Select the Right Tools

Understanding, developing, and nurturing customer relationships require a strong flow of information across the enterprise. Having the right information at the right time and enabling effective interaction across all channels is critical for CMR. The selection of the right tools becomes more specialized.

My good friend, Bernice Grossman, president of database marketing company DMRS Group, has been advising both B-to-B and B-to-C marketers on their database marketing, integration systems, and CRM projects since 1983. She has lead companies through the process of finding just the right technology vendors for their integration needs and gives this advice:

> Examine your needs first, not the technology. It's easy to get swept up by information on hot new technologies and vendors; however, your starting point for the Request for Proposal (RFP) process should be your own company's needs. You must be able to detail the following basics before beginning to examine solutions:
> —What you really want to be able to solve and/or do using the solution
> —How you expect it will solve or do it (e.g., functionality of the solution)
> —How it will interface with all the various users and uses in your organization, including how different departments will interface with the solution
> —How (if at all) customers and prospects will interface with it.[17]

A caveat for CMR: There are dozens of technology providers offering CRM solutions these days. Few, if any, have had the experience of managing customer interactions based on the proposition that the customer should have the power. You will have to be very specific about things (like the new measurements discussed above in Step 3) to be sure the prospective supplier's tool can actually deliver your needs.

Many software solutions are capable of measuring campaign expense reduction and incremental sales. Metrics, like the strength of your customer dialog and the quality of the information you are gaining from the customer, will require new algorithms. Moving from product measures to customer measures will mean creating new definitions of success. Grossman advises against an RFP with a simple check-off column where potential vendors can say whether they comply or not. She says, "It's useless. It doesn't mean anything!" She compares a check-off box to asking people if they dance. "If they say yes," Grossman says, "how much do you really know about their ability? Instead, you should ask that vendors provide either a software screenshot or a very detailed explanation to support every single answer they give you so you are sure they really can provide the tech you require."[18]

CRM represents an entirely new way of looking at the profitability of the organization, and therefore of looking at customers, marketing, information, and strategy. It starts with new thinking, new questions, new evaluations of customers, and new metrics. It requires a new business strategy, reengineered processes, and appropriate tools. As these eight steps show, CRM will require a lot of changes. Just don't try to make them all at once.

There's No Free Lunch **17**

But CMR should not be an added expense

T HE QUESTION I AM MOST OFTEN ASKED, when talking about CMR, is, "Yes, but how can we afford to cater this much to our customers? It seems as though you're talking about a lot more communication expense."

The answer is that evolving your customer relationship initiatives to true CMR does not involve additional expense. It entails new prioritizing of existing expenses. Even CRM attempts can be wasteful if priorities are misunderstood. Most companies waste money in their communication with customers. This is true in both a company's proactive and reactive communications. The process of learning what is important to your customers and developing customized communications and services will involve new marketing expense, but these costs need not be additional.

When business priorities change in order to shift investments to what is critical for the customer, the value of each marketing dollar spent must be measured in terms of its value to the customer. This means dollars saved as well as dollars spent.

WHERE TO SPEND AND WHERE TO SAVE

To learn when to spend and when to save, you have to start with the discovery of what is important to each customer. Once you have this knowledge, you can then adjust your investments to spend only in the media relevant to your target customer—what she reads, watches, and listens to. Beyond that, it becomes a matter of targeting the right customers and limiting your offers, whether they be by mass media, direct mail, e-mail, or telemarketing, to those customers you know will be interested.

You can also tailor your level of service to reflect the individual needs of each customer (as discussed in Chapter 14). Scaling back or eliminating wasted efforts will produce substantial savings—more than enough to support your CMR customization.

Media

The proactive side starts with media investments. The move to CMR doesn't mean abandoning mass media, but rather letting the most valuable customers guide you to their preferred sources of information. Customers will tell you how and where they want to get their information if you take the time to ask them.

Package goods manufacturers are getting better and better about making use of trading area data for defining shoppers by store and interacting with retailers for use of their customer knowledge. It's a good start to measure market share by geographical subsets and regions, but a bigger opportunity exists in sorting stores and advertising investments by consumer preferences. This improved media targeting will not only save marketing dollars that can be used for CMR, it will also add value for the brand managers who care about loyalty, the sales managers who care about cases by chain, and the media service people who have traditionally cared only about eighteen– to fifty-four–year-old women.

Target Marketing

Unless under exceptional circumstances, customers will only accept products that fit their needs and their lifestyles, so the process of communicating means truly knowing your customer. The biggest wins come when you know enough about your customers to offer products that will be received willingly. You will not only have a reason for the offering, but you can also explain the reason in your communication. You can convince customers that you are offering personalized solutions as part of the product or service.

Yet marketers continue to saturate the mass media trying to offer a broad selection of products to everyone. One Sunday my local newspaper included twenty-seven free standing inserts from retailers and ninety-eight free standing inserts or pages from manufacturers. Less than two percent of all these advertisers were of any interest to me.

I'm told that struggling Kmart distributes 75 million inserts every week of the year. It's possible that more than a third of those are reaching homes with little or no interest in the chain. If Kmart were to sharpen their customer and prospect targeting by eliminating just a few million of the wasted distribution they would save more than enough to fund a formidable CMR initiative to retain their most valuable customers, so desperately needed for their survival.

CUSTOMER RELEVANCY

By understanding customer relevancy—what really matters to customers—companies can develop programs for mass marketing programs that are more productive while, at the same time, reserving the funding required for CMR.

It's not just mass media investments that suggest waste that could be reapplied for CMR projects. Seklemian/Newell studies have shown that most firms, even those who profess to be practicing CRM, are over-mailing and are spending significant telemarketing dollars to contact the wrong customers. Profitable proactive marketing requires understanding the desired customer experience and putting the customer in control.

There is waste on the reactive side of the communication equation as well. As a company adapts to customers' needs and requirements, it reduces costs while enabling customers to get better, easier access to the information and services they care most about. AT&T, planning to spend $2.6 billion, and Nextel, planning to spend $1.2 billion to bolster customer service, may not understand this.

In late 2002, after extensive customer research, Saks Department Stores learned that customers do not require the same levels of service in all departments. As a result, they maintained one-on-one personalized service in the cosmetics, shoes, men's tailored clothing, intimate apparel, fine china, and furniture areas of all stores. They also maintained this high level of service in the women's better sportswear and men's better sportswear areas of selected stores where they know customers expect it. These departments have transitioned to a more CMR type of service. The remaining departments of the stores offer fast, friendly, and efficient service at centralized service centers. Customer response to this new bifurcated service strategy has been very positive.

Companies trying to provide best customer service to all of their customers are misspending on these initiatives. Empowering the customer to manage the relationship allows him to decide the level of service he wants from your firm. Companies exploring this opportunity are finding they can save enough by eliminating wasted investments to finance all of their CMR activities.

CUSTOMER EQUITY

One of the best analyses of the process of learning where to spend and where to save marketing dollars for best return on your investments to turn customers into assets can be found in *Driving Customer Equity: How Customer Lifetime Value is Reshaping Corporate Strategy* (Rust, Zeithaml, and Lemon, The Free Press, 2000), named Marketing Book of the Year by the American Marketing Association. If you are serious about CMR, I suggest reading this book. The authors stress "managing according to Customer Equity (the value of a firm's customers) rather than Brand Equity (the value of a firm's brands) and focusing on customer profitability instead of product profitability."

This concept of customer equity is so central to the accomplishment of CMR goals and objectives I have asked the authors to contribute the following:

Marketing ROI: Where to Spend and Where to Cut Your Marketing Efforts for Maximum Return on Investment[1]

If you had an extra $500K in your marketing budget, how would you spend it? Would you:

- Run more television advertising?
- Invest in your loyalty program?
- Lower prices?
- Bring in exciting new merchandise?
- Develop new products or services?
- Hire more sales associates?
- Sponsor a local community event?

How would you decide? Now it's unlikely that you have an extra five hundred grand sitting around waiting to be spent. But think of it this way: if you had to *cut* your marketing budget by $500K, what would you cut? Wouldn't it be great to be able to determine the value of each dollar spent on marketing, and to be able to invest in the efforts that will result in the greatest return?

Recently, new research has been done to develop a model and mechanism to figure out which investments (e.g., CRM programs, brand building, price discounts, merchandising enhancements, quality improvements) are worth the cost. These new models help you figure out where the next marketing dollar should go.

To understand how this new approach, called the Customer Equity Framework, works, it's important to understand the critical questions facing marketers today:

- What do my customers want?
- How can I get my customers to come back more often? To buy more? To tell their friends about my company?
- How do I convince customers to spend more money with my firm than with my competitors'?
- Most important, how do I do this at a profit?

In answering these questions, you have to understand what truly drives your customers to do business with you and with your competitors. You also have to understand how your marketing actions impact the buying behaviors of your customers. Our research suggests that the key to understanding these issues and the metric that will help you maximize your return on marketing dollars is Customer Equity. *Customer Equity* is defined as the aggregate discounted lifetime values of all your customers. Without going deeply into the underlying math here, the key "asset" that you're trying to "grow" is the value of the future stream of profits that you'll receive from the customers in your market (those who buy from you now, and those who buy from your competitors). The greater your share of this "asset," the greater your long-term profitability.

Now, just because Customer Equity deals with customer lifetime value (CLV), don't think we're talking about customer relationship management. We're not.

Think about how you might grow the long-term profits from your customers and gain more share of your competitors' customers—in other words, how you might increase your Customer Equity. You can:

■ Improve the value your customer receives (we call this Value Equity)
■ Strengthen the customer perceptions of your brand (we call this Brand Equity)
■ Deepen the relationship the customer has with you (we call this Relationship Equity)

By breaking up the major drivers of Customer Equity into these three areas, you can then begin to understand what is most important to you customers. Your Customer Equity will grow or shrink based upon (1) how well you understand which of these drivers is most important to your customers, and (2) how well you manage—and invest in—those drivers that are critical to your customers.

A bit more about each driver:

■ **Value Equity** is defined as the customer's objective assessment of the utility of a brand based on perceptions of what is given up for what is received. In essence, your customer's objective evaluation of your products and services. Think about this as the customer's *head*. The critical, actionable steps you can take to strengthen your store's Value Equity are in three areas: quality, price, and convenience.

▪ **Brand Equity** is defined as the customer's subjective and intangible assessment of your brand, beyond its objectively perceived value. Brand Equity represents the customer's emotional connection with your store—the customer's *heart*. Action steps you can take to strengthen Brand Equity are: improving customer awareness, improving the customer's attitude toward your store, and investing in actions to improve your firm's corporate citizenship reputation. Not surprisingly, marketing communications play a critical role in growing Brand Equity.

▪ **Relationship Equity** is defined as the customer's tendency to "stick" with your store, beyond the customer's objective and subjective assessments of your firm. Think of Relationship Equity as your firm's social connection or *glue* with the customer—built up over time through the interactions the customer has with you. The key action steps to strengthen Relationship Equity are: loyalty programs (with both soft and hard benefits), community-building programs, and knowledge-building programs.

Right now, many firms *try* to do all of these tasks simultaneously, without differentiation, and always with limited budgets. We're not sure that's possible. But we are certain it's not the best use of your resources. The key to growing long-term profits is determining where to best invest your efforts—based upon what is most important to the customer.

So, how do you begin to determine where you should invest your marketing efforts for maximum return? The decision support system, *Customer Equity Driver*™, takes you through the following steps to determine the best use of your marketing dollars:

▪ **First,** you must determine what is the most important driver to your customers in their future purchasing decisions. Brand Equity? Value Equity? Relationship Equity?

▪ **Second,** you need to understand which actionable subdrivers are most effective in growing the value of your customer base. In other words, what actions will be most effective in getting your current customers to buy more, increase the likelihood that your current customers come back, and increase the probability that your competitors' customers switch to your store.

▪ **Third,** evaluate where you are on each driver relative to your competitors. For example, you may find out that your firm is perceived as "average" on a subdriver of Value Equity that customers really care about (e.g., knowledgeable sales staff, convenient hours)—and your key competitor may be performing much better on that dimension. A good candidate for marketing investment!

▪ **Finally,** invest where the payback is highest. You will actually be able to compare the potential returns from very different strategies—a loyalty program versus a price reduction; a community involvement program versus a merchandising initiative.

The Customer Equity framework provides an actionable approach to marketing that is customer centered, yet competitor cognizant. You will finally be able to understand, as the old adage suggests, which half of your marketing efforts are "wasted." New levels of efficiencies and effectiveness (not to mention accountability) for marketing investments are possible. Are you ready?

In our research on Customer Equity and in the writing of our book, *Driving Customer Equity: How Customer Lifetime Value Is Reshaping Corporate Strategy* (McGraw-Hill, 2000), we have learned some key lessons about how to grow Customer Equity in a variety of business environments. Here's what we've learned.

1 It's not always about price.
2 It's not always about having the right brands.
3 Loyalty programs are not the key driver for all retailers (you may be giving away unnecessary margin).
4 Soft benefits can be as (or more) important as hard benefits in loyalty programs.
5 You can't overlook the importance of assortment and convenience to your customers.

6 Most important: It's not just about brand. It's not just about quality, convenience, and price. It's not just about CRM. *It is about finding out what's important to your customers*—what "drives them" to do business with you—and making sure that you're the best at what matters most to them! Best in your region. Best in your specialty area. Continue to deliver on what is most important to your customers. It's not rocket science. But it is hard work.[2]

THE BOTTOM LINE

Finding the money to fund your CMR initiatives means prioritizing your marketing investments based on the new rules to improve the value your customer receives, to strengthen the customer perception of your brand, and to deepen the relationship your customer has with you. There is no free lunch; CMR will have its cost. But, in most cases, the cost can be more than offset by saving otherwise wasted marketing dollars.

The New Rules of CMR

- Determine the value of each dollar spent on marketing based on what is most important to the customer.
- Make media selections by letting customers guide you to their preferred source of information.
- Spend only to offer products or services you know will be of interest.
- Don't waste money on the wrong customers; invest in the ones who can be profitable for you.
- Don't try to offer the same service benefits to all customers. Learn the level of service each individual customer wants and deliver no more and no less.

Don't Boil the Ocean 18

Be wary of the big-bang approach

YOU HAVE MADE THE CASE FOR CMR. You've gotten budget approvals and senior management sign-offs. You have the right software in place to manage your customer knowledge, and you have integrated your customer data from all of your multichannel customer interactions. Now you're in the hot seat to deliver results. Where do you start?

Some companies will come into the CMR initiative from a solid base of a good CRM program with some personalization tools and activities already in place. Others will be making the broader leap from basic database marketing. It would appear that the former would provide the easier step and that the original CRM initiative would have brought everyone on board for an easy acceptance of CMR. If that were true, we would not be seeing so many CRM failures.

Most companies' CRM programs were designed to make business better for the company. It's a big jump from an inward focus on benefits to the concept of trying to make business better for the customer. It may be easier to move people within the company from the simple tracking of customer transactions in database marketing to the development of a program based on understanding customers' unique needs. In either case, there are two basic rules to consider at the start of shifting to CMR:

▪ **Rule 1:** Don't underestimate the skills, tools, time, budgets, and process changes that will be required to begin to allow the customer to benefit from having a strong voice in the management of the relationship.

▪ **Rule 2:** Think big but start small. Plan for incremental learning as you go.

Skill sets will involve some training and lots of internal communication to assure an enterprise-wide understanding of the new objective. All customer-facing personnel will have to learn new customer communication skills.

TOOLS AND PLANNING

It will not be enough for the company simply to have the appropriate tools; the ability to absorb new technology will be critical to success. This will require creating new guidelines and training to be sure everyone in the workforce uses the new tools effectively. Whatever time line you project, double it. Take into account the fact that key players will not always be available the moment you need them. Process changes will be greater than you have planned. Vacations, other priorities of the business, and delays in vendor deliverables will also stretch your time line.

Working with a large retail client, Seklemian/Newell established a plan to develop new CMR initiatives in two phases. We projected that Phase 1, developing the strategy, would take nine months, and that Phase 2, testing the implementation, would take six months. As we progressed we soon realized that Phase 1 would take twelve months and that, even then, we would not be ready to make the leap to Phase 2 without adding a new step. We revised the schedule to include an interim Phase 1.5, which added six months to the process. This is a classic example of the why it's important to factor in extra time.

Break the budget into specific project tasks for best control. There have been cases, even in rather simple CRM deployments, where, because of poor project structure, the budget is consumed before projects are ready and without consideration of what is being delivered. Not only does that result in cheap and rushed implementation, but also starts the program off on the wrong foot. Early investments in expensive software and hardware can diminish the start-up budgets before a company is ready to implement its program, resulting in a rushed and weak rollout. It is imperative to keep each expense category separate and controlled from the start.

STARTING SMALL

All of these caveats bring us to Rule 2. If you try to change the whole way of doing business on an enterprise-wide basis, quick wins are unlikely to happen. Any big-bang approach causes masses of change requests and your framework will not be strong enough to cope at the start. Projects of a large scale all too often become long drawn-out affairs with no real results until near the end. Quick wins will keep the project alive and funded. Limit your pilot to a controllable area of the business while looking ahead to the bigger projects that can make use of what you've learned. This was the principle involved in the BancoRio example in Chapter 15, where the six-stage CMR project was tested in just three of the bank's 267 branches before enterprise-wide rollout.

Starting with projects that address narrow business goals and produce high impact will begin to create the structure that will serve as the foundation of broader projects. At the start the most important goal is to prove the concept and to get everyone within the company to believe in the project. These beginning stages should be carried out in the most cost-effective manner.

There will be pressures to add on to the starting projects. Even after you have prioritized projects based on their impact on customer perception and their income revenue potential, others within the company will press for their own personal agendas. Tom Kaneshige, a senior editor at e-business magazine *Line56*, explains:

> A project often starts out filling a specific need. But CRM means many things to many people, thanks to its wide-ranging functionality and cross-enterprising nature. It's not unusual for a highly placed executive to catch wind of the project and become star-struck at the vast potential it represents, creating conditions in which a stream of

add-ons results in an initiative that is over ambitious. Potentially even more problematic is that CRM touches customers, so even minor hiccups can damage key relationships, and major problems can have lasting negative implications.[1]

We've seen this happen all too often, and it will be even truer for CMR, where we are asking the customer to get more involved. Pressures will come from outside your company as well. It's easy to be led astray by vendors and system integrators. Vendors will often press for the installation of functions you haven't asked for. Make sure that you get what you want without any unnecessary extras. If you find you need other features later, you can have them added then.

Start with simple prototypes that demonstrate the business case for CMR and quickly deliver measurable business value to your CMR stakeholders. When Verizon started into CRM they chose limited projects to pilot in small regions. Maura Breen, senior vice president and CMO of Verizon's Retail Markets Group, had this to say at a Conference Board session on strategic management:

> An important question we had to answer was how to size CRM for a $22 billion business with 25 million customers without boiling the ocean. We're taking a phased approach, defining manageable projects in specific geographies that can be measured for ROI, and then using the learning to expand the effort. The first phase creates an experience for high value customers in the call center, our most heavily trafficked channel. We're looking at how to make it easier to provide more of Verizon's products and services on one call to customers who need them.[2]

While Verizon is concentrating more on efficient cross-sell rather than on turning the management of the relationship over to the customer, the lesson is clear: Start with a limited customer group (high value customers), a single business process (the call center), and a limited area (specific geographies), all selected so that they can be measured for ROI.

At this pilot stage, it is important to be sure that your efforts complement the long-range plans of the program. Elements that are beyond the scope of the early pilot should not be addressed, but they should be identified and prioritized for later inclusion in the initiative.

Joseph Colletti, executive vice president of consulting services at CRM firm ANALYTIC*i*, explains this need for forethought with an analogy. "If you are building a car and you know that one eventual goal is to use the car to tow a boat, you should understand the ramifications of that up front. You will want to make sure the blueprint of the car takes into account this long term need."[3]

What he means is that you don't have to attach the trailer hitch yet, but you do have to be sure that the engine size and suspension of the car will support the longer-term objective. This kind of planning will assure that the incremental learning from the pilots will deliver everything you need when rolled out across the enterprise. In the pilot you may be able to work only with customer information from the transaction database. It may be that customer interactions from the Web or from the call center will not be added until later, but you will want to prioritize these for later inclusion and be certain, at the start, that the systems and processes in the test will be robust enough to deliver your later needs.

PROTECT YOUR PRESENT BUSINESS

CMR is so sexy that it can take everyone's attention away from business as usual. One of the first things to confirm, at the start, is that the things that are driving the business today will continue to get attention and the funding they deserve. If database marketing has been driving the business, don't ease off on that as you start your journey into CMR. Fine tune it, as required, to see that it doesn't interfere in the customer's acceptance of your new strategies, but don't lose its driving force. If CRM has been your strength, add on but don't reduce your CRM investments. Protect what you have.

As this book is being written, our consulting company, Seklemian/Newell is in the process of helping a large retail client company move from database marketing through CRM to CMR. We started by separating the challenge into three activities:

- the current database marketing
- the proposed CRM
- the ultimate CMR

For the existing database activities we established plans and reserved funding to assure continuation of the database marketing activities that were driving important parts of the business. We would take small risks within the pilot projects, but would be careful to maintain most of the driving force of the existing database marketing.

For the new CRM initiative we designed a pilot, carefully selecting a region that could be isolated for the test. Within that region we looked for the company's most enthusiastic personnel at management and front-line level to lead the pilot. Further refining the process, we selected representative customer segments and control groups within the pilot region.

One of the objectives was to move customers from discount shopping to higher margin sales. Studies of the customer transaction files showed that customers who shopped in the major sale events—after being targeted in our database marketing activity—did not shop in the same pattern later in the same month. Our hypothesis was that if we sent these customers details of new merchandise and other information with special relevance for them instead of just sale notices, we could interest them in shopping at full price. To meet our objective we had to eliminate the test customers from one of the database marketing sale mailings, a calculated risk.

We moved into the CMR phase of the initiative with the same careful controls. Again we isolated a test group of customers and control group to try to learn what difference it would make if we could really build a relationship that would put more power in the hands of the customer.

Early results show the CRM activities are keeping customers at the same or better spending levels at higher margins; preliminary CMR findings show we are increasing the quality of the dialog with these customers. As the selected customers share more personal information with us, we are beginning to see increased cross-sell and customer retention.

It is imperative in any test to be certain that every action of the test and every aspect of the test base can be replicated in the rollout. In a small test you can do a lot of one-on-one training to get sales associates or other front-line employees to change work habits. If you won't have the time or the manpower to do exactly the same training for the thousands of employees that will be involved in the rollout, you won't see the same results. For the test project use only tools that will be workable on the larger scale. Seklemian/Newell once saw a retailer test a customer relationship program using a store in a tourist resort market in high season. After a successful test, they rolled it out only to learn that the experience with the resort market's tourist customers was not applicable to their broad customer base.

The message for anyone starting the CMR journey remains: Don't try to boil the ocean. Think big but start small. Your start must be a testing or pilot stage. This stage is all about finding what is going to work. The pilot stage gives your team time to learn, minimizes up-front investment and risk, and builds credibility for the CMR concept. Once you have tested economically the hypothesis that CMR can add depth to the customer relationship and profit to the company, it becomes a simple matter to scale it to broader goals.

As Herb Kelleher, former chairman of Southwest Airlines, is reported to have said, "Think small and act small, and we'll get bigger. Think big and act big, and we'll get smaller."

PART FOUR

A Look
Ahead

There's No There, There 19

Can customer relationships survive
Internet ubiquity?

THE INTERNET HAS BEEN TRANSFORMED beyond what anyone
could have foreseen thirty years ago. The Internet has become
ubiquitous and unavoidable. It's no longer just an icon on a personal
computer—it's everywhere. Gertrude Stein made a famous comment, "The problem with Oakland, California is that there's no
there, there." Like Oakland, the Internet has no center. There is no
way to pinpoint its place; it is everywhere.

THE INTERNET AND CUSTOMER RELATIONSHIPS

Internet-supported customer relationship activities are emerging as
one of the fastest growing areas of Web use. Customers are moving
from the call center to Internet interactive channels because of the
higher degree of control and accessibility these channels provide. As
Internet terminals for general use are becoming more common, your
customers will have greater opportunities for interaction.

A recent study by market-analysis firm Datamonitor reveals that
Internet access is spreading like a virus through European retail
establishments. Stand-alone Internet terminals are appearing in locations such as bars, cafés, telephone boxes, and gas stations. BP's British

gas stations plan to provide consumers with the chance to check out Internet information during the short window of time spent filling the tank. BP is betting that during the two minutes it takes to fill up you would rather log on than stare at the pump ticker or other patrons.

It's not just a European phenomenon. At Schlotzsky's Deli, the Austin, Texas–based fast food chain, customers can surf the Net in one of its new cyber delis while they savor their muffuletta-style sandwich with a side of salt and vinegar chips.[1]

One Inner-City Internet Initiative

In Boston, entrepreneur Eric Bobby has instituted a campaign to expand access to retail services and the Internet for a large and underserved market—the nation's inner cities. His product, known as CityKi, hopes to give Web access to people who ordinarily wouldn't have it. Bobby is seeking to address the dearth of physical stores in inner-city neighborhoods by providing consumers with broadband access to selected merchants, service providers, financial institutions, government agencies, and community generated content. The Initiative for a Competitive Inner City (ICIC) estimates that inner-city neighborhoods represent nearly 8 million households, or approximately 12 percent of total U.S. households, and that the inner-city retail market in the United States is worth about $90 billion. But this is more than just e-commerce. With CityKi customers can set up and access their own personal e-mail accounts at the kiosk.

As of early 2002, about twenty companies are featured online at the CityKi kiosk. They include eBags, Staples, PETsMART, Proflowers .com, Amazon.com, Toys "R" Us, Target, Best Buy, Dell Computers, Tower Records, Barnes & Noble, and Overstock.com.[2] Because of such initiatives, companies can reach people who wouldn't ordinarily have access to computers at home or even at work.

WLANs

Research from Analysys predicts that 21 million people in the United States will be using public wireless local area networks (WLANs) in 2007. Analysys estimates that the use of public WLANs will generate over $3 billion in service revenue by 2007.

As part of its report "Public Wireless LAN Access: U.S. Market Forecasts 2002–2007," Analysys finds hotels currently dominate the public WLAN scene providing roughly 1.67 million access locations in the country. However, Analysys believes that by 2007, restaurants and cafes will provide roughly 14.18 million access locations, surpassing the amount provided by hotels (10.35 million).[3]

A Glimpse of the Future

This ubiquity of the Internet will be dizzying. Douglas McWirter, the writer who first reviewed the Datamonitor study calls it sensory overload, "Think of the Internet as a strobe light at a dance club. At first it seems cool, but after a few minutes it makes you dizzy and gives you a headache." He asks, "Does anyone really need to be connected this much?"[4] A better question might be, what will this ever-present customer access mean for customer relationships?

Just how up-close and personal are we talking? Consider this. To speed the process of meeting and greeting at the Internet Everywhere CEO Summit 2000, a company called Charmed.com gave away boxes that attendees could hang around their necks to swap contact information with one another just by standing in front of each other and chatting. These "badge boxes," put together from boxes of Altoids Mints bought at the local Sam's Club, enabled hands-free, no-hassle schmoozing. These were no ordinary Altoid boxes. Charmed .com had transformed them into wireless interactive communication devices that allowed participants to share information. The boxes exemplified the kind of immersive Internet experience those at the conference were seeking to build in the future.[5]

Others at the Summit added their comments. Science-fiction writer Gregory Benford said, "Comfy culture will be the end result of putting the Internet everywhere. IP-enabled devices will eventually care for the inhabitants of the industrialized world, making everyday activities like shopping or walking down the street into personalized experiences."[6]

It will also make civilization an increasingly familiar place, said science-fiction writer David Brin, author of *The Transparent Society*

(Perseus Publishing, 1999). He said the ability to use Internet devices to call up information on anyone, anywhere as users travel will recreate small villages—where everyone knows everybody else by reputation—like most inhabitants of villages hundreds of years ago.[7]

Professor Alex Pentland, academic head of MIT Media Laboratory, predicts that the technical infrastructure will be with us in the clothes we wear and on the products we buy. He said, "We see the technology 'on the person.'" He showed a slide of a student who had developed eyeglasses that allow the wearer to call up information as he looks at the world around him. While others converse with him, the wearer can look up the backgrounds of those he talks with, or pull up Web pages related to the conversation.[8]

Add to this ubiquity the fact that e-mail isn't waiting anymore for people to boot up their PCs. More people, every day, are taking advantage of wireless technology. Microsoft is moving closer to realizing its Net vision of ubiquitous access to Web-based content and services with the next version of its Windows CE operating system, designed to provide support for the delivery of Web-based services and content to mobile devices.

In February 2002 IBM Research announced the building of a computer the size of a stack of index cards. Although it has no plans to market the device, IBM is testing the three-inch wide, five-inch long, three-quarters of an inch thick machine to find out how people will react when they can carry their PC with them everywhere they go. Users will be expected to customize the machine to fit their needs. The device can be transformed into a handheld, desktop, laptop, tablet, or wearable computer in seconds without having to be rebooted. IBM plans to build about 100 of the devices and loan them to various customers in a number of different industries and see how people's use changes when they have a full PC with them all the time.[9]

THE INTERNET AND CMR

What does this type of development mean for CMR? The Internet's omnipresence will be dizzying, but the good news is it will allow for more personalized interaction. The bad news is that some companies claiming to be "doing" CRM, but really just targeting customers for special offers, will push what they want to sell to customers wherever they are. My fear is that too many will try to capitalize on that two minutes waiting for the gas tank to fill by flashing more and more generic banner ads, in effect creating more spam.

Firms will be able to capitalize on the Internet being "everywhere you are" to help customers manage the relationship anytime, from anywhere. In the traditional brick-and-mortar retail setting we have always taught sales associates not to greet customers with the phrase, "May I help you?" It made it easy for the customer to say no. Perhaps now, if we're really trying to let customers manage the relationship, it's time now to greet that customer who is trying to get something done in his two minutes at the gas station with a cheery, "How may I help you today?"

Some firms are finding new ways to let customers manage the relationship from wherever they are. For example, the Golden Paw, a San Diego luxury boarding resort and spa for pets, does this with Web cams placed throughout its 11,000-square-foot center. They allow customers to log on and see how their pets are during their absence. Customers call it "a nice, comforting feeling."[10] As trivial as this example may seem, The Golden Paw's service to customers is a perfect example of CMR in action. They have found a way to empower customers by reacting in real time to customers' needs.

To meet customers' current needs we have to have the same memory as the customer. That will require integration of back-office and frontline activities using information originating from and communicating in real time with every other sales and communication channel for that customer. The sources of customer information will include brick-and-mortar stores and offices, sales associates, mail, fax, e-mail, phone, the Web, wireless, and interactive TV. Most companies still have a long way to go for capturing that sort of customer information.

PwC Consulting queried 2,000 global companies and found that:

- 74 percent said their companies "need to do more" to improve back-to-front integration
- 64 percent said their companies "need to do more" to integrate data from multiple channels

- Only 17 percent regarded back-to-front integration as "achieved"
- Only 24 percent rated cross-channel integration as "achieved"[11]

This integration is no longer an option. As customers continue to move from your call center to your Internet interactive channels for control and accessibility, and as their opportunities for interaction become available everywhere they are, your opportunities for CMR expand to influence more of their everyday activities. The "villages" David Brin predicted will become communities of customers where your reputation will be on the line every day. Anything that stands in the way of the customer managing the relationship, anything that hinders customers' ability to help themselves, will stand out. You won't have any choice. You will have to reengineer your business processes from the outside in, starting with the customer and the things that will make her life easier.

Electronic Empowerment **20**

How will electronics revolutionize customer communication?

T HE ELECTRONIC TRANSFORMATION started with the Internet. However, as one writer says, "The Internet isn't a revolution; it simply revolutionizes the way we send and receive information. People now focus more on the information *on* the Internet than information *about* the Internet."[1]

What does this mean for the Internet's place in helping us to empower customers? You can use your Internet communications to involve your customers, rewarding them, and using dialog to let them control the relationship. When customers come to your website, they have chosen to come and have given you permission to communicate with them. This new communication opportunity is about trust.

How do you use the Internet for CMR? Build dynamic websites that will create dialog, will work for the customer, and will build trust. This goal is not easy to achieve, since, according to a survey by Forrester Research, only 14 percent of adults trust ads that appear on the Internet. This figure is opposed to 30 percent for magazine ads, 25 percent for radio, 23 percent for TV, and 18 percent for direct mail.[2]

The longevity of the medium correlates directly to its perceived trustworthiness. Newspapers are the oldest medium; the Internet is the newest. While direct mail has been around for at least 130 years, its ease of use makes it available to less-than-honest hawkers and has compromised its credibility. So, it takes more than longevity to build trust. Trust is developed by customer experiences.

The Bridgestone/Firestone success story in Chapter 12 was the result of the company learning that customers determine where to have a vehicle serviced, in large part, on the trust factor. To help create trust, Bridgestone/Firestone store managers send personal e-mail communications to customers after each service visit. The notes provide helpful information to customers about what can go wrong with their vehicles, with the goal of avoiding major repairs. It was this trust, built upon past experiences, that reinforced the relationship between customers and stores and kept customers loyal to the Firestone brand during the tire recall.

THE PURPOSE OF WEB COMMUNICATION

At the beginning, most companies' websites provided little more than one-way information, known as brochureware. As companies began to use their sites to create dialog, customers told the companies what they liked about them, what they didn't like, and what companies could do to improve things. For example, companies began to realize that faster download time is more important than flashy graphics. They noticed that they were losing visitors due to complicated online forms. They simplified the experience for the customer and placed more emphasis on structure and navigation efficiency than they had before. You can learn a lot from your customers when you empower them, and the Internet is the place to start the learning.

Web communication is not just about commercial messages. The Roman Catholic Church uses the Internet to webcast papal addresses live from St. Peter's Basilica. A company named Medtronic has developed a customer-based initiative to save time for physicians and patients by enabling "virtual office visits." The product, called Carelink, is an Internet-based service enabling patients to download a full range of current "condition data" relating to their use of a cardiac device, such as a pacemaker or defibrillator. A small mouse-sized receiver captures current heart and device function information and transfers it over a standard phone line to the Medtronic Carelink

Network, enabling the physician to evaluate the patient's condition without the need for an office visit.[3] Carelink is a great example of a company empowering customers with value-added services. Not only does it save the customer's valuable time, but it also helps make his life less stressful.

A Look at Some Trends

As you develop your CMR communications it is also important not to try to force things to the Web if there is a simpler solution. Keep in mind the story of the man who was quietly reading his newspaper when his wife asked him if he thought it was going to rain. He walked to his computer, pointed his browser to the local weather page, and was about to answer his wife, when she stood up, opened the door, and stuck her head outside. "It's raining," she announced, as her husband tapped away.[4] Sometimes it's easier just to open the door and look. Just because a bank offers online services, doesn't mean all of its customers will want to do their banking online. Some customers may still find it easier to visit the drive-thru window during their lunch hour to deposit a check. It all comes down to giving the customer the choice.

Beyond the Internet, there are some things in the electronic transformation that will revolutionize our customer communication opportunities. Some are simple.

Customer Comment Cards

In some restaurants today you'll find an electronic customer comment card tucked inside the holder that delivers your check. This small, wireless surveying device permits you to share your opinion on how well the restaurant is fulfilling your needs. The device allows the restaurant owner to get a real-time view of customer concerns and act on them right then, right there. For example, negative feedback to questions such as, "Would you recommend this restaurant to a friend?" or "On a scale of one to ten, rate your overall experience," will trigger an alert to the manager on duty. He then can approach the table and perhaps offer an incentive for the customer to give the restaurant a chance to improve the dining experience. It is reported that the electronic comment cards are increasing customer participation in surveys. One restaurant that used to get about fifteen to twenty completed paper surveys each day now gets more than 100 electronic survey results each day.[5] Of course there's a lot more to this than the restaurant getting a better return on surveys; the instant gratification also makes the customer feel empowered.

Unified Messaging

Another opportunity for customer relationship building comes from Unified Messaging systems. They offer conferencing capabilities, call forwarding, call routing, and a service typically referred to as Find Me Follow Me—a number portability function that allows you to be reached, no matter which of your phones you're using. To offer empowered personal service to customers, a firm's representative can give his or her customers a virtual local number to call. Whenever a customer calls, Find Me Follow Me finds the rep based on preset schedules and criteria. You can create a rule that works a certain way on weekdays and another way on weekends. You can also create rules for special customers, so a call from a most important customer will blast you on all your phone lines, including your car phone and other mobiles.[6]

Video

A new Panasonic phone comes complete with a camera for making video calls. When the phone is held at arm's length, the camera can either point at the user or be rotated 180 degrees to transmit what the user is seeing or a product a user wants to show to a customer on the line. Camera phones won't be ubiquitous overnight, but they will change the way we communicate with customers.

There are other ways we'll gain the gift of sight. A Silicon Valley start-up has embarked on an effort to let computers see the world in three-dimensions—to look out at the world through a small lens and create a 3-D picture of the objects around it. The company hopes that by early 2003 some manufacturers will place a lens the size of a fingertip in the ends of their cell phones and handheld computers. The lens would project a keyboard in front of the user that would process hand movements, allowing a person to type "virtually," without the need for a physical keyboard. Users would type just by moving their fingers above the handheld.[7]

How will camera phones and 3-D pictures enable CMR? It may be easier to build trust when we can see customers, and they can see us. Customers will be empowered when they can type messages to companies without the need for a keyboard. And, savvy marketers will be looking for any new tools to help empower customers.

Translations

Help is on the way as well for companies that must communicate in languages other than English, for customers in other countries or for non-English-speaking American consumers. A natural language engine from Banter, Inc. can take messages from customers—such as e-mail or chat—and extract from them what the customer is trying to say. Banter's technologies are helping organizations to cut costs, improve service, and increase revenue by answering free-form questions on websites. This lightens the labor load for agents by suggesting responses to customers' e-mails, providing automated responses, and routing messages to the people with appropriate skills. The technology finds patterns in e-mail and other text-based messages that used to require human analysis; thus shortening response time to make life easier for the customer.[8]

Television

Even television is getting in the personalization game. After decades of false starts, interactive television (iTV) is creeping into millions of American homes. Forrester Research estimates that by the end of 2002, about 15 percent of the 105 million U.S. households with TV sets will have some kind of interactive service—almost double the number for 2001.[9] How can iTV help build closer relationships between companies and consumers? Instead of a passive ad, iTV enables an active, individualized relationship-building campaign.

For example, the first time a viewer is shown an offer for a financial services company, the overlay might include a new account kit. If the viewer has already taken the initial offer, the next overlay will change. Instead of an icon asking if the customer wants that same brochure, the message asks, "Did the material arrive?" Messages can be adjusted to individual households based on previous behavior.[10] It's not quite a dialog, yet, and it's not quite CMR, but with companies like Ford, American Airlines, and Charles Schwab testing it, it is another important trend to keep an eye on.

Computer Power

So how far might we go in the sphere of customer electronic empowerment? Computer power seems limitless. As companies collect more and more data from multiple sources to strengthen customer relationships, the experts are talking about petabytes. Although a petabyte of data is difficult to fathom, the editors of *Information Week* tell us to think of it as the equivalent of 250 billion pages of text, enough to fill 20 million four-drawer filing cabinets, or a 2,000 mile-high tower of 1 billion diskettes. Sears Roebuck & Co. is already combining its customer and inventory data warehouses to create a 70 terabyte system. The retailer will hit the 1 petabyte threshold—1,000 terabytes—within four years.[11]

Will computers be able to cope? It would appear so. In 2002 scientists studying nuclear weapons detonated the first E-bomb (a computer simulation of a nuclear explosion) as part of the National Nuclear Security Administration's Stockpile Stewardship Program, which manages the safety, security, and reliability of America's nuclear deterrent. The researchers at Los Alamos and Lawrence Livermore National Labs detonated two of the largest computer simulations ever. The computation used more than 6.6 million CPU hours, which would take today's home computer more than 750 years to complete. The data consumed was equivalent to thirty-five times the information available in the Library of Congress.[12] And now some see supercomputers the size of pencil erasers that will work ten times faster than the fastest computers today.[13]

WHAT'S NEXT?

What might we expect next that may help us communicate with and empower customers? Applied Digital Solutions is seeking the FDA's permission to market a computer ID chip that can be embedded under a person's skin. The device, called a VeriChip, is about the size of a grain of rice and would be difficult to counterfeit or transfer to another person. Imagine the possibilities: no worry about lost credit cards; quicker boarding at the airport without having to show photo ID three times; and the ability electronically to recognize customers the minute they enter your store.[14]

What will marketing (and CMR) be like when computers can sense customers' emotions? "E-motional" technology is already being developed by researchers at the University of Southern California's Integrated Media Systems Center. The project is aimed at understanding customers' needs and creating smart self-service systems that can adapt to emotional signals.

Researchers are creating templates of facial features, expressing emotions such as joy, surprise, anger, fear, and sadness. Then, smart cameras that operate on sophisticated modeling techniques map customers' facial features against a base of known facial reactions and match them to an emotional state. The modeling process will allow self-service devices to make appropriate offers in real time. If you forget your glasses and are forced to squint to read the ATM monitor, the ATM will increase the type size, or if you smile at a product ad on a store kiosk the device can print out a coupon just for you.[15]

What does all this technology have to do with allowing customers to manage their relationships with your company? Empowerment tools are changing fast. They will continue to change faster than we can now imagine. Some will say this technology borders on invasion of privacy; customers will be receptive to this new sharing of information only if we continue to find ways to respect their wants and needs. Our responsibility will be to use these new tools carefully, judiciously, and with great respect for our customers and our world.

What Do Customers Want from Mobile Messaging? **21**

Do customers really want to order groceries while driving home from work?

THERE'S NOT MUCH YOU CAN'T DO wirelessly today. In early 2001, an official in the Malaysian government confirmed that divorces via SMS (short message service) mobile messaging were indeed legal. Thus, Malaysia joined several Muslim countries and the city of Dubai where the use of this simple 160 character communication tool is valid as a means of regaining single status. A husband can send a message containing the words "I divorce you." His wife is then obligated to report to a court and have the divorce made effective. Later in the year, the religious councilor to the prime minister decided to override the ruling saying that Malaysian law does not permit SMS divorce even though Islamic law does.[1] At the time of this writing, the SMS divorce process was still legal in Dubai.

MOBILE COMMUNICATION

It takes little more than the sight of American figure skater Sasha Cohen, at the opening ceremony of the 2002 summer Olympics in Salt Lake City, handing her cell phone to President Bush so he could say hello to her mother to realize the anytime, anywhere power of mobile communication. The convergence of the two fastest-growing communications technologies of all time—the mobile phone and the Internet—suggests dramatic opportunities for marketers. But these may not be the opportunities we anticipated.

M-Commerce

In March 2000, Jeff Bezos of Amazon.com predicted that by 2010 all of his customers would be using wireless devices to make purchases. He called m-commerce (mobile commerce) "the most fantastic thing that a time-starved world has ever seen," and claimed that within five or ten years, "almost all e-commerce will be on wireless devices."[2] With the promise of 3G networks the talk was all about people watching video clips on the train or videoconferencing in a taxi; but now, consumers are concentrating on more realistic goals such as using phones to access e-mail, download news and weather reports, and call up location-specific information.[3]

Content Is Not King

What it turns out people want from their wireless devices is person-to-person communication. Andrew Odlyzko, a former AT&T researcher who is now at the University of Minnesota, says, "Content is not king—connectivity is more important. The killer app for 3G phones might turn out to be increased voice traffic."[4] For CMR, connectivity will be the key to increased dialog with customers, and dialog—person-to-person communication—is the power that drives the customer management of relationships.

A survey report by *The Economist* makes the point that "it should come as no surprise if the killer app for the mobile Internet, at least for consumers, turns out to be person-to-person communication. That, after all, has been the golden prize of all previous technologies, from telegraph to telephone to mobile phone. Whether it's transmitting speech, words, pictures, or graphics, all are social activities, and mobile phones are primarily social devices."[5]

All this suggests that this new technology presents the greatest opportunity for businesses to develop richer, more profitable relationships with individual customers by giving them what they actually want—person-to-person verbal communication. The latest research by NOP Research Group in the U.K. clearly indicates that "the one-size-fits all approach to mobile Internet use will miss the mark by a country mile."[6] Wireless communication, whether by voice or by instant messaging, offers businesses the ability not only to interact with customers, but also to create rich dialog for learning more about their individual needs and finding ways to give them more control over the business relationship.

Strengthening Consumer Ties

Keebler Co., a subsidiary of The Kellogg Co., is the first consumer packaged goods company to use instant messaging to strengthen ties with consumers of company brands, including Keebler, Harvest Bakery, Club, Toasted, Vanilla Wafers, Sunshine, Murray Sugar Free, and Town House. The service, called RecipeBuddie, allows consumers to request recipes based on their mood or food preferences.

The service is open to consumers on the AOL Instant Messenger, AOL/CompuServe, and MSN platforms and does not proactively contact consumers or collect personal information; the consumer initiates the dialog. To participate, consumers send an instant message to the screen name RecipeBuddie. Responses are immediate, delivered in the voice of Becky, a thirty-five-year-old mother of two from suburban Chicago.

Anna Murray, principle of New York–based eMedia Inc. and creator of RecipeBuddie, says, "Through Becky, Keebler can establish a kind of trust relationship with consumers. RecipeBuddie isn't meant to compete directly with the vast database sites such as AllRecipes.com and others. This is instant messaging, after all. It's meant to give good recipe ideas quickly in the most convenient, fun way possible."[7]

Pull Technology

There will still be value in pushing individual messages such as sports scores, stock quotes, and weather to customers who have signed up for such alerts. But the real CMR opportunity is what some are calling "pull" marketing, with which customers can request specific information through their phones. The problem with "push" technology is that it's all one-way traffic. "Pushing is no big deal; pulling is the future," according to Stanislas Chesnais, chairman and CEO of Netsize, a French start-up that offers SMS technology.

He uses the example of a theater with two mobile phone numbers that mobile users can call to send text messages—one for show times and one for film reviews. Theater-goers send a message with the film name to the first number and receive the show times for the day, then another message to the second number, again with the film name, for a short review of the film—all via SMS.[8]

Catalog retailer Lands' End moved to "pull" technology when on-line customers told them they would shop more frequently online if they could get real-time answers to their questions. Lands' End launched a new service called "Lands' End Live," which enables customers to use instant messaging to talk with customer service representatives. The average customer who uses the service spends 8 percent more than one who doesn't and is 67 percent more likely to buy than an online customer not using it.[9] Lands' End has since added another customer empowerment technology they call "Shop with a Friend," which lets two customers exchange messages as they shop. Siblings can converge on the site and discuss which sweater would be best for Mom's birthday present.

In addition to empowering customers, these services give Lands' End new options for customer feedback. Shoppers were already providing some comments on the phone, by mail, and by e-mail, but Sam Taylor, Lands' End vice president of international and e-commerce, says, "Instant messaging makes it even easier for online customers to convey their thoughts about Lands' End products and services."[10] The folks at Lands' End understand the CMR process of developing richer, more profitable relationships with individual customers by giving customers more of the power.

Wireless Empowerment

Safeway, in the U.K., is empowering customers by giving them Palm-powered handheld devices with small magnets on the back of them so customers can put them on their refrigerators. As customers empty the orange juice carton or the milk carton they just tick off the product and brand and the request gets transmitted wirelessly to their nearest Safeway store.[11] Customers are more apt to stop off at their Safeway store when they know their order is ready than they are to stop elsewhere to buy food on the way home. This sounds even better than ordering groceries while driving home from work.

Real-Time Information

In 2002 *Computerworld* named its choices for wireless innovators who found ways to empower their customers. Customer-led, Fidelity Investments was one of the first to launch its wireless service. At that time, a survey of Fidelity customers revealed that 40 percent believed they had missed out on investment opportunities because they were away from a wired channel and didn't have access to market information. Knowing that the right information at the right time can be worth millions to its customers, Fidelity launched Instant Broker. The wireless service empowers active traders by allowing them to monitor activities affecting their accounts through pagers, and enables traders to initiate transactions.[12]

Based on the success of Instant Broker, Fidelity added to its customer empowerment with Fidelity Anywhere which allows customers to manage their 401(k) accounts, charitable donations, insurance, and more. Fidelity plans to expand Fidelity Anywhere to include a limousine and hotel service, enabling users to book and confirm reservations. Fidelity Anywhere supports devices from Palm Inc. as well as General Motors' OnStar system. Joseph Ferra, Fidelity's chief wireless officer, says, "We want to be on as many devices as possible. Fidelity Anywhere's primary value is to draw customers into deeper relationships and increase customer loyalty."[13]

It hardly needs to be said, when you empower your customers and get them to use your proprietary technology for services beyond those of your firm, you are building the kind of relationships that will keep customers loyal to your brand.

In 1999, United Airlines started to empower customers when it became the first airline to offer real-time flight information on the Palm VII. The company now offers Proactive Paging that notifies passengers of changes in their flight status and a Wireless Application Protocol-based (WAP) phone application that gives up-to-date flight and frequent-flyer information and offers domestic booking. United tracks flights through its systems and notifies passengers based on specified preferences. Passengers may be alerted to delays or changes in departure gates—whatever they specify. According to Niru Shah, United Network's director of application development, "The wireless users are frequent flyers. They want control and appreciate timely information. The customers have really embraced this, showing a 2,800 percent increase in usage in 2001."[14]

Hotels such as Six Continents, Holiday Inn, InterContinental, and Crowne Plaza offers wireless reservations systems and allows guests to request driving directions and local weather forecasts with SMS messaging. Next, some wireless vendors are talking about what they believe will be the application for hotels that will make guests go "Wow!"—wireless check-in. Instead of forcing incoming guests to wait at a check-in desk, hotels will deploy employees with handhelds into the lobby, on the hotel entrance driveway, or into parking areas, or even the bar. With a few taps on the screen they will be able to check in the guest and issue a key from a portable printing device.[15]

Business-to-Business

CMR is taking hold in the business-to-business arena as well. Hewlett-Packard's drive towards creating the "ultimate total customer experience" is capitalizing on mobile opportunities to give more power to HP customers. Ian Brooks, HP's head of Internet Strategy, says,

> Mobile is giving us the chance to satisfy our customers more than ever before. With mobile technology, customers really want to do business with you. You can transmit sales data, live, from the field; customers can ask you about anything: what happened with the support call we logged last week, has my payment gone through yet; have the parts I ordered arrived; and all you do is whip out your PDA to give them the answer, right there and then. The last thing we want is an unanswered question, because instant, accurate information is a major factor in satisfying customers.[16]

BEYOND WIRELESS COMMUNICATIONS

What may be beyond wireless communications as we know them today? We already have communication through radio frequency identification tags (RFIDs)—the technology now in use in Exxon-Mobil's Speedpass and the E-ZPass highway tollbooth systems. Futurists see the time when billions of these plastic tags, the size of postage stamps, will be out there communicating, infiltrating business and everyday life to a greater extent than today's personal computers, cell phones, or e-mail. In decades to come, they say, the impact of the RFID might be as fundamental as the invention of the light bulb. Arno Penzias, a Nobel Prize-winning scientist and one-time head of Bell Labs, has this microcosmic scenario:

> You lose your eyeglasses. They've fallen under the family room couch. The tag on your eyeglasses connects with a reader in the family room. You sit at your computer and type in a search box: "Where are my eyeglasses?" A reader sends out a signal looking for tags. The signal excites the tag on your eyeglasses. The computer responds: "Under the couch."[17]

We don't have to wait for Penzias's scenario to play out. Products like The i-SPOT Personal Items Locator by Digital Innovations and FINDIT an electronic locator device made by Ambitious Ideas are already on the market, and the Sharper Image has a product called, The Now You Can Find It Electronic Locator. All of these use radio frequencies to pinpoint the location of lost items within twenty to forty feet, emitting a tone when a button is pressed on the transmitter. With the average American spending sixteen minutes a day looking for lost items, this could be a big market.[18] The Personal Items Locator and FINDIT can't yet be credited with CMR, but ideas like this often lead to innovative customer relationships.

IT'S A LONG JOURNEY from a digital divorce in Malaysia, to an Olympian's phone call from Salt Lake City to her mother, to "pull" technology in Lands' End's home in Dodgeville, Wisconsin, to a supermarket in London, to the Friendly Skies. There is not much you can't do wirelessly today. Lands' End, Safeway, and United Airlines are truly beginning to allow customers to manage the business relationship through the use of new technology. Whether your customer wants to shop online with her sister, order groceries from a magnet on her refrigerator, manage a 401(k) plan, find out if a parts order has arrived, or use a PC to find his eyeglasses, it will be vital for marketers to understand these new wireless tools and learn to use them to give the customer the power to do what the customer wants to do—on the customer's terms.

Will Wall Street Care? **22**

Relationships as a corporate asset

Your CMR INITIATIVE has defined customer typology based on customer process differences. You have developed a deep understanding of the unique wants and needs of individual customers. You have identified opportunities to let your customers manage their relationship with your firm. You have invested a lot of resources—both time and money. Is the result an expense or an asset?

CUSTOMER LIFETIME VALUE

When we think of corporate assets we typically think of equipment, buildings, accounts receivables, and other old-world balance sheet listings. For most businesses the most valuable business asset isn't on the balance sheet. It is the value of the customer base and the strength of the customer relationships.

One of the best studies I have seen on the subject came from Kaj Storbacka, founder and chairman of CRM Group Ltd. and a board member at the Center for Relationship Marketing and Service Management at the Swedish School of Economics. In his study, "Customer Relationships as Assets," he says, "The most important asset in the future is customer relationships. Increased relationship value leads to increased shareholder value."[1]

Why is this so? Customer lifetime value is a measurable asset. And everything we're talking about concerning CMR strengthens customer loyalty, which results in an increased lifetime value of your customer base. Being able to develop lifetime customers and to maximize their profit potential can increase the capitalized value of the company. Perhaps we will see companies valued one day on their price-to-customer-relationship ratio, when people come to accept Storbacka's premise that increased relationship value leads to increased shareholder value.

The Bottom Line

A stock's price to earnings (P/E) ratio is calculated on current earnings, whereas the expected future prices are calculated based on expected future earnings. Investors bid the price up now because they expect the prices to be even higher later. When expectations of a company's future are high, the multiplier applied to future expected earnings increases dramatically. For example, Amazon.com maintained a very high capitalization before it even made a profit because expected earnings were high. The more loyal the customer base, the higher the multiplier.

Customer relationships as a company asset is not a new thought. It was first addressed by Frederick Reicheld in his now famous book, *The Loyalty Effect: The Hidden Force Behind Growth, Profits, and Lasting Value* (Harvard Business School Press, 1996). He pointed out that U.S. corporations lose half their customers in five years, half their employees in four, and half their investors in less than one, and that disloyalty stunts corporate performance by 50 percent. Two quotes from *The Loyalty Effect* make the best case for investing in CMR as a way of increasing your base of loyal customers as a corporate asset:

- ▪ "Today's accounting systems mask the fact, but inventories of experienced customers, employees and investors are a company's most valuable asset."[2]
- ▪ "There is a secret to success. You cannot *control* a human inventory, which of course has a mind of its own, so you must

earn its loyalty. People will invest their time and money loyally only if they believe that their contributions to your company will yield superior returns over time. The secret is therefore to select these human beings carefully, then teach them how to contribute and receive value from your business system—or better yet, give them incentives to learn these lessons for themselves. The key to decreasing inventory losses is to manage a virtuous cycle of loyalty, learning and value creation."[3]

When Reicheld says you can't *control* a human inventory he makes the case for CMR. That's exactly why it is arrogant for a company to think it can manage relationships with customers who have minds of their own. CMR is a process of selecting the right customers carefully and teaching them how to contribute to and receive value from your business system. That's the process that will optimize customer relationships, earn loyalty, and create customer lifetime value as a corporate asset.

Optimization

The founders of PreVision Marketing suggest the way to drive customer relationship efforts to the bottom line is through what they call Customer Relationship Optimization. They believe success is more than building a process in which a customer can interact with a company via any one-to-one medium (telephone, the Internet, or in person) without needing to repeat his or her history and profile at each point of contact, and more than delivering cohesive messaging across channels. Although critical to company operations, they say, such activities are just the beginning for true Customer Relationship Optimization.

They believe this optimization requires new financials:

To optimize your business economics you need deep insight into the trade-offs associated with different customer investment strategies. And you need to leverage your customer information beyond marketing to identify business productivity improvements across the organization. Today's most innovative leaders are not only organizing their businesses around their customers, but creating customer-driven business plans and new customer financials.[4]

Customer-driven business plans are what we're talking about when we empower the customer, and it is financials we're talking about when we ask if Wall Street will care.

To help view customer relationships as an asset, the following are some of the effects on shareholder value:

- effective cross-sell and up-sell
- larger share of customer
- premium pricing
- lower acquisition costs
- lower costs to serve
- faster cash flow
- steadier cash flow
- increased future earnings from customer lifetime value

Beyond that, stronger relationships often result in customers recommending the firm to others.

The Competitive Gap

Some say customer lifetime value has decreased in relevancy and that the concept is an anachronism. Today's customers have ever rising expectations, the pace of new product and service offerings is accelerating, and corporate America is in an upheaval with companies regularly acquiring and divesting operations—literally jumping in and out of product areas and industries. There is also an increased mobility of consumers in switching jobs, moving, and changing lifestyles.[5] In this environment the only way companies will be able to develop the kind of loyalty that will increase customer lifetime value is with the use of CMR initiatives, which make the company more important to the customer. For CMR the model is turned around and measures the company's lifetime value to the customer. The power of CMR restores the viability of customer lifetime value and its effect on a company's capitalization value.

Kaj Storbacka's study showed customer relationships drive shareholder value because a firm's market capitalization is based on evaluations of future earnings. He believes it is management's task to grow market capitalization in two ways:

1 **by increasing competitive gap:** using the relationship initiative to differentiate the firm from its competitors and create superior returns

2 **by creating sustainable cash flow:** creating barriers to competitor entry and customer exit, developing believable new business models, and sustaining superior returns

MEASURING LOYALTY

Meeting both financial and CMR goals will require more than measuring lifetime value, more than tracking today's typical metrics—satisfaction and defection. A McKinsey study furthers this point:

> Despite all the money invested to promote loyalty among high-value customers, it is increasingly elusive in almost every industry.
>
> A better appreciation of the underlying forces that influence the loyalty of customers—particularly their attitudes and changing needs—can help companies develop targeted efforts to correct any downward migration in their spending habits long before it leads them to defect. Such appreciation also helps companies improve their current efforts to encourage other customers to spend more. Our recent two-year study of the attitudes of 1,200 households about companies in 16 industries as diverse as airlines, banking and consumer products shows that this opportunity is surprisingly large. Improving the management of migration as a whole by focusing on not only defections, but also on smaller changes in customer spending, can have as much as ten times more value than preventing defections alone. Companies taking the approach we recommend have cut downward migration and defection by as much as 30 percent.[6]

The McKinsey study reminds us that measuring degrees of loyalty is an evolving craft. Companies first tried to measure and manage their customers' satisfaction in the early 1970s, on the theory that increasing it would help them prosper. In the 1980s, they began to measure their customers' rate of defection and to investigate its root causes. McKinsey makes the point that these ideas are still important but, "They are not enough. Managing migration—from the satisfied customers who spend more to the downward migrators who spend less—is a crucial next step."[7]

The study goes on to say, "This step is so important because large amounts of value are at stake. Many more customers change their spending behavior than defect, so the former typically account for larger changes in value." McKinsey cites the example of a retail bank where 5 percent of checking account customers defected annually, taking with them 10 percent of the bank's checking accounts and 3 percent of its total balances. But every year, the 35 percent of customers who reduced their balances significantly cost the bank 24 percent of its total balances, whereas the 35 percent who increased their balances *raised* its total balances by 25 percent. This effect showed up in all sixteen industries studied and was dominant in two-thirds of them.[8]

The McKinsey study backs up its argument with two more examples:

> A local phone company found that more than 90 percent of its loyalty opportunities came from reaching out to customers dropping business features such as second lines and call waiting. A financial institution aimed all its loyalty efforts at increasing its customers' satisfaction. It made major investments to cut down on service failures (such as unanswered phones) and reduced the number of closed accounts. But the effect on overall growth was marginal.[9]

Relative Numbers

Brand futurist Nick Wreden makes the same point in his book, *FusionBranding: Strategic Branding Models for the Customer Economy … and Beyond* (Accountability Press, 2002), "People spend way too much time worrying about 'absolute' numbers, like lifetime value.

(customer lifetime value) of an existing customer base.[15] Whenever a company can show that its customer relationships can drive value going forward and make the company less dependent on new customer acquisition, the company's stock should earn a higher multiple. Increased relationship value leads to increased shareholder value. Wall Street will care.

A<small>T THE START OF THIS BOOK</small>, our customer asked why CRM isn't working for her. Despite the fact that she has given personal information to companies, she continues to receive irrelevant and unwanted offers. Trying to manage customer relationships—targeting specific customers for specific product or service offerings—has done little to enrich the lives of our customers, and it's clear that moving to a CMR way of doing business will make customers' lives easier. Initiating this change requires fresh ways of learning to understand the values that are important to your individual customers, and then integrating that knowledge to create a single view of the customer.

THE CHALLENGES AHEAD

There are many challenges you will encounter as you transition to CMR. Being able to answer "yes" to the following questions will help assure confidence in your success:

Are you ready for a world turned upside down?

In the world of CMR the power of defining the relationship transfers to the customer. Customers will engage in different types of dialog with suppliers, often being the ones to initiate the search for a solution. The concepts of self-service give the customer more control; the seller no longer mandates the process. There will still be targeting, but the customer may choose the target firm. In this topsy-turvy CMR world, the customer will tell us what she is interested in and not interested in, what kind of information she wants, what level of service she wants to receive, and how she wants us to communicate with her—where, when, and how often. Remember: CMR is all about making the customer feel like a human being and not like a number.

Can you avoid the two most frequent mistakes companies make?
First, don't confuse a CMR strategy with a technology implementation. CMR is not technology. Of course, you will require technology applications to enable your CMR strategy—software for the customer database, customer-friendly Web applications, and call center technology, perhaps even interactive mobile devices. All these technologies are secondary. The critical issue is to get your CMR business process right before trying to implement the technology. Remember the advice from Marion Howard-Healy in Chapter 16, "A poor business process that is automated remains just that—a poor process."

Second, don't allow your CMR initiative to be seen as an IT project. Everyone in the enterprise must understand that your CMR program is not a technology upgrade. It must be seen as a fundamental change in the quality of your interactions with your customers, designed to make these interactions more effective, better for your customers, and more profitable for the company. You will need technology because understanding, developing, and nurturing customer relationships all require a strong flow of information across the enterprise. Having the right information at the right time and enabling effective interaction across all channels is critical. Make it clear at the start to everyone involved that CMR is a new way of doing business.

Can you change your business strategy?
CMR will require modifying your traditional marketing efforts. It will demand more than promotions and advertising, and will require new tools for customer communication. A challenge for some companies will be getting a CMR strategy in line with the need to grow customer value when the advertising agencies (and their media planners) are more interested in customer acquisition and giving the brand image a makeover. Instead of fighting against CMR projects that appear to threaten their power base, marketing directors will have to recognize the transferability of their skills to CMR and learn to use these tools for more profitable media investments. Your strategy will have to include training programs to teach all personnel the objective of passing control of the relationship to the customer and the effective use of CMR tools. Product

managers, sales managers, sales personnel, and others will need to develop customer service strategies, and even product offers, based on customer needs.

Can you retrain the monkeys?

It's easy to laugh over the story of the monkeys in Chapter 16, but every company does have its culture, and the switch from a company-centric firm to a customer-centric company will require a serious shift in culture. Some in your company will resist the transformation because "We've always done it this way," others will fear loss of power and will resist change to protect their turf, and still others will hold back because they don't believe that CMR will work. You will need something better than spraying cold water on these folks to change they culture they have lived with for so long. Enlisting associates at all levels in the reengineering process—not just those who are enthusiastic about the project, but the naysayers as well—will help solve this. Once those who start off with negative attitudes become believers, they will become a driving force behind the project and communicate a positive message to others in the company.

Are you ready to let your customer own the information?

Privacy is still a customer concern. Moreover, the privacy fire is constantly fanned by columnists such as William Safire of the *New York Times*, writing about what he calls "an intrusion explosion." Safire goes so far as to suggest that privacy advocates should create a simple "privacy index" [of political representatives] so voters can see which politicians are on their side and which don't care.[1]

We have always believed we owned the information we collect about customers. When we tell customers we are giving them the power to control the relationship, they will expect ownership of the personal information they share with us. CMR can work only with the customer's permission. Tell your customers your privacy policy in a straightforward and easy-to-understand manner. Give them—and stick to—your promise that you will never share their personal information with third parties, and they won't think of you as "Big Brother arriving with a grin and a fistful of coupons."

Don Schultz had it right. For your customer information to have value for your customers, it should simplify and improve their lives. If it's really working for the customer—not just the marketer— privacy would not be the issue that it is.

Columnists aren't going to stop fanning the flames. Politicians aren't going to miss this easy chance to win votes. Any failure to respect a customer's privacy—any violation of trust—will turn your customer away.

How will you measure success?

There will come a day when you will have to prove the value of all your CMR efforts. Reviewing the failure rate of customer relationship initiatives, Liz Shahnam, VP and director of CRM, META Group, reports, "When I look under the covers, these folks who experience failure are not talking about technology failure. It's more about failing to focus that goal that addresses metrics, ROI."[2]

It is important to establish up front what will constitute success. Achieving CMR is not just better direct mail targeting to reduce mail costs or service center efficiencies to produce savings. You must prioritize existing expenses and reallocate them for more effective customer development. Measure all of your marketing investments against customer relevancy—things that really matter to your customers.

WHERE DO YOU START?

The questions above suggest big-picture changes that will have to occur. But how do you get from here to there? The eight steps in Chapter 16 will guide you toward an overall strategy, but what actions can you take today to begin the process of switching to CMR?

Create a Task Force

Start with the creation of a CMR task force led by a senior executive with enough power and influence to sell your program at every level of the enterprise. At your first meeting have the team come to an agreement on your business objectives and the reasons for your CMR project. Spell out clearly what you want to achieve and resolve the important question of what will constitute success. With this understanding you can develop the business case to support your plan. Begin with an impartial assessment of where you are now and what processes must change to enable you to empower customers. With these goals established, dig into your customer database to find out which customers are the most important to keep and which customers have the greatest potential for growth. Remember you can't empower every one of your customers—and you shouldn't try.

Evaluate Your Customer's Experience

Before you can define the CMR experience you want to deliver to your customers, you need to evaluate their experience with your firm today. This will require some research. There are some simple things you can do that will teach you a lot without requiring thousands of dollars on third-party studies. For years, retailers have hired mystery shoppers to gauge the shopping experience. Expand on that concept and find out what things are like from the customer's viewpoint. Contact your call center, as a customer would, to get help or information. Navigate your website to place an order or get the answer to a question. You will find that you are doing some things well, and that some things will have to change. Only after finishing your own tests should you bring aboard researchers such as Brickstream (see Chapter 8) or Message Factors (see Chapter 15) to help gather more information.

Talk with Your Customers

Finally, it's time to talk with your customers to find out which of your business processes matter to them and what you can change to make their lives easier. This will not require formal surveys; you will learn more by asking questions and listening to customers at every point of interaction. This process must include allowing your customers to choose which channel they prefer for reaching you and for your company to reach them. Take a fresh look at your marketing communications strategy from the customer's perspective. William McEwen, global practice leader at Gallup Brand Loyalty Management, offers some good advice:

If companies seek to engage their customers, and not just sell to them, then they must view the customer relationships not from a marketing perspective, but from the customer's viewpoint—because that is what truly matters. Increased customer communication doesn't ensure that the company's messages will be either welcome or relevant. More entries into a customer database won't ensure that the company's employees will have any idea what to do with this information, or what to focus on, when they access that database.

Inundating customers with increased sales opportunities won't create stronger emotional connections any more than doubling an advertising budget means the campaign will be more compelling or that it will result in a more powerful brand.[3]

With this foundation established, it's time to turn your task force into a change management team to identify how each department within the company will be affected by these initiatives. Revisit Sandra Gudat's seven questions in Chapter 16 that have to be answered to assure success.

At the start of this journey you will have set a timeline for the completion of the project. Don't hesitate to revisit this often to revise as necessary. Seklemian/Newell's experience suggests that most companies underestimate the time required.

In addition to all of this internal effort, have key members of your task force attend conferences to learn what others are doing. The value of these conferences goes far beyond the case studies presented by the experts. The best conferences provide an opportunity to share one-on-one and learn from others who are looking for the pot of gold at the end of the CMR rainbow. Two of the best sources to start with are Seklemian/Newell's annual Customer Relationship Management Conference (www.loyalty.vg) and The Peppers and Rogers Group, which holds several conferences throughout the year (www.1to1.com).

Concepts to Get You Started

The following concepts are at the heart of CMR. Keep them in mind as you strive to meet the challenges. They will help you keep your thinking on the larger goals and set you on the best course for letting customers manage the relationship.

What CMR is:
- A philosophy of doing business that will affect the entire enterprise
- Creating an experience, developing relationships, and personalizing the interaction with individual customers in ways directed by the customer
- Commitment to changing results by changing what you really do and what you really believe
- A combination of processes, people, and technology that develops intelligence about the customer
- Learning what the customer wants and delivering no more, no less
- Investing in the customers that represent the greatest growth for your business, those you can best turn into assets
- Letting your customers tell you what they care about
- Prioritizing customer investments to grow your business

What CMR will require:
- Customer engagement, enablement, and empowerment
- Dialog: listening to customers and letting customers connect to each other
- Aligning your strategy with your company's profitable growth objectives, and getting the strategy right before searching for the technology
- Driving the vision down to the execution level, making sure the entire workforce believes in your CMR initiative and can effectively use the tools
- An open exchange of information, not just with customers but within the enterprise
- Customized services and messages that are timely and relevant for your customer
- An ROI model with measurable metrics in place
- Customer permission
- Intense leadership from the top of your organization

Afterword

We dance 'round in a ring and suppose.
But the secret sits in the middle and knows.
Robert Frost, *The Secret Sits*

ONE OF MY FAVORITE PEOPLE is Elinor Frost Francis Wilber, one of Robert Frost's granddaughters. We have been close friends and neighbors for many years and when our children were young, they would sit in her living room and listen as the poet laureate said this poem. They didn't know he was a poet laureate; he was just a grandfather. In this poem, Frost could have been talking about twenty-first-century marketers dancing around the altar of customer relationship building, making suppositions about why so few companies are getting the return they expected on their CRM initiatives.

The secrets do, indeed, sit at the center of customer-oriented CRM initiatives. The cases and examples in this book are meant to show you how companies are beginning to find ways to empower their customers. You don't have to be in the same business as in the examples; the concepts in each case are the important lessons.

Change is never painless, and the progression advocated in this book will not be simple to achieve. The practice of CMR is a journey, as yet uncharted. I hope you will find this book to be a road map that makes it easier for you to pioneer this new frontier.

Notes

Chapter 1 Why Doesn't CRM Work?

1. "Gartner Dataquest Forecasts CRM Services Revenue to Increase 15 Percent in 2002," Gartner, Inc. press release, April 9, 2002, p. 1.

2. "Retailers Say CRM Is Crucial But Few Are Implementing Initiatives," *Direct Marketing*, October 2001, p. 12.

3. Gary Lemke, "CRM: The Perfect Storm," *Customer Support Management*, November 1, 2001, p. 2.

4. "Great Expectations," Annual CRM Roundtable, *Direct*, March 15, 2002, p. 28.

5. "The More Things Change," *Retail Ad-Week*, September 24, 1990, pp. 4–5.

6. Richard H. Levey, "Consumers: A User's Manual," *Direct*, August 2002, p. S7.

7. Ibid.

8. *Direct*/Yankelovitch survey presented at the National Center for Database Marketing Conference, Philadelphia, August 2002.

9. Sheryl Nance-Nash, "Let Them Lead," *Direct*, May 15, 2001, p. 50.

10. "CRM Stumbles on the Catwalk," *Internet World*, April 2002, p. 14.

11. Susan Fournier, assistant professor Harvard School of Business; Susan Dobscha, assistant professor marketing, Bentley College; and David Glen Mick, Endowed Chair of Marketing, Dublin City University, "Preventing the Premature Death of Relationship Marketing," *Harvard Business Review*, January/February 1998, p. 43.

12. Richard Forsyth, "Six Major Impediments to Change and How to Overcome Them in CRM (and Politics)" CRM-Forum, June 11, 2001.

13. Dick Lee, "Getting to 'Duh'," *Customer Relationship Management*, November 2002, p. 28.

14. "A CRM Blueprint: Maximizing ROI from Your Customer-Based Strategy," Peppers and Rogers Group & Microsoft Great Plains Business Solutions, 2001, p. 4.

15. Richard Forsyth, "CRM Doesn't Add Up for UK Plc," CRM-Forum Weekly, March 28, 2002, p. 1.

16. Ruth Stevens, "Analyzing the Recipe for Success," 1to1.com, January 3, 2002, p. 1.

17. Anonymous, posted November 17, 2001 on www.datahighways.net (and several other websites).

Chapter 2 It's Not a Question of the Chicken or the Egg

1. National Center for Database Marketing Winter Conference, New Orleans, December 2001.

2. Jeremy Epstein, "Report from CRM Expo: Strategy First, Technology Second," marketingprofs.com, September 17, 2002, p. 1.

3. "IT Success Depends on Quality of Spending, Not Quantity," information-week.com, December 24–31, 2001, p. 62.

4. Philip B. Clark, "Rapp Collins Exec Defends CRM Spending," *BtoB*, September 17, 2001, p. 14.

5. John Radcliff, "Eight Building Blocks of CRM: A Framework for Success," *Gartner, Inc.*, December 13, 2001, p. 2.

6. Ibid., p. 1.

7. Adrian Payne, "Building a Strategic CRM Programme," CREDO, Paris, March 15, 2001.

Chapter 3 "One Girl in a Convertible ..."

1. Steve Luengo-Jones, *All to One—The Winning Model for Marketing in the Post Internet Economy* (New York: McGraw-Hill, 2002), Chapter 5.

2. Ibid.

3. Brian McManus, "10 Steps to Customer Intelligence Success," crmguru.com, fall/winter 2001, p. 2.

4. "Personalized, Proactive Customer Service is Key to Satisfaction," *iccmweekly*, March 7, 2002, p. 1.

5. Denny Hatch, "Delight Your Customers," *Target Marketing*, April 2002, p. 33.

6. Eric Yoder, "Improving their CRM Game," *1to1 Magazine*, March 2002, p. 35.

7. Kenneth L. Kanady, "Confessions of a Loyal Customer ... When Being Satisfied Is Just No Longer Satisfying," CRM-Forum, April 8, 2002, p. 2.

8. "Bermuda Case Study," blau.com, January 22, 2002.

9. "Seller Beware: Some Marketing Practices Are Driving Customers Away," *Brann-News*, May 16, 2001, p. 1.

10. David Post and Bradford Brown, "Peer Production Promises to Leap in Importance," informationweek.com, January 7, 2002, p. 74.

11. "Using User Forums to Improve the Product," *3D-DMA Daily Digest*, February 11, 2002, p. 5.

12. Michael Lowenstein, "On-Line Community: A Potentially Significant, but Underutilized, Internet CRM and Customer Loyalty Tool," crm-forum.com, January 14, 2002, p. 2.

13. Kim Peterson, "Service with a J," *San Diego Union-Tribune*, March 26, 2002, pp. C1, C4.

14. Jennifer Kirby, "Accessing Value Groups Through Online Communications," CRM-Forum, April 8, 2002, p. 1.

15. Scott Robinette and Claire Brand with Vicki Lenz, *Emotion Marketing: The Hallmark Way of Winning Customers for Life* (New York: McGraw-Hill, 2002), p. xiv.

16. Fred Crawford and Ryan Mathews, *The Myth of Excellence: Why Great Companies Never Try to Be the Best at Everything* (New York: Crown Publishing, 2002).

Chapter 4 Why Do We Have Two Ears and Only One Mouth?

1. "Navigate the Maze," *Advertising Age*, October 30, 2001, p. S1.
2. Kris Oser, "CRM Best Medicine for Prescription Drug Sector," *DIRECT Newsline*, March 21, 2002, p. 1.
3. Don Peppers, "A Prescription for CRM Pharma Karma," *INSIDE 1to1*, January 12, 2002, pp. 2–3.
4. Don Peppers, "A Healthy Base for E-Customer Relationships," *INSIDE 1to1*, January 12, 2002, p. 6.
5. For more detailed information on the ideas in this chapter, read *Wireless Rules: New Marketing Strategies for Customer Relationship Management Anytime, Anywhere* by Frederick Newell and Katherine Lemon (New York: McGraw-Hill, 2001).

Chapter 5 It's No Longer Good Enough to Ask Forgiveness Rather Than Permission

1. Brett Anderson, "Privacy Protection In a Wireless World," *The Insider*, June 20, 2001, p. 22.
2. Richard Barlow, "Loyalty Marketing: Six Trends to Watch in 2002," the-dma.org, January 9, 2002, p. 5.
3. Lisa Vaas, "Customer Privacy Lockdown," *eWEEK*, October 16, 2001, p. 2.
4. "Privacy Guru Joins IBM," crm-forum.com, November 30, 2001, p. 1.
5. "Profitable Privacy," computerworld.com, February 18, 2002, p. 1.
6. Lisa Vaas, "Customer Privacy Lockdown," *eWEEK*, October 16, 2001, p. 3.
7. Kate Kaye, "Could Price Personalization Be Next?" brandera.com, January 26, 2002, p. 2.
8. Ibid., p. 4.
9. "DoubleClick Settles All Class Action Privacy Lawsuits," *DigitalCoast-Reporter*, March 29, 2002, p. 2.
10. Alex Simmons, "Opinion: Say 'So Long' to The Wild West," CRM-Forum, April 5, 2002, p. 1.
11. Matt Berger, "Microsoft Recasts .Net My Services to Allow Customer Control," computerworld.com, April 12, 2002, pp. 1, 2.
12. "Online Survey Shows Progress on Privacy," *The DMA Interactive*, March 28, 2002, pp. 1, 2.
13. Don E. Schultz, "Some Comments on the Absolute Value of the Database," *Journal of Direct Marketing*, 1994.
14. "Permission Boosts Consumer Response, Study Finds," *DM News*, December 17, 2001, p. 2.
15. James R. Rosenfeld, "Lies, Damned Lies, and Internet Statistics," *Direct Marketing*, November 2001, p. 62.
16. "E-Mail to Beat Out Direct Mail: Study," *Direct Newsline*, March 20, 2002, p. 3.
17. Nick Usborne, "It's Not About Permission, It's About Trust," *ClickZ*, August 14, 2000, p. 2.

Chapter 6 Permission in Action

1. Jan Strupczewski, "Study Shows Mobile Phone Marketing Power," *Yahoo!-NEWS*, January 22, 2002, p. 1.

2. Todd R. Weiss, "Wireless Devices to Help Cut Visitor Waits at Nine Six Flags Parks," computerworld.com, February 1, 2002, pp. 1, 2.

3. Tig Tillinghast, "Gator—Good or Evil?," *OnlineSPIN*, January 9, 2002, p. 1.

4. "Gartner Calls Gator Digital Wallet Market Leader," Gator press release, December 11, 2001.

Chapter 7 Type, Point, Click, and Send Now

1. "Maybe This Internet Thing Is Going to Stick Around for a While, After All," *Newsbytes via COMTEX*, December 6, 2001, p. 1.

2. Todd Campbell, "The First E-Mail Message," *PreText Magazine*, pretext.com, March 1998, pp. 1–5.

3. "Harness E-Mail: How it Works," learnthenet.com, January 7, 2002, pp. 1–2.

4. "E-Mail Helped Companies Grow in 2001: DMA Study," *Direct Newsline*, April 4, 2002, p. 4.

5. *The American Heritage Book of English Usage*, 1996, Chapter 9, p. 2.

6. Ibid., pp. 3, 4.

7. Jennifer B. Lee, "A Different Type of English," *The San Diego Union-Tribune*, September 23, 2002, p. E3.

8. Charles Schwab: Improving Customer Satisfaction for AOL E-Mail Users," *Quris, Inc.*, February 2001, p. 2.

9. Mark Elpers, "Managing Migrating Subscribers: Keeping Your E-Mail Lists Clean," *The DMA Interactive*, April 1, 2002, p. 1.

10. Bob Brand, "E-Mail Pet Peeves," thebee.com, November 2001, pp. 1–6.

11. Kim Peterson, "Spam Overload," *The San Diego Union-Tribune*, April 1, 2002, p. E1.

12. Christine Tatum, "Unwanted E-Mails Are Clogging the Internet, with New Remedies Available for Users and Service Providers," *The San Diego Union-Tribune*, January 21, 2002, p. C3.

13. Linda Formichelli, "When Spam Burns You: Why Unsolicited Bulk E-Mail Is Bad Business," *The Network Home Journal*, as reprinted by twowriter.net, March 30, 2002, p. 2.

14. Ibid., p. 2.

15. Charles Schwab, "Improving Customer Satisfaction for AOL E-Mail Users," *Quris, Inc.*, February 2001, p. 1.

Chapter 8 Who's Minding the Store?

1. Jay A. Scansaroli and David M. Szymanski, "Who's Minding the Future?" *Retailing Issues Newsletter*, Center for Retailing Studies, Texas A&M University, January 2002, Volume 14, Number 1, pp. 6–7.

2. Beth Negus Viveiros, "Novel Approach," *Direct*, March 1, 2002, pp. 37–38.

3. Paco Underhill, *Why We Buy: The Science of Shopping* (New York: Simon & Schuster Books, May 1999), Chapter 1. Reprinted with the permission of Simon & Schuster Adult Publishing Group. Copyright © 1999 by Obat, Inc.

4. Don Peppers, "Putting the "E" in Sears," 1to1.com/inside1to1, February 17, 2002, pp. 6–8.

Chapter 9 Personalization Technology—Boon or Bust?

1. "What is Personalization?" personalization.org, January 26, 2002, p. 1.

2. Michael Rosenberg, "The Personalization Story," itworld.com, January 26, 2002, p. 2.

3. Christopher Saunders, "Survey: Personalization Crucial to Scoring New Customers, Data," internews.com, May 11, 2001, pp. 1, 2.

4. Jack Aaronson, "Welcome Back, Mr. Lesbian!: Pitfalls of Perceived Personalization," *ClickZ*, April 4, 2002, pp. 1–2.

5. Chuck Paustian, "Online Account Management: Time to Start Getting Personal," *CARD Marketing*, January/February 2002, pp. 18, 19.

6. Mickey Alam Khan, "All Owner Uses Net For Sales News," *iMarketing News*, February 25, 2002, pp. 1–2.

7. Angela Karr, "Questions About Personalization," *Customerinterface*, December 2001, pp. 32, 33.

8. Ibid.

9. Ibid.

10. Ibid.

11. "Mitchells/Richards," *Retail Ad World*, February 2002, pp. 16, 17.

12. "Multi-Channel Customers Most Valuable: Study," *Direct Newsline*, January 29, 2002, pp. 2, 3.

13. Jason Compton, "On Time, On Target," destinationcrm.com, November, 2001, p. 2.

14. Lenny Liebman, "Personalization Branches Out," internetweek.com, November 6, 2001, p. 5.

15. Sandeep Krishnamurthy, "The Main Problem with Personalization," digitrends.net, June 15, 2001, p. 2.

16. Jesse Berst, "Why Personalization Is the Internet's Next Big Thing," *ZDNet AnchorDesk*, April 14, 1998, p. 2.

17. Michael Pastore, "Valuable Consumers Demand Personalization," *Cyber-Atlas*, May 9, 2001, p. 1.

18. "Back to Levy Story," webcmo.com, January 26, 2002, p. 6.

19. Susan Cohen, "Plan Before Personalizing," sas.com News and Events, January 26, 2002, pp. 1–3.

Chapter 10 But What About the Loyalty Card?

1. Brian Woolf, *Loyalty Marketing—The Second Act* (Greenville, South Carolina: Teal Books, 2002), p. 5.

2. Carol Parenzan Smalley, "Butterflies and Barnacles: Re-writing the Rules of Loyalty," crmguru.com, September 13, 2002, p. 8.

3. Ibid., p. 10.

4. Garth Hallberg, *All Consumers Are Not Created Equal* (New York: John Wiley & Sons, 1995), p. 40.

5. Ibid., p. 118.

6. Richard G. Barlow, "Loyalty Marketing: What Is Its Role in a CRM World?," crmcommunity.com, January 9, 2002, p. 3.

7. James Cigliano, Margaret Georgiadis, Darren Pleasance, and Susan Whalley, "The Price of Loyalty," *McKinsey Quarterly*, 2000, Number 4, p. 1., www.mckinsey quarterly.com (January 15, 2003).

8. Richard Barlow, "Loyalty Marketing: Six Trends to Watch in 2002," *The DMA Interactive*, January 9, 2002, p. 2.

9. Peter Leech, "Can Stored Value Cards Drive Loyalty?" *Know Thy Customer*, March 2002, p. 2.

10. Richard Barlow, "Loyalty Marketing: Six Trends to Watch in 2002," *The DMA Interactive*, January 9, 2002, p. 2.

Chapter 11 No Card? No Problem!

1. James Lawson, "Don't Touch That Dial," *Direct*, March 1, 2002, pp. 30–31.

Chapter 12 All Cows Look Alike

1. Crm-forum.com, August 29, 2001.

2. Michael Bayler and David Stoughton, *Promiscuous Customers: Invisible Brands* (New York: John Wiley & Sons, December 2001).

3. "Watchin' the Game, Havin' a Bud," *Brand Strategy*, March 2001, p. 11.

4. "From the Store to the Web and Back Again," *1to1 Magazine*, January/February 2002, p. 24.

5. William Arruda, "The Brand Connection—The Link Between Corporations and the Executives That Lead Them," www.marketingprofs.com, August 2002, pp. 1–2.

6. Kate Maddox, "Survey Finds HP, Compaq, Cisco Most 'Bruised and Battered' Brands," *BtoB*, January 2002, p. 2.

7. "Marketing Trends," www.darwinmag.com, July 2001, p. 63.

8. Richard Rosen, "Interaction: The Bridge Between Awareness and Prospect Involvement in Brand-Building Advertising," *DMA, in Case You Missed It*, Volume 2, Issue 3, p. 3.

9. Ibid., p. 66.

10. Ibid., pp. 67, 68.

11. Ibid., pp. 66, 67.

12. Naomi Klein, *No Logo: Taking Aim at the Brand Bullies* (New York: Picador USA, 2002), Chapter 15.

13. Paul Twivey, "Follow the Rules of Engagement," *Brand Strategy*, March 2001, p. 15.

Chapter 13 Before You Build a Better Mousetrap

1. Frederick Newell, *loyalty.com—Customer Relationship Management in the New Era of Internet Marketing* (New York: McGraw-Hill, 2000), p. 300.

2. Erica Morphy, "The Cost of Not Deploying CRM," ecommercetimes.com, March 26, 2002, pp. 1–2.

3. Ibid., p. 2.

4. Matt Hines, *SearchCRM*, March 21, 2002.

5. Don Peppers, "Customer Relationship Management: Delivering the Benefits, *INSIDE 1to1*, August 13, 2001.

Chapter 14 Customer Service—Who Cares?

1. "Convenience Trumps Price for Online Shoppers," 1to1.com, December 24, 2001, p. 5.

2. Lou Hirsh, "Customer Service—Who Cares," crmdaily.com, December 19, 2001, p. 2.

3. Lou Hirsh, "No Customer Service Please," ecommercetimes.com, May 28, 2002, pp. 1–2.

4. "CRM in 2002: Redesign from the Customer's Perspective," gartner.com, January 7, 2002, p. 2.

5. "60 Percent of B2B Firms Not Following Up With Prospective Customers," *Direct Marketing*, November 2001, p. 10.

6. Richard Forsyth, "Banana Skins and Gold Stars," CRM-Forum, January 20, 2002, pp. 1–2.

7. Elaine Cascio, "Is Self-Service Driving Your Customers Away?," *ICCM Weekly*, January 17, 2002, p. 1.

8. "New DMA Report Finds Increasing Use of Web Sites To Manage Customer Service Fulfillment Functions," *The DMA Interactive*, March 28, 2002, p. 1.

9. Ibid.

10. Melanie Howard, "Wake up Business—Smell the Coffee," www.bt.com/insight-interactive, March 2002, p. 1.

11. "CFO Mind Shift: Technology Creates Value," *CFO Research Services*, August 2002, p. 4.

12. "Billion-Dollar Customer Care Deals Announced," *ICCM Weekly*, January 24, 2002, p. 1.

13. Kimberlee Roth, "TaylorMade Golf Improves Its Service Game," *1to1 Magazine*, March 2002, pp. 15–16.

14. "The Customer View of the Business," crm-forum.com, January 9, 2002, p. 5.

15. "60 Percent of B2B Firms Not Following Up with Prospective Customers," *Direct Marketing*, November 2001, p. 10.

16. Greg Gianforte, "The Insiders Guide to Next-Generation Customer Service on the Web," rightnow.com, April 9, 2002, p. 2

17. "The Importance of Customer Histories," *ICCM WEEKLY*, March 21, 2002, p. 1.

18. Melanie Howard, "Wake up Business—Smell the Coffee," www.bt.com/insight-interactive, March 2002, p. 2.

19. Scarlet Pruitt, IDG News Service, "E-Tailers Missing Mark on Customer Service," pcworld.com, January 8, 2002, pp. 1–2.

20. Blake Rohrbacher, "Serving Customers Online," my.ckz.com, January 29, 2002, p. 2.

21. "Couriers Deliver Customer Service," informationweek.com, June 3, 2002, p. 60.

22. Lou Hirsh, "Multichannel Magic: Who's Doing It Right?" crmdaily.com, April 1, 2002, pp. 1–2.

23. "Online Customer Service Catches Up," *ICCM Weekly*, January 24, 2002, p. 1.

24. Allison Linn, "New Xbox Gets Flak for Waits on Service," *The San Diego Union-Tribune*, January 5, 2002, p. C2.

25. Kathryn Balint, "Too Much Too Fast," *The San Diego Union-Tribune*, January 14, 2002, p. C1.

26. Ibid., p. C7.

27. "EasyRentaCar Expanding Online Service for Online Services," right now.com, April 9, 2002, pp. 1, 2.

28. Susan Carstensen, "The Savings of Web-Based Self-Service," *RightNow Technologies, Inc.* White Paper, 2001.

29. Martha Rogers, Ph.D., "How Good Customer Relationships Go Bad," *INSIDE 1to1*, January 5, 2002, p. 2.

30. Jo Bennett, "Sports Authority Hits a Home Run with Technology and Training," *1to1 Magazine*, January/February 2002, p. 16.

31. Ibid., p. 19.

32. Ibid., pp. 2–3.

33. John Berry, "Vrrrooom—How Companies Can Rev Up Rules Engines to Drive Up Profits," destinationcrm.com, March 2002, pp. 1–2.

Chapter 15 Which Customers and Why

1. Sandeep Kirshnamurthy, "A Comprehensive Analysis of Permission Marketing," *Journal of Computer-Mediated Communication*, 2001, pp. 13, 14.

2. Ibid., pp. 6, 7.

3. "Opinion: Business Intelligence Is the Strongest Link," crm-forum.com, March 20, 2002, p. 1.

Chapter 16 Crossing the Chasm—What Will You Need to Change?

1. "Why Some Sectors Are Stymied by CRM," *E-Commerce Times*, January 10, 2002, p. 4.

2. Adrian Payne, "British Telecom Survey: CRM at the Crossroads," crmcommunity.com, March 7, 2001, p. 2.

3. Francis A. Buttle, "Is It Worth It? ROI on CRM," CRM-Forum, May 7, 2002, p. 4.

4. Brad Cleveland, "Rethinking Service Level and Quality," *Call Center Magazine*, April 2002, p. 66.

5. James G. Barnes, *Secrets of Customer Relationship Management: It's All About How You Make Them Feel* (New York: McGraw-Hill, 2002), Chapter 5.

6. John Radcliffe, "Eight Building Blocks of CRM: A Framework for Success," gartner.com, January 10, 2002, p. 2.

7. David Simms, "More with Less: Counting CRM Calories," crmguru.com, September 16, 2002, pp. 2, 3.

8. Anonymous.

9. Sandra Gudat, "What Makes CRM Work?" *The DMA Interactive*, April 4, 2002, p. 2.

10. Ibid.

11. Jennifer Zaino, "Employee Collaboration on the Upswing," information week.com, February 11, 2002, p. 88.

12. Lou Hirsh, "The Inside Story on Customer Loyalty," ecommerce-times.com, April 8, 2002, pp. 1–3.

13. "Customer Focused Empowerment Pays at Ritz-Carlton," serviceexcellence.com, April 10, 2002, pp. 2–5.

14. Marion Howard-Healy, "CRM to CMR—A Paradigm Shift for Customer Care," quoted in Richard Forsyth, "Deliver the Benefits from CRM by Putting the C into CRM—Part 1," CRM-Forum, March 4, 2002, p. 1.

15. Jerry Sparger, "Eight Steps to a Successful CRM Project," crmcommunity .com, July 11, 2001, p. 4.

16. Kimberly Hill, "CPR for CRM," *E-Commerce Times*, March 26, 2002, p. 1–3.

17. "Your CRM/eCRM Data Integration Project," *Relationship Marketing Report* (reprinted from marketingsherpa.com, Volume IV, Issue XI, 2001), pp. 1, 2.

18. Ibid., p. 9.

Chapter 17 There's No Free Lunch

1. Roland T. Rust, Valarie A. Zeithaml, and Katherine N. Lemon, *Driving Customer Equity—How Customer Lifetime Value is Reshaping Corporate Strategy.* Copyright © 2000 by Roland T. Rust, Valarie A. Zeithaml, and Katherine N. Lemon. Reprinted with permission of The Free Press, an imprint of Simon & Schuster Adult Publishing Group.

2. Katherine Lemon is assistant professor of marketing at the Carroll School of Management, Boston College. She can be reached at lemonka@bc.edu. Roland Rust is the David Bruce Smith Chair in Marketing and director of the Center for E-Service at the R. H. Smith School of Business at the University of Maryland. Valarie Zeithaml is Roy and Alice H. Richards Bicentennial Professor and Area Chair of Marketing at the Kenan-Flagler School of Business at the University of North Carolina.

Chapter 18 Don't Boil the Ocean

1. Tom Kaneshige, "Surviving CRM," line56.com, November 2, 2002, p. 2.

2. Jacqueline Allen, "Talking CRM Shop with Industry Execs," *INSIDE 1to1*, February 16, 2002, pp. 3–4.

3. Joseph Colletti, "A Crawl, Walk, Run Approach to CRM," *DM News*, December 10, 2001, pp. 26, 30.

Chapter 19 There's No There, There

1. "Schlotzsky's Gets Serious About Customer Technology," *Stores*, February 2002, p. 44.
2. "Kiosk Project Targets Inner Cities' Online Needs," *Stores*, February 2002, p. 38.
3. "Wireless LAN Provide Net Access," *BizReport*, February 13, 2002, p. 1.
4. Douglas McWirter, "Here, There and Everywhere," crm.com, December 7, 2001, p. 2.
5. Brian Caulfield, "A Glimpse Into Our Future, When the Net is Everywhere," *Reporter's Notebook*, April 1, 2000, p. 1.
6. Ibid., p. 1.
7. Ibid.
8. Ibid., p. 3.
9. "Update: IBM Deals a Card-Size Computer," computerworld.com, February 7, 2002, p. 1.
10. Kim Peterson, "Look Who's Watching," *The San Diego Union-Tribune*, January 2001, p. C7.
11. Adam Klaber and Dan Hirschbuehler, "The Alchemy of CRM," line56 .com, February 9, 2002, p. 3.

Chapter 20 Electronic Empowerment

1. Blake Rohhrbacher, "As Users Get Smarter, Marketers Must Keep Up," clickz.com, February 26, 2002, p. 1.
2. James R. Rosenfeld, "Lies, Damned Lies, and Internet Statistics," *Direct Marketing*, November 2001, p. 61.
3. Bill Millar, "Getting to the Heart of CRM," *INSIDE 1to1*, February 10, 2002, pp. 8–10.
4. Richard Louv, "Technology Hasn't Freed Us; We're Under Its Spell," *The San Diego Union-Tribune*, February 3, 2002, p. A12.
5. Jo Bennett, "Customer Feedback for the Hands That Feed," *INSIDE 1to1*, January 28, 2002, p. 3.
6. Michael Cohn, "Messages from Anywhere," *Internet World*, April 2002, p. 50.
7. Ashlee Vance, "Canesta Lets Computers See," IDG News Service-idg.net, March 26, 2002, p. 1.
8. John Ziooerer, "Sprechen Sie Deutsch," *Internet World*, April 2002, pp. 52–53.
9. "Interactive TV Arrives, Sort of," nytimes.com, April 4, 2002, p. 2.
10. Bill Millar, "Smart TV's Implicit Bargains," *1to1 Magazine*, January/February 2002, p. 33.
11. "Tower of Power," informationweek.com, February 11, 2002, pp. 1, 2.
12. George V. Hulme, "Simulations Go Nuclear," informationweek.com, April 8, 2002, p. 1.
13. David M. Ewalt, "The Next (Not So) Big Thing," informationweek.com, May 13, 2002, p. 1.

14. Robert M. Rubin, "Business Case: Will We Reach 1984 by 2004?" informationweek.com, March 25, 2002, p. 1.

15. Jo Bennett, "The E-Motional Rescue of Self-Service Devices," *INSIDE 1to1*, May 5, 2002, p. 3.

Chapter 21 What Do Customers Want from Mobile Messaging?

1. Øystein Meland, "A Ban on SMS Divorce," wap.com, July 13, 2001, p. 1.

2. "Survey: The Mobile Internet—The Internet Untethered," *The Economist*, October 11, 2001, p. 11.

3. Ibid., p. 4.

4. Ibid., p. 13.

5. Ibid., p. 14.

6. Colin Strong, "How Mobile Internet Segmentation Can Deliver Customer End Value," *Customer Management*, March/April 2001, p. 67.

7. Mickey Alam Khan, "Keebler Aims to Be Buddies with Customers," dmnews.com, October 16, 2002, pp. 1–6.

8. Kristi Essick, "Sending Out an SMS," *The Industry Standard*, August 6–13, 2001, p. 48.

9. "Not Just Kid Stuff," informationweek.com, September 3, 2001, p. 38.

10. Ibid.

11. "Market Successes," computerworld.com, May 17, 2001, p. 3.

12. Alan Radding, "Leading the Way on Wireless," computerworld.com, September 24, 2002, p. 5.

13. Ibid., p. 6.

14. Ibid.

15. "Hospitality Checks Out Wireless," mbusiness daily.com, March 2002, pp. 21, 22.

16. "CRM in a Wireless World," *HP CRM*, autumn 2001, p. 14.

17. Kevin Maney, "New Chips Could Make Everyday Items 'Talk'," *eCommerce Times*, April 12, 2002, pp. 2, 4.

18. Katherine Balint, "Nothing to Lose," *The San Diego Union-Tribune*, May 13, 2002, pp. E1, E14.

Chapter 22 Will Wall Street Care?

1. Kaj Storbacka, "Customer Relationships as Assets—Evaluating the Impact of CRM on Your Organization's Profitability and Shareholder Value," *CREDO*, Paris, March 15, 2001.

2. Frederick F. Reicheld, *The Loyalty Effect: The Hidden Force Behind Growth, Profits, and Lasting Value* (Boston: Harvard Business School Press, 1996), p. 3.

3. Ibid., pp. 4, 5.

4. "Are You Simply Managing Your Customer Relationships, or Are You Optimizing Them," *PreVision Executive Briefing*, spring 2001, p. 1.

5. Arthur O'Connor, "New Thinking About Customer Value Metrics, Part 2," ecrmguide.com, July 11, 2001, p. 2.

6. Stephanie Coyles and Timothy C. Gokey, "Customer Retention Is Not Enough," The McKinsey Quarterly.com, 2002, Number 2, p. 1.

7. Ibid.

8. Ibid.

9. Ibid., pp. 2, 5.

10. Nick Wreden, *FusionBranding: Strategic Branding Models for the Customer Economy ... and Beyond* (Atlanta: Accountability Press, 2002) as excerpted in *Relationship Marketing Report*, Volume IV Issue XII, p. 2.

11. Jeffrey Kosnett, "Ready for Long-Term Commitment?," *Investing Kiplinger's*, November 2001, p. 1.

12. Steve Skinner, "Sprint PCS Wireless Reports Customer Value to Shareholders," *INSIDE 1to1*, January 19, 2002, p. 4.

13. Ibid.

14. "Looking Beyond the Numbers for Company Value," *INSIDE1TO1 @1to1.com*, October 19, 2002, p. 6.

15. Steve Skinner, "Sprint PCS Wireless Reports Customer Value to Shareholders," *INSIDE 1to1*, January 19, 2002, p. 3.

Conclusion

1. William Safire, "Witnessing an Intrusion Explosion," *San Diego Union-Tribune*, May 3, 2002, p. B10.

2. Jim Ericson, "The 'Failure' of CRM," line56, *E-Business Executive Daily*, August 2, 2001, p. 3.

3. William J. McEwen, "Is CRM All Hype?" destinationcrm.com, May 2, 2002, pp. 2, 3.

Index

About Bloomberg

Bloomberg L.P., founded in 1981, is a global information services, news, and media company. Headquartered in New York, the company has nine sales offices, two data centers, and 87 news bureaus worldwide.

Bloomberg, serving customers in 126 countries around the world, holds a unique position within the financial services industry by providing an unparalleled range of features in a single package known as the BLOOMBERG PROFESSIONAL® service. By addressing the demand for investment performance and efficiency through an exceptional combination of information, analytic, electronic trading, and Straight Through Processing tools, Bloomberg has built a worldwide customer base of corporations, issuers, financial intermediaries, and institutional investors.

BLOOMBERG NEWS®, founded in 1990, provides stories and columns on business, general news, politics, and sports to leading newspapers and magazines throughout the world. BLOOMBERG TELEVISION®, a 24-hour business and financial news network, is produced and distributed globally in seven different languages. BLOOMBERG RADIO℠ is an international radio network anchored by flagship station BLOOMBERG® 1130 (WBBR-AM) in New York.

In addition to the BLOOMBERG PRESS® line of books, Bloomberg publishes *BLOOMBERG MARKETS*™ and *BLOOMBERG WEALTH MANAGER*®. To learn more about Bloomberg, call a sales representative at:

Frankfurt:	49-69-92041-280	São Paulo:	5511-3048-4506
Hong Kong:	852-2977-6900	Singapore:	65-6212-1100
London:	44-20-7330-7500	Sydney:	612-9777-8686
New York:	1-212-318-2200	Tokyo:	813-3201-8910
San Francisco:	1-415-912-2970		

About the Author

Frederick Newell is a leading international marketing consultant who has helped giant multinationals as well as small businesses around the world develop customer relationship management strategies to strengthen customer loyalty and increase profitability. He works with large companies in the United States, Canada, the U.K., Brazil, and Argentina and is a sought-after keynoter for conferences around the world.

Newell is a member of the Board of Directors of the Retail Advertising and Marketing Association, International; a former member of the Operating Committee of the Direct Marketing Association's Retail Marketing Council; an associate member of the CRM Forum; and serves on the Board of Directors and Advisory Boards of several start-up companies in the United States.

He is the author of *Wireless Rules* (McGraw-Hill, 2001), *loyalty.com* (McGraw-Hill, 2000), and *The New Rules of Marketing* (McGraw-Hill, 1997). Newell's awards include the PR News Public Relations Award, Advertising Professional of the Year, and election to the Retail Advertising Hall of Fame.

He can be reached at frednote@aol.com.